THE FIRST INSTITUTION

THE FIRST INSTITUTION

A THEOLOGICAL AND PRACTICAL GUIDE

FOR THE REFORMATION OF GOD'S INSTITUTION

OF MARRIAGE AND FAMILY

- FOR THE GLORY OF GOD -

Published by:

The
Armoury
Ministries
www.thearmouryministries.com

The First Institution
Copyright © 2004, 2005 by Michael J. Beasley.
ISBN (Softcover) 978-1-935358-01-5

Library of Congress Cataloging-in-Publication Data

Michael John Beasley

> The First Institution
> Includes bibliographical references and index.
> Library of Congress Registration: TX 6-218-372
> DREG: 22 JULY 2005

Printed in the United States of America

~ *Dedications* ~

To my precious Savior, Who is the faithful Bridegroom

of His chosen people...

And to my beloved bride whom I desire to love even more as Christ

loves the church...

And to my dear children, whom I desire to love even more

like our precious Heavenly Father

Who loves His children in His great

grace and mercy.

~ Soli Deo Gloria ~

Hosea

2:19-20

"I will betroth you to Me forever; yes,

I will betroth you to Me in righteousness

and in justice,

in lovingkindness

and in compassion,

and I will betroth you

to Me in faithfulness.

Then you will know

the Lord."

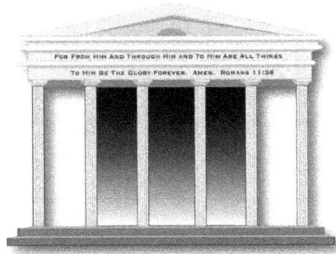

THE FIRST INSTITUTION

CONTENTS

CHAPTER 3
RESTORING THE GENESIS 2 MARRIAGE - 101

CHAPTER 4
REFORMED PARENTING
FOR THE GLORY OF CHRIST - 191

CHAPTER 5
TRAINING CHILDREN
FOR THE GLORY OF CHRIST - 227

CHAPTER 6
CONCLUSION: THE GLORY OF GOD
IN MARRIAGE - 288

APPENDIX - 293

FOR FROM HIM AND THROUGH HIM AND TO HIM ARE ALL THINGS
TO HIM BE THE GLORY FOREVER. AMEN. ROMANS 11:36

THE FIRST INSTITUTION

PROLOGUE:

ONE UNIVERSE

UNDER GOD

Our whole world is at war.

The countless skirmishes seen around the globe, whether small or great, reveal a systemic disease of unrest in our world. But what truly plagues our planet is far more grave than such physical conflicts, and this is even evident in the contests often seen here in America: contests that deal with fundamental questions concerning human freedom, mankind's destiny, theism, and atheism. Even the petty and frequently recycled debate over America's pledge of allegiance, which asserts that America is *one nation under God,* reveals this same spiritual disease plaguing our entire globe. As to this latter point, we can learn much from those who complain about our nation's pledge: when the words *under God* were first added to the nation's pledge in 1954, it was accepted without question; after all, our nation's *Declaration of Independence* has always affirmed that all men are endowed with certain *unalienable rights by their Creator.* But in recent years such words and concepts, which affirm God's *sovereign authority,* have become fodder for several legal battles that have further polarized an already divided nation. While such controversies have been disheartening, they have unveiled some important truths about the culture in which we live. What we learn from such contests is that beneath this small tip of legal wrangling and enmity lurks a deadly iceberg of rebellion against God and His authority. Thus, this controversy over the nation's pledge of allegiance has proven to be a small illustration of a much deeper problem within mankind. The terrifying reality is that those who deny the Creator have no real concept of the judgment that

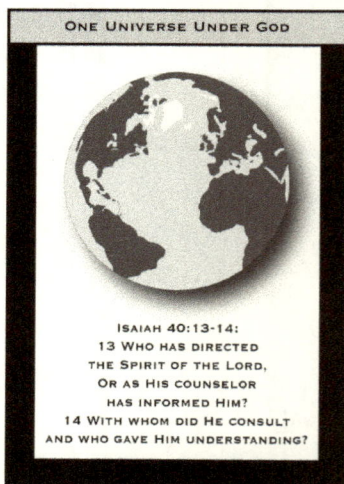

ONE UNIVERSE UNDER GOD

ISAIAH 40:13-14:
13 WHO HAS DIRECTED
THE SPIRIT OF THE LORD,
OR AS HIS COUNSELOR
HAS INFORMED HIM?
14 WITH WHOM DID HE CONSULT
AND WHO GAVE HIM UNDERSTANDING?

10

awaits them.[1] The Scriptures remind us that one day all creation will bow in submission to the risen Son of God, and in that day every created thing in Heaven and on the earth[2] will bow in submission and confess the absolute Lordship of Jesus Christ to the glory of God the Father.[3] In that final judgment of mankind, all creation will make this universal declaration of God's unquestioned authority, whether as a final confession unto judgment, or as an act of genuine worship by the disciples of Jesus Christ unto eternal glory.[4] When His judgment is complete, there will be no petitions heard, no protests permitted, and not a single appeal will be entertained. The only sound that will fill God's Supreme Court of justice will be the song of the Lamb, which will yield the eternal celebration of Christ's victory and dominion *over the entire Universe*. As the disciples of Jesus Christ, we long for that day with great yearning, but until that glorious day comes we must remember that we are in the midst of a fierce battle; a war that has endured from the time of creation to the present. Therefore, knowing the fear of the Lord we must *persuade men*[5] to give an account to the sovereign Creator.

When considering the world in which we live one must remember that the very battles faced today are not at all new. Ever since the beginning of the human race our world has endured *constant warfare*. Of course, I speak not of guns, bombs, and artillery *per se*,

---

[1] Romans 1:18-25.

[2] Revelation 5:12-14: 12 saying with a loud voice: "Worthy is the Lamb who was slain to receive power and riches and wisdom, and strength and honor and glory and blessing!" 13 And every creature which is in heaven and on the earth and under the earth and such as are in the sea, and all that are in them, I heard saying: "Blessing and honor and glory and power be to Him who sits on the throne, and to the Lamb, forever and ever!" 14 Then the four living creatures said, "Amen!" And the twenty-four elders fell down and worshiped Him who lives forever and ever.

[3] Philippians 2:10-11: 10 ...at the name of Jesus every knee should bow, of those in heaven, and of those on earth, and of those under the earth,11 and that every tongue should confess that Jesus Christ is Lord, to the glory of God the Father.

[4] Matthew 25:31-46.

[5] 2 Corinthians 5:11.

instead I speak of the spiritual battle that has raged from the beginning of the human race. It is this perpetual battle that involves different kinds of weapons and opponents; and behind the enemy line of such a battle stands the Devil with his demonic hoard as he maniacally opposes the will and good pleasure of God. In reality, there has never been a moment when this enemy of God has ceased from his warfare[6] and neither will he ever surrender. Thus, it is alarming to consider that while this spiritual world-war continues to take place, most people in our present day and age just go on living their lives completely unaware of its reality. This deception is especially strong here in America where we have an abundance of food, wealth, resources, education, civil structure, and national peace. But our abundant resources have in some ways masked the reality that we are in a severe struggle, and our enemy is far more powerful and clever than any terrorist on earth. Though the enemy's tactics and battlefronts are many, there have always been four key targets of the Devil's wrathful opposition, and they are: *Christ; The Elect; the Scriptures; and God's Institution of Marriage.* This fourfold front of attack is evident throughout the pages of God's Word, and with bitter irony, constitutes the basis and context for God's final judgment of the Devil himself.[7]

It is my firm belief and conviction that there is a great need in our day for the people of God to be awakened to, and strengthened for, these aforementioned lines of battle. It is for this reason that I have written *The First Institution (TFI),* the main focus of which centers on this particular battle line of marriage – with this important qualification: *While the subject of marriage is indeed central to this work, the reader must not assume that the other lines of battle will be ignored. In fact, it is impossible to discuss the qualities of a God-glorifying marriage without presenting the centrality of Christ, the*

---

[6] 1 Peter 5:8.

[7] Revelation 19:7-9, 20-21.

necessity of God's redemption, as well as the indispensable nature of His Holy Scriptures in everything. Thus, every aspect of marriage and family will be explored in order to magnify all of the battlefronts that confront believers today. I am convinced that the neediness of this age is great because the values of our world are falling to a new all-time low. Therefore, if we are to understand our need for a study on marriage and family, we must also consider this world's relentless enmity against the Creator and what it is that He has *joined together.*[8]

WAR OF THE WORLDVIEWS

The modern valuation and understanding of God's institution of the family is returning to a level of corruption that is barely rivaled by the most depraved cultures of past time. During the completion of this work our nation has witnessed the anarchy of many judges, governing authorities, and politicians who have pressed an agenda to redefine the institution of marriage without any regard to law - *whether the law of men or especially of God.* The corruption of our culture has become so excessive, that it is actually considered to be a matter of debate as to whether men should marry men and women should marry women! But this pattern of corruption is the very earmark of a society that is being given over to its own wickedness:

> **Romans 1:26-27**: 26 For this reason God gave them over to degrading passions; for their women exchanged the natural function for that which is unnatural, 27 and in the same way also the men abandoned the natural function of the woman and burned in their desire toward one another, men with men committing indecent acts and receiving in their own persons the due penalty of their error.

In light of this societal degradation, a very important question must be addressed: *exactly who has the authority to define marriage and*

---

[8] Matthew 19:6.

family? Judges and legislators in our own nation are laboring diligently to redefine what the nuclear family is, but do these individuals actually have the authority to establish the standards that define the family? The very simple answer from Scripture is: No. Only God has the authority to define the institution of the family, for He is the *Author* (Latin – *auctor*; Creator) of all things. This Latin word [*auctor*] is the foundation of our English words *author* and *authority*. Therefore, when we say that God has authority, we are acknowledging His office as the Creator and governor of all things. The ramifications that accompany this truth are vast, because when we speak of *any earthly authority* we must recognize that God is their ultimate source. The Word of God repeatedly affirms this important truth:

> **Isaiah 40:13-17:** 13 Who has directed the Spirit of the Lord, or as His counselor has informed Him? 14 With whom did He consult and who gave Him understanding? And who taught Him in the path of justice and taught Him knowledge, and informed Him of the way of understanding? 15 Behold, the nations are like a drop from a bucket, And are regarded as a speck of dust on the scales; Behold, He lifts up the islands like fine dust. 16 Even Lebanon is not enough to burn, nor its beasts enough for a burnt offering. 17 All the nations are as nothing before Him, they are regarded by Him as less than nothing and meaningless.

The reality is that God's authority is absolute and is therefore unquestionable. In fact, all of Holy Writ begins with a simple, yet compelling, stipulation regarding God's absolute authority: *"In the beginning God created the heavens and the earth" Genesis 1:1*. By this statement alone we have scriptural evidence that all governing authorities, all powers, dominions, and earthly institutions (including the institution of marriage) *subsist beneath the unquestionable authority of the Creator.*[9] Thus, this simple and obvious conclusion

---

[9] Romans 1:20.

14

from God's Word has been the very target of opposition in our culture for some time, and those who name the name of Christ must be prepared to give a sound defense on behalf of God's authoritative Word.

MANKIND'S CREATED PURPOSE

The philosophies of secular humanism and Darwinism have so affected the world's culture that any discussion today about the Creator is instantly dismissed as extremist rhetoric. One of the many tragedies of secular humanism is that it has reduced mankind to an insignificant mass of biological phenomena, and therefore within the scope of this philosophy, mankind believes that he answers to no absolutes *because they do not exist.* By such a premise as this, life, morality, truth, and reality are to be defined by man's subjective judgments and perceived needs. In a universe such as this mankind answers to no one but himself, while at the same time the true value of God's creation is utterly lost. As Steve Weinberg said (author of *The First Three Minutes*):

"The more the universe seems comprehensible the more it also seems pointless."[10]

Such a hopeless statement as this reminds us that scientific research does not necessarily lead men to a knowledge of the truth.[11] In fact, with each and every discovery that is made in this vast Universe, many have further deduced the absence of God; but such reasoning is based upon the false foundation of human reason. It is quite popular

---

[10] Steve Weinberg, The First Three Minutes (1977), quoted in Donald B. DeYoung, Astronomy and the Bible, (Baker Book House, Grand Rapids, Michigan), p. 117.

[11] 2 Timothy 3:1,2,7 1 But realize this, that in the last days difficult times will come. 2 For men will be lovers of self, lovers of money, boastful, arrogant, revilers, disobedient to parents, ungrateful, unholy...7 always learning and never able to come to the knowledge of the truth.

to conclude, by human reason, that the miracle of life on earth was merely a spontaneous and inconsequential event. There are even some who, in their desperation to explain the miracle of life on earth, have resorted to the fictional fantasies of *exogenesis* and *panspermia* – neither of which have a basis in empirical science. Such forms of thinking may be increasing in popularity, but they are nothing more than belief systems that contradict the empirical realities of general and special revelation. But if we are to understand God's purposes in creating the heavens, mankind, and even marriage, then we must begin with the empirical evidence that is supplied within the book of beginnings: *Genesis*. This book is so foundational that we will invest nearly half of our study in it, especially as we examine the doctrines of marriage and family.

The word *Genesis* itself comes from the Greek word *gegenētai* which means to be born or begotten. It is no wonder that this book of beginnings brings us immediately to the scene of all beginnings whereby *in the beginning God created the heavens and the earth and all things in them*. But this miracle was no strenuous event for the omnipotent God, requiring vast epochs of time, rather "...by the word of the Lord the heavens were made, and by the breath of His mouth all their host."[12] On the first day of creation we see that the Lord created, out of nothing,[13] all the heavens and the earth as a kind of cosmic sermon that continually declares the vast wisdom and glory of God: "The heavens are telling of the glory of God; And their expanse is declaring the work of His hands..."[14] The Scriptures

---

[12] Psalm 33:6.

[13] The Hebrew word *bār'ā* [created], in this context, denotes a creation that is made *ex nihilo* [out of nothing] rather than it being formed from other, pre-existing materials. The root *bār'ā* has the basic meaning "to create." It differs from *yāṣar* 'to fashion' in that the latter primarily emphasizes the shaping of an object while *bār'ā* emphasizes the initiation of the object. Harris, R. L., Harris, R. L., Archer, G. L., & Waltke, B. K. Theological Wordbook of the Old Testament (Electronic Edition Moody Press, Chicago, 1999, c1980) p. 127.

[14] Psalm 19:1.

repeatedly teach us that all of God's creation is full of purpose, for all things exist for His glory. However, it is clear that mankind's foolishness is inclined towards the belief that he is insignificant in view of the expansiveness of the universe. We can see this tendency in the reflections of the psalmist David in Psalm 8:3-4:

"When I consider Thy heavens, the work of Thy fingers, The moon and the stars, which Thou hast ordained; What is man, that Thou dost take thought of him?"[15]

When David considered the vastness of space itself, he felt small and insignificant. Compared to the Universe we are indeed small and seemingly insignificant! Yet, this was not the end of David's meditation, for he recalled the miracle of creation as recorded in the first chapter of Genesis and as a result David's meditation was recalibrated by Holy Writ. This is apparent when he says in Psalm 8:5-6:

"Yet Thou hast made him a little lower than God, and dost crown him with glory and majesty! Thou dost make him to rule over the works of Thy hands; Thou hast put all things under his feet."

David's thoughts were corrected in the following manner: he realized that his human assessment of creation was inadequate to understand its true meaning and purpose, for as miniscule as man is, he is at the center of a cosmological stage upon which the eternal God is displaying the magnitude of His wisdom, mercy, and grace.[16] Yes, mankind is inestimably miniscule in the vast cosmos, *but he is the very centerpiece of all that God has made,* therefore he is under obligation to answer to the One who created everything for His ultimate glory.

---

[15] Psalm 8:1-2.

[16] Romans 1:33-36, 9; Rev. 4:11.

This understanding of man's centrality in God's creation has clashed much with modern philosophies and sciences, and as a result many in our society believe that the Bible has nothing helpful to say about man or the Universe. This conflict has accelerated even more over the last 150 years as evolutionary theory has effectively steam-rolled the world's epistemology into a flat and godless humanism. Such an overwhelming acceptance of evolutionary theory has infiltrated nearly every discipline of study and has thereby polluted the minds of men in our generation. Consider the following summary of secularism's destructive legacy:

- **Mankind's Value:** According to humanism, man is an insignificant product of chance in this vast, self-existing universe. Man is therefore manifesting his own authority in the earth as the most highly developed of all animal species and plant life. *But according to Scripture the heavens and the earth were made in order to provide a glorious habitat for mankind. Man was made as the pinnacle of His creation, bearing God's own image and being made in order to manifest His authority in the earth and to display His wisdom and glory.*

- **Mankind's Nature:** According to human wisdom man is ascending as a species, improving, evolving, and developing into something better through the process of natural selection. In a universe void of an absolute and holy God, man is not thought to be sinful nor totally depraved. *However, according to Scripture, man fell from his function and nature as being the pinnacle of God's creation and is now deemed, along with Satan and the fallen angels, as the very enemy of God. Man went from being the most prized object of creation to being an object of God's wrath.*

- **Mankind's Purpose:** According to human wisdom, man is a self-authority, therefore the human race is endowed with the right to

18

define the value of human life and the purposes of human servitude. Role distinctions among men and women have no place in a society of absolute relativism. In addition, the process of procreation is a mere biological function, having no moral constraints. The procreative processes can be manipulated in whatever way is necessary to support the propagation of the species. *But according to Scripture, God made the man and the woman to worship Him and to reflect His wisdom and glory, endowing them with the ability to procreate within the context of a monogamous marriage union.*

- **The Institution of Marriage and Family:** According to human wisdom, a family is deemed as any assembly of people who can provide a means of survival for its associates. There are no reasonable standards for defining the marriage union to include the subjects of monogamy, sex pairings, or the purpose of their union. Children are to be cared for physically and educationally with the intent of having them develop a high esteem of themselves. *But according to the Scriptures a family, by God's original design, is defined as being the monogamous union of a man and a woman in marriage and it includes, by God's blessing, children who are to be deemed as gifts from the Lord. The family was made for the sole purpose of the worship and servitude of the Lord God, the Creator.*

By these secular influences, the values and beliefs in our world continue to rot, however, these epistemological differences between the world and Scripture are not new in any way, for men have brandished their imaginary autonomy in the presence of God throughout all generations:

"Man is just as much a natural phenomenon as an animal or plant; that his body, mind and soul were not supernaturally created but are products of evolution, and that he is not under the control or guidance of any supernatural being or beings, but has to rely on himself and his own powers."[17]

This humanistic confession ought to remind the reader of one very important truth: Satan's strategies have never changed throughout history, for he has always opposed the wisdom of God covertly and overtly. He will use any means necessary in order to deceive men and lead them away from the worship of the one true God. But *do not be deceived*, the aforementioned differences are not merely academic, rather they represent the difference between sound doctrine and the doctrines of demons; the difference between heaven and hell; *the difference between lauding Satan for his lies and praising God for His holy wisdom and glory.*

THE FIRST OF ALL INSTITUTIONS

No matter how small the first man and woman were with respect to the Universe, they were the centerpiece of all that the Lord made, because they bore His image and were created in order to rule the earth through their ministry as the family of God. Such a realization as this elevates our understanding of the importance of the first institution of marriage and family. *It is therefore important to understand that the institution of the family was created for a great and wonderful purpose: the worship of God.* Fathers, mothers, and children are called to this unique privilege of worshipping the Creator who made all things for His good pleasure and glory. The real question that we must answer is this: *how are fathers, mothers, and children to serve and worship the Lord?* The answer to this

---

[17] Henry M. Morris, <u>The Biblical Basis for Modern Science</u> (Baker Book House, Grand Rapids, Michigan), p. 391: "Sir Julian Huxley, as quoted in a standard American Humanist Association promotional brochure. Huxley, on of the founders of the A.H.A., was probably the most influential scientific evolutionist of the twentieth century, chief founder and promoter of neo-Darwinism as well as first Director-General of UNESCO."

question constitutes the very focus of *The First Institution* as summarized in the following three principles:

1. Men are to render worship to God through their calling as the leaders of their home. As such, they are called to shepherd their households as humble servants of God, patterning their lives after Jesus Christ, the Good Shepherd, who sacrificially loves and protects His bride the Church (Ephesians 5:22-33).

2. Women are to render worship to God through their calling as a loving companion and helper. She is to love her husband, her children, and she is to minister to them in the home with humility and reverence as she follows the example of Christ in all His humble servitude (Ephesians 5:22-33).

3. Children are to render worship as unto the Lord through the obedience and honor that they render to their parents. They are to listen to the instruction of their parents and seek out the profit of God's Word as it is taught to them (Ephesians 6:1-3).

These three principles may seem to be too simple to be effectual, but like the Gospel itself, its simplicity is quite compelling such that even a child can embrace its important message. It is for this reason that the reader will not find any "12 Secrets to a Happy Marriage" in this book for the simple reason that there are no hidden "secrets" when it comes to God's institution of marriage. God has not hidden Himself from us such that we would be forced to *innovate* principles for marriage on our own. It is a dangerous business when men attempt to formulate their own wisdom based upon the art and thought of human reason,[18] therefore the fortresses of man-made speculation must be torn down by the powerful Word of God.[19] And since our

---

[18] Acts 17:29.

[19] 2 Corinthians 10:3-5.

whole world is at war it behooves the people of God to employ only those weapons deemed powerful in any conflict.[20]

It is my sincere desire and prayer that this work will be a clear representation of Biblical truth and nothing else. May Jesus Christ increase, while this author, along with all other human contributors, decrease. May the family of God indulge in God's Word alone, being satisfied with it and nothing else, for the words of the Lord are finer than much fine gold,[21] refined like pure silver,[22] sweeter than honey and the drippings of the honeycomb.

Taste and see that the Lord is good... Psalm 34:8.

---

[20] Ephesians 6:10-18.

[21] Psalm 19:10a.

[22] Psalm 12:6 The words of the Lord are pure words; As silver tried in a furnace on the earth, refined seven times.

THE FIRST INSTITUTION

FOR FROM HIM AND THROUGH HIM AND TO HIM ARE ALL THINGS.
TO HIM BE THE GLORY FOREVER. AMEN. ROMANS 11:36

CHAPTER 1

THE GLORY OF

GOD'S CREATION

As noted in the previous section, the harsh reality of our present society is this: the modern world stands firmly against the important duties of the husband, wife, and family. Principally, through the lack of godly male leadership in our nation, along with the rising influences of feminism, the institution of the family has degraded at an alarming rate. The gaping wounds in the American family are many, being clearly illustrated through the exaltation of materialism, the emasculation of men, the devaluation of children, and the rebellion of women against the God-ordained roles found in the creation account in Genesis. Yet these *symptoms* point to a more fundamental and systemic problem: the outright rejection of God's authority. It is no wonder that our American culture has become like Vanity Fair:[23] a culture that exalts the possession of things over the procession of godliness. Thus, with such an over-emphasis on materialism and a de-emphasis on the priority of the family, American homes are drowning in the morass of money worship as is evidenced in that simple confession offered in the *National Study of the Changing Workforce*:

> "In dual-earner couples, there is a significant third job that has to be done at home—family work."[24]

What exactly has happened in American culture such that family life now constitutes *the third job* of parents? The honesty of this statement clearly unveils the prevailing attitude of our income-centered society. However, I can assure the reader that the greatest challenge for the American family has nothing to do with the acquisition of more wealth. Instead, the greatest challenge facing the

---

[23] The use of the name *Vanity Fair* has in mind that fictional town in Bunyan's work of The Pilgrim's Progress, where Christian and Faithful walked amongst the town's inhabitants who were guilty of "thefts, murders and adulteries." John Bunyan. The Pilgrim's Progress: From this world to that which is to come. (Oak Harbor, WA: Logos Research Systems, Inc., 1995).

[24] James T. Bond, Cynthia Thompson, Ellen Gallinsky and David Prottas, The National Study of the Changing Workforce, 2002 [italics mine].

family today is in a return to the simple principles of Scripture pertaining to the distinct callings of husbands, wives, and children. There is a great need for revival in families throughout America and across the world, but who can lead this revolution of the family? Our much needed revival can only come by means of the Holy Spirit as He works in the hearts of women and in the hearts of men who are uniquely called to lead their households for the glory of God. May the Lord raise up a new generation of men who will resolve to serve the Lord like Joshua, who was willing to stand alone in order to secure his family's devotion to the Lord God:

> **Joshua 24:15** If it is disagreeable in your sight to serve the Lord, choose for yourselves today whom you will serve: whether the gods which your fathers served which were beyond the River, or the gods of the Amorites in whose land you are living; but as for me and my house, we will serve the Lord.

The tides of public pressure often press firmly against the biblical definitions of the family, but men must resolve to stand in the boldness of the Spirit and serve the Lord without compromise. Thus, in order for men to be revived to their true calling as leaders, they must wholly embrace their unique calling as shepherds and priests of their homes. Therefore, with the humility and prophetic leadership of Elijah, men must (with repentance in their own hearts) call their families back to the Scriptural standards of God:

> **Malachi 4:5-6**: 5 Behold, I am going to send you Elijah the prophet before the coming of the great and terrible day of the Lord. 6 And he will restore the hearts of the fathers to their children, and the hearts of the children to their fathers, lest I come and smite the land with a curse.

The Scriptures repeatedly teach us that the husband/father has a remarkable amount of responsibility as the leader of his household; a responsibility that he must embrace with all seriousness. His ordained authority in the home has a very ancient beginning, going all the way back to the first few passages of the book of Genesis where we learn about God's creation of the *first man, ministry and, commandment.*

THE FIRST MAN, MINISTRY, AND COMMANDMENT

The creation account has a very important context which spans from Genesis chapter 1 to 2. Because of this, both chapters must be carefully examined *together* lest we fail to understand the full continuity of man's beginning. Such a chronological analysis as this is crucial and will keep us from the pitfalls of a *casual* approach to this book of beginnings. For example, we understand that the man and the woman were entrusted with significant roles and responsibilities when they were created; but Genesis chapters 1 and 2 offer very different levels of detail concerning such roles. Consider, for example, the creation narrative in chapter 1:

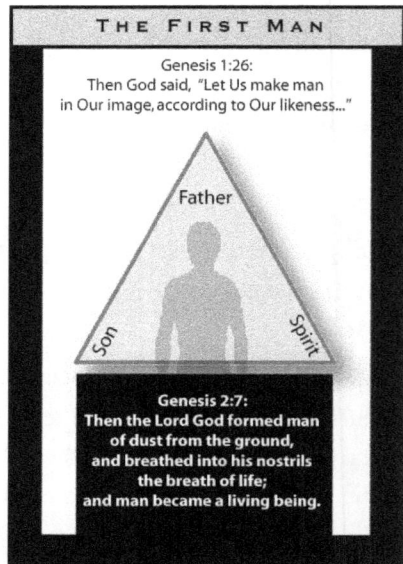

THE FIRST MAN

Genesis 1:26:
Then God said, "Let Us make man in Our image, according to Our likeness..."

Father

Son   Spirit

Genesis 2:7:
Then the Lord God formed man of dust from the ground, and breathed into his nostrils the breath of life; and man became a living being.

Gen. 1:27-2:4: 27 And God created man in His own image, in the image of God He created him; male and female He created them. And God blessed them; and God said to them, "Be fruitful and multiply, and fill the earth, and subdue it; and rule over the fish of the sea and over the birds of the sky, and over every living thing that moves on the earth." Then God said, "Behold, I have given you every plant yielding seed that is on the surface of all the earth, and every tree which has fruit yielding seed; it shall be food for you; and to every beast of the earth and to every bird of the sky and to every thing that moves on the earth which has life, I have given every green plant for food"; and it was so. And God saw all that He had made, and behold, it was very good. And there was evening and there was morning, the sixth day. 2:1-4: 1 Thus the heavens and the earth were completed, and all their hosts. 2 By the seventh day God completed His work which He had done, and He rested on the seventh day from all His work which He had done. 3 Then God blessed the seventh day and sanctified it, because in it He rested from all His work which God had created and made. 4 This is the account of the heavens and the earth when they were created, in the day that the Lord God made earth and heaven.

Genesis 1:1-2:4 gives us a general description of the roles and responsibilities of the first man and woman, however, the question regarding *how* these roles and responsibilities were to be executed could be missed if we failed to incorporate the context of what follows in Genesis 2:5-25. Genesis 2:5-25 is not a mere repeat of chapter 1:1-2:4, but is an advancement of revelation. These sections (among others in Genesis) are distinguished by the Hebrew word *tôlĕdôt* - which are most likely colophonic markers of the records of original eyewitnesses – a pattern of revelation repeated throughout the book of Genesis (2:4, 5:1, 6:9, 10:1, 11:10, 11:27, 25:12, 36:1, 37:2).[25] These individual sections reveal an important harmony and unity within this first book of Moses. If we were to divide and isolate them, then their harmony would be lost. Because of this, we will examine the first *man, ministry, and commandment* through a careful examination of both sections found in chapters 1 and 2, yet with a special emphasis on the more robust detail revealed in the latter. The importance of these initial sections in Genesis is apparent when we examine their contents, side by side:

---

[25] While I hold to the view which states that the *tôlĕdôt* markers are colophonic in purpose, it must be noted that this is not critical to the broader argument presented in this book. In any view, there is a harmony and concordance between all the sections of Genesis that must not be ignored. This is in keeping with the perspicuity and harmony of all Scripture.

• The first couple's order of Creation:	
Genesis 1:26-27 May appear to speak of a simultaneous creation of the man and woman...	*...but Genesis 2:7-23 reminds us that there is a certain order – the man was created first and then the woman.*
• The first couple's relationship:	
In Genesis 1:28 we have a simplified description of their relationship, summarized in the function of procreation...	*...but Genesis 2:5-25 gives us a more complete statement of their relationship – that the woman was a suitable helper to the man and that the man would cleave to his wife in devotion to her.*
• The first couple's freedoms:	
Genesis 1:29 says that they were to partake from every plant and tree...	*...but Genesis 2:17 reminds us that they had the one limitation respecting the tree of the knowledge of good and evil.*
• The first couple's ministry:	
In Genesis 1:26 the God-head declared "...let them rule..." Such a statement reminds us that as a couple, they were to subdue and rule over the earth. This verse is oftentimes used in order to try to nullify any role distinctions between the man and the woman...	*...but Genesis 2:5-25 reminds us that their authority is distinguishable, explaining that Adam was entrusted with the responsibilities of serving in and protecting the garden, naming the animals and exercising his responsibilities by means of the ministry of the Word which was entrusted to him. The woman was to be Adam's helper, aiding and supporting him as he conducted this ministry.*

It should be quite clear from this brief comparison that Genesis chapter 2:5-25 will be crucial for a more thorough understanding of the institution of marriage as it was originally created. The most important elements gleaned from the 2nd chapter have to do with the first couple's distinctive roles, as well as the nature of their union in marriage. But for now, we will introduce our study of chapter 2 by carefully looking at the *first man, his ministry, as well as the first commandment which the Lord entrusted to him:*

- **The First Man:** Genesis 2:7 Then the Lord God formed man of dust from the ground, and breathed into his nostrils the breath of life; and man became a living being.

- **The First Ministry:** Genesis 2:8…15 8 And the Lord God planted a garden toward the east, in Eden; and there He placed the man whom He had formed…15 Then the Lord God took the man and put him into the garden of Eden to cultivate it and keep it.

- **The First Commandment:** Genesis 2:16-17 16 And the Lord God commanded the man, saying, "From any tree of the garden you may eat freely; 17 but from the tree of the knowledge of good and evil you shall not eat, for in the day that you eat from it you shall surely die."

From Genesis 2:7-17 we have several significant firsts: man himself was made before the woman (she was made from his side later in the chapter 2, v. 22). While Adam existed alone in this unique garden, he was entrusted with two leadership responsibilities: *1. The ministry of cultivating and protecting the garden and 2. The spoken commandment of God which prohibited him from eating from the tree of the knowledge of good and evil.* These duties, as entrusted to Adam, are filled with important lessons concerning the role of the man. You see, Adam's duties in the garden went well beyond his having a green thumb. Ultimately, the responsibilities entrusted to him, by means of the Lord's commandments, teach us a great deal about the first man's obligation to serve as a leader. Consider first the contents of the Lord's instructions to Adam:

God's Positive Command: Genesis 2:16 And the Lord God commanded the man, saying, "From any tree of the garden you may eat freely..."

God's Prohibitive Command: Genesis 2:17 ...but from the tree of the knowledge of good and evil you shall not eat, for in the day that you eat from it you shall surely die.

We see here that Adam was entrusted with *positive and prohibitive laws*, the simplicity of which is compelling. By these commandments it is quite evident that Adam's ministry of the Word was not complex *per se*, for his simple obligation was to enjoy the vast expanse of the garden while observing only one prohibition. Within the scope of his duties to God, Adam was to cultivate (*serve*) and keep (*guard*) the garden as follows:

- **Cultivate (serve):** The Hebrew word translated as "cultivate" is the common word for serve (H. *ebed*). This would denote all aspects of ministry in the garden relative to Adam's instructions.[26] He was to enjoy freely all that the garden had to provide by the Lord's ordained authority. This calling of servitude in the garden was based upon the liberty which was given to Adam, as well as the bounty of provisions that the Lord had supplied for his every need.[27]

---

[26] The very nature of Adam's ministry in the garden cannot be entirely known, for this pre-fall garden may not have had the same service needs as in the case after the fall (Genesis 3:17-19). It's need was more than likely centered on satisfying the man, as he freely enjoyed its produce, rather than requiring some great measure of husbandry.

[27] Adam lost his privilege as a servant of God in the garden through the sin that he committed (Gen. 3). Through one act of sin, Adam forsook his stewardship, but he was a mere type of the One who, through one act of righteousness (Romans 5:19) would regain paradise for His own: Revelation 22:14 Blessed are those who wash their robes, so that they may have the right to the tree of life, and may enter by the gates into the city.

- **Keep (guard):** The Hebrew word translated as "keep" is perhaps better represented by the English word "protect" or "guard."[28] The word "keep" is not an improper choice either, however when we are reminded that this word, in its primitive form (H. *šāmār*), speaks of the guardianship afforded by a soldier or watchman (Psalm 130:6),[29] then we realize that we are speaking of something more than just plant husbandry. In fact, this word is used again in Genesis 3:24 to speak of the cherubim's guardianship of the garden when Adam and his wife were driven out.[30] This *transfer of guardianship (šāmār)* clarifies the nature of Adam's original stewardship in the garden which was lost by means of his one transgression.

What is particularly revealing, regarding the Lord's instructions to Adam, is this word which speaks of guardianship *(šāmār)*. When we say that Adam was assigned to *keep* the garden, we understand that he was to *guard* it like a soldier, or as the sword-wielding cherubim in Gen. 3:24. But what was Adam supposed to guard in the garden? What exactly was there to protect? Answer: nothing, except *the tree of the knowledge of good and evil*. Besides this tree, there was nothing else that would require such protection. This delineation of Adam's responsibilities is no trivial matter; nor is the order in which he was created unimportant. What Genesis chapter 2 teaches us is that Adam, who was first, *was given exclusive responsibilities in the garden and that his duties were clearly established before the creation of the*

---

[28] The Hebrew word *šāmār* most often speaks of some form of watch, protection or guardianship as provided by a soldier. In Genesis 2:15 the LXX (the Greek translation of the Old Testament) predictably uses the Greek word *phulassein* which is identical in meaning. Harris, Archer, & Waltke, Theological Wordbook, #2414.

[29] This word is also used in relation to the Lord's *guardianship* over our path: Proverbs 3:26 For the Lord will be your confidence, And will *keep* your foot from being caught.

[30] Genesis 3:24 So He drove the man out; and at the east of the garden of Eden He stationed the cherubim, and the flaming sword which turned every direction, to guard (*lišmōr*) the way to the tree of life. By this and the immediate context of Adam's responsibility to uphold the prohibition concerning the tree of the knowledge of good and evil, it suits the context to say that his work of "keeping" was specifically that of guardianship. It would be this particular form of duty that Adam would fail in when the woman and he both ate the forbidden fruit.

woman; even before the existence of original sin. As to this latter point, it must be remembered that the role distinctions presented in Genesis 2 *are not the result of sin.* Perhaps to some, the fact that Adam was created first may not seem to be important; however the Apostle Paul depended on this truth in order to address the important matter of the roles of men and women:

> **1 Timothy 2:11-13**: 11 Let a woman quietly receive instruction with entire submissiveness. 12 But I do not allow a woman to teach or exercise authority over a man, but to remain quiet. 13 For it was Adam who was first created, and then Eve.

There are some who have supposed that Paul spoke about the roles of men and women in this verse from the reasoning of the culture and circumstances of his day. However, nothing could be further from the truth; for he immediately drew from the truths of the book of Genesis in order to establish the basis for his instruction. Contextually, we are reminded that Paul wrote this letter to Timothy who was shepherding the church in Ephesus. In this epistle Paul addressed the priorities for the church to include the roles of men and women.[31] Paul taught Timothy that women were to *receive* authoritative instruction rather than *give* it.[32] He then presented a

---

[31] That these instructions had application to Timothy at Ephesus does not forestall their relevance for all churches of all time: Paul's instructions to Timothy were for all the people of God of all time: 1 Timothy 3:15 but in case I am delayed, I write so that you may know how one ought to conduct himself in the household of God, which is the church of the living God, the pillar and support of the truth.

[32] It is often the case that people will mention the occasion of Deborah in order to renounce the prescriptive texts that deal with the roles of men and women. Calvin confronts this error well in his commentary on 1 Timothy: "If any one bring forward, by way of objection, Deborah (Judges 4:4) and others of the same class, of whom we read that they were at one time appointed by the commend of God to govern the people, the answer is easy. Extraordinary acts done by God do not overturn the ordinary rules of government, by which he intended that we should be bound. Accordingly, if women at one time held the office of prophets and teachers, and that too when they were supernaturally called to it by the Spirit of God, He who is above all law might do this; but, being a peculiar case,37 this is not opposed to the constant and ordinary system of

reason for this instruction in verse 13[33] by citing a most important event in the creation narrative: "*Adam was first*, and then Eve." By referring to this *first man* Paul was reminding Timothy about the unique responsibility of leadership that has been entrusted to all men. What he states explicitly in 1 Timothy 2:11-13, he teaches implicitly in his follow-up letter to Timothy, whereby he taught that men are to be entrusted with the authoritative responsibility of the ministry of the Word:

> **2 Timothy 2:2** *And the things which you have heard from me in the presence of many witnesses, these entrust to faithful men, who will be able to teach others also.*

In both of these texts, we see that Paul had repeatedly instructed Timothy regarding the man's role as a *guardian and leader through the ministry of the Word*. These are the same duties and responsibilities that are patterned after *the first man and his ministry*. But had it been Paul's intention for Timothy to pass along the baton of leadership to men *and women*, then he would have simply said so. However texts like 2 Timothy 2:2 remind us that the progeny of leadership, in all generations, must be entrusted *to men* who are faithful guardians by the authority of the Lord's commandments;[34] for it was Adam who was first created and who was uniquely entrusted with the first ministry and commandment. Adam's role as the leader and federal head of the human race will be examined more thoroughly in chapter 2 *The Shame of Adam's Sin (The First Deception and Transgression)*, but for now we must embrace this

---

government." John Calvin, <u>Calvin's Commentaries</u> Vol. XXI, (Baker Books, Grand Rapids, MI 1996), p. 67.

[33] Paul employed the conjunction *gar* in order to establish the ground or basis for his instruction to Timothy concerning the role of women in the church. The very simple construction here leaves no doubt that Paul was teaching Timothy concerning the roles of men and women from the O.T. book of Genesis and not from the popular culture of the day.

[34] See also 1 Timothy 3:1-7 and Titus 1:5-9.

important principle of Adam's headship. His office as a leader and guardian was clearly distinct from the role and calling of the woman who would later be formed from his side.

This discussion of role distinctions, between men and women, generates no small amount of debate; especially in our modern, feministic world. Philosophically it can become a matter of endless speculation as to why it is that God was pleased to make men and women so similar in some ways; yet so distinct in many other ways. But such a reality is a matter to be left to the transcendent wisdom of God. We could also speculate endlessly over why He made the elect angels to consist of the distinctions of archangels, seraphim, and cherubim; but this too is a mystery. What we can conclude, with absolute certainty, is that it simply pleased Him to create creatures who serve Him according to their created distinctions, similarities, and ordained purpose in life.[35] The very fact that Adam was first, serving in the garden and upholding God's Word, points to his role as the leader. He was God's ordained representative in the garden who would need *help* from one who would be drawn from his side and fashioned by the Creator. God therefore created the woman for the man's sake so that His ordained purposes would be fulfilled.[36]

---

[35] It should be noted that the reality of our created order and the overall ministry of the Gospel is a pre-occupation of and mystery to the angels as well – we all serve a transcendently wise God! 1 Peter 1:12, 1 Cor. 11:10.

[36] 1 Corinthians 11:3, 9: 3 But I want you to understand that Christ is the head of every man, and the man is the head of a woman, and God is the head of Christ...9 ...indeed man was not created for the woman's sake, but woman for the man's sake. Calvin is correct when he comments on the implications of God's created order: "Since, therefore, God did not create two chiefs of equal power, but added to the man a helper the Apostle justly reminds us of that order of creation in which the eternal and inviolable appointment of God is strikingly displayed." The order of creation played in important role in Paul's instruction to the Corinthians which had no small amount of problems within their worship services: This was evidenced by the men who failed to lead like men (1 Corinthians 16:13) and the women who failed to submit to God ordained authority (1 Corinthians 14:35). As he did in 1 Timothy 2:13, Paul pointed to the order of creation in order to signify that God has ordained the man and the woman with differing roles. It becomes a very important matter to accept: that a man's leadership and a

From what we have examined so far, it should be quite obvious that this book of beginnings is crucial and essential in the matter of understanding marriage and family. Additionally, the importance of these texts is also seen with respect to the sanctity of marriage, for the Lord Jesus Christ taught from Genesis 2:24-25 in order establish the value and nature of the marriage union.[37] Such a point reminds us that our interpretations of Genesis must be governed by the inspired teachings of Christ and His Apostles, rather than in the vacuum of our own speculations. Genesis 2 clearly shows us that the institution of marriage was to be led by the first ordained leader - Adam. His ministry of leadership even included the responsibility of naming of the animals, a duty that again connotes authority.[38] But Adam was not created to be alone; rather he was made in order to abide with a special and wonderful helpmeet. Adam named her *'iśāh* because she was made, not from the dust of the ground, but from his own side. As the handiwork of God she was a wonderful creation and gift from the Lord, who would complement Adam in every way.

THE FIRST WOMAN

As we now consider the Lord's original creation of the first woman, we must remember that this important design of His has been grossly maligned within this fallen world. Women today are surrounded by a culture that is obsessed with *external appearance,* by means of stylish fashions and physical beauty. This obsession is clearly displayed through most contemporary movies, television programs, the music industry, and many magazines. In fact, one can hardly avoid entering a grocery store without passing magazine racks adorned with

---

woman's submission to that leadership are role responsibilities that were established before the fall.

[37] Matt. 19:1-6.

[38] Psalm 147:4 He counts the number of the stars; He gives names to all of them.

pictures of malnourished and scantily clad models who look like they could use a solid meal and a few extra stitches of clothing. Along with this, the retail industry's unstoppable deluge of trendy clothing, shoes, hair styles, and designer trinkets reminds us that most businesses understand this principle of fashion-obsession; even more than the consumer does. But America's love affair with looking good isn't only for the rich and famous. According to the U.S. Census Bureau of 2002, Americans spent over six and a half billion dollars on cosmetics, beauty supplies, and perfumes; and this figure does not include the exploding industry of plastic surgery. It is ironic that a culture which is so consumed with the pursuit of beauty, actually knows very little of the subject! For example, who would ever expect a major fashion show in L.A. or New York to sport the following as their program's theme?

> **Proverbs 31:30** Charm is deceitful and beauty is vain, But a woman who fears the Lord, she shall be praised.

The beauty that the world pursues, with all its energy and finances, is *fleeting, deceitful*, and *vain*. It is preoccupied with that which is external, but fades away so quickly; and it is lured by the glamour produced by a make-up brush which temporarily covers imperfect complexions. Yet despite this world's misperceptions, there *is* such a thing as beauty. True beauty is that which does not fade away, but endures in the One who created all things that are beautiful. In fact, it is the Lord Himself who is the source of everything beautiful, and He delights in all things that are holy and genuinely fair. All things that are good, pure, and holy come from the Lord who is beautifully holy, for the Scriptures declare: "...Worship the LORD in the splendor of his holiness. Strength and beauty are in His sanctuary."[39] Even Christ Himself delights in the beautiful purity and holiness of

---

[39] See Psalm 96:6-9. *The Holy Bible : New International Version*. 1996, c1984 (electronic ed.) (Ps 96:9). Grand Rapids: Zondervan.

His own bride who will be presented before Him one day, without a spot, wrinkle, or the blemish of sin. That day will be characterized by bounteous joy and the exuberant praise of God:

> **Revelation 19:7** Let us be glad and rejoice and give Him glory, for the marriage of the Lamb has come, and His wife has made herself ready.

Here is *true beauty* indeed: Christ Jesus the Lord being joined in eternal matrimony to His bride who was made beautiful through His effectual sacrifice for her. It is this same heavenly scene that the Lord illustrated when He created the first institution of marriage by joining Adam to his beautiful, *holy* bride. Despite what our world considers to be beautiful, the Word of God gives us the only true portrait of beauty, and it is clearly seen when the first woman was created in God's own image:

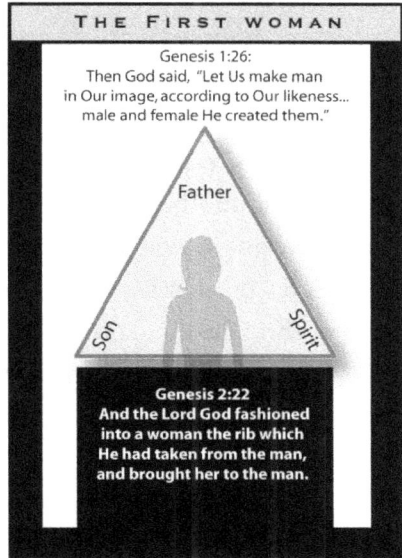

THE FIRST WOMAN

Genesis 1:26:
Then God said, "Let Us make man in Our image, according to Our likeness... male and female He created them."

Father

Son

Spirit

Genesis 2:22
And the Lord God fashioned into a woman the rib which He had taken from the man, and brought her to the man.

Genesis 2:18-25: 18 Then the Lord God said, "It is not good for the man to be alone; I will make him a helper suitable for him." 19 And out of the ground the Lord God formed every beast of the field and every bird of the sky, and brought them to the man to see what he would call them; and whatever the man called a living creature, that was its name. 20 And the man gave names to all the cattle, and to the birds of the sky, and to every beast of the field, but for Adam there was not found a helper suitable for him. 21 So the Lord God caused a deep sleep to fall upon the man, and he slept; then He took one of his ribs, and closed up the flesh at that place. 22 And the Lord God fashioned into a woman the rib which He had taken from the man, and brought her to the man. 23 And the man said,

> "This is now bone of my bones,
> And flesh of my flesh;
> She shall be called Woman,
> Because she was taken out of Man."

24 For this cause a man shall leave his father and his mother, and shall cleave to his wife; and they shall become one flesh. 25 And the man and his wife were both naked and were not ashamed.

Without the taint of sin, the first couple was joined together *as a type of Christ's future union with His holy bride.* We see that the declaration of the Lord, in Genesis 2:18, established an important fact: it was *not good* that Adam should remain alone in the garden. This same Hebrew word translated as "good" (*tôḇ*) is used in the creation account in Genesis 1, verses 12, 18, 21, 25, 31. The primitive concept of *tôḇ* speaks of something that is full of abundance, wholesome, or *complete.* Thus, Adam was created *so that* he would be joined to another, in the holy union of marriage, so that God's eternal purposes would be complete; this included Adam's need to fulfill God's purposes of populating the earth, subduing it, as well as thriving through the fellowship and friendship of one who would be his equal in essence, and yet be wonderfully different in many ways. Adam needed a helper, but not just any helper. He needed a suitable helper; one who was very much like him; one to whom he could relate; one with whom he could have an intimate union unlike any other. It is fascinating that God's fashioning of the woman did not follow quickly in the next verse, but occurs four verses later. The omniscient God of the Universe could have fashioned the woman immediately, instantly resolving the apparent dilemma of Adam's isolation, but He did not. Why? Because the Lord, in His wisdom, was about to guide Adam through a process that would clearly illustrate his *unique* need. Adam needed more than a functional partner; he needed someone who would come *from* him and be an *inseparable* part of his life and ministry. Therefore the next verse begins, not with the fashioning of the woman from his side, but with God's formation of "every beast of the field and every bird of the sky."[40] Imagine this remarkable scene for a moment: Adam had the privilege of witnessing the Lord's miraculous formation of the beasts and birds. The Lord then *brought* the animals in a lengthy procession before Adam so that he would examine them and name them. This part of the narrative may not seem all that apparent to the modern mind, because in our culture we have in many ways lost the significance and purpose of names. Ancient cultures often gave names to their offspring in order to confer a description of the one named, and this is probably reflected in the garden account since Adam was to name the animals *based upon his observation of their creaturely distinctions.* This is not only evident in Adam's naming of the animals, but is especially obvious when the man (*'iyś*) named his wife *'iśśăh*.[41] Adam examined a very long procession of marvelous but *unsuitable* creatures; and what a massive project this was! With each beast of the field, and bird of the air, came the reflection to Adam's mind: *"Not suitable!"* Each animal further illustrated for

---

[40] Some have argued that Genesis two speaks of a second phase of creation in an epochal process of theistic evolution and that this is evidenced by the expression regarding God's forming animals after the formation of man. This is argued in light of the fact that the birds of the air were made on the 5th day and the beasts of the Earth were mentioned before the creation of man, Genesis 1:20-26. However, the simple observation is typically missed, that God was performing these acts in the midst of a unique garden that was especially established for Adam, the specific location of which is clearly given in Genesis 2:8-14. The formation of each kind of animal to be presented to Adam in the garden does no violence to Genesis 1, but affirms the understanding that Genesis 2 offers more detail to the creation account. It makes sense that Adam was supernaturally given a sampling of *every* beast and bird so that he could witness God's creative power and wisdom, while being reminded of his own unique need for a helper.

[41] Once Adam does this in Gen. 2:23 and again in 3:20 after the judgment account. In each case, Adam gives his ordained helper a name that describes her created distinctions: She was woman (H. *'iśśăh*) formed from the man (H. *'iśś*). The addition of the feminine ending (*ah*) to the word for man (H. *'iś*) denotes that the woman was derived from the man, being very similar (as a member of humanity) and yet very distinct (as a woman).

Adam that his needs were unique and would require a special work of God. As magnificent as these creatures were, they in no way compared to what the Lord would create:

Genesis 2:21-22: 21 So the Lord God caused a deep sleep to fall upon the man, and he slept; then He took one of his ribs, and closed up the flesh at that place. 22 And the Lord God fashioned into a woman the rib which He had taken from the man, and brought her to the man.

Adam had been through a very long and guided discovery, *directed by the hand of God*,[42] and what a climactic ending! Here we see that the Lord brought, not another creature formed from the ground, but a precious helper who came from Adam's own flesh. This special mode of God's creation made it quite clear to Adam that the woman had an unparalleled relationship with the man. Note Calvin's observations on this important point:

"...it was not from any necessity on God's part that He borrowed from man the rib out of which he might form the woman; but he designed that they should be more closely joined together by this bond..."[43]

The woman was the fulfillment of God's promise to make a suitable *helper for Adam*. The very concept of the word *helper (ezer)*,[44] as it is correctly translated, speaks of one who comes to the aid or support of another. In the Old Testament Scriptures it is frequently used to

---

[42] God *brought* (H. *Bo'*) each animal to Adam, one by one, and He also *brought* the woman as well. The repetition of the verb here seems to indicate that the woman was at the end of a long line of creatures to be observed by Adam. She was last, but she was the greatest, without comparison.

[43] Calvin, Commentaries, p. 134-135.

[44] H. *ezer* – a helper, or assistant. One who is before another in a place of submission and openness - Psalm 119:168 I keep Thy precepts and Thy testimonies, For all my ways are *before* (H. *ezer*) Thee. "While this word designates assistance, it is more frequently used in a concrete sense to designate the assistant. (Cf. Gen 2:18, 20 where Eve is created to be Adam's help[er].)" Harris, Archer, Waltke, Theological Wordbook, p. 661.

speak of the Lord's *help* given to His people in time of need.[45] This same word, *ezer*, is frequently rendered in the LXX (Septuagint, the Greek translation of the Old Testament) as *boēthos* and is used on several occasions in the New Testament. These New Testament uses of *boēthos* (along with the verbal form *boētheō*) affirm this concept of help or support. For example, Paul was called upon *to help* those in Macedonia through a vision;[46] in the book of Revelation John beheld a vision in which the earth is called a *helper* to the woman;[47] and Luke supplies a very helpful use of the word to describe Paul's journey to Rome by sea, such that when a violent wind began to overpower their ship, protective measures were taken in order to preserve the ship from destruction:

Acts 27:17: ...they used supporting cables in undergirding the ship.

These supporting cables (*boētheias*) provided strength and help to the ship's overall structure and function. Illustratively, it is in this sense that the Lord had created and provided a helper for Adam. Her role was to provide help and support to her husband in order to uphold and strengthen him in his duties. Such a role as this does not denote inferiority, for the Lord is the believer's *help par excellence!*[48] As Adam's helper, the woman was created in order to fulfill an ordained role that was no less significant than his. Through the creation of the man *and the woman*, God's creative purposes could now be fulfilled in keeping with His eternal decree.

It is very clear from every aspect of the Genesis narrative that the man was created to provide leadership and the woman was given to

---

[45] Ex 15,2; 18,4; Dt 33,7.

[46] Acts 16:9.

[47] Revelation 21:16.

[48] G. *Boēthos* is used in both the Old Testament and the New Testament to speak of the Lord's help given to His people: Mt 15:25; Mk 9:22, 24; Ac 21:28; 2Co 6:2; Heb 2:18.

the man in order to *support him as his loving helper*. This will be further developed in the chapters to come, but for now it must be stated that the roles of the man and the woman were clearly established in the pre-fall union of the first man and woman.

THE FIRST INSTITUTION

In a courtship and marriage sequence that was practically instantaneous, the first man and woman were established in their marriage union at the very moment of their introduction. Their matchmaker was the holy and infinite God of the Universe who made them in His image and likeness for His good pleasure and glory. By God's sovereign ordination, the first man and first woman were truly "meant for each other" without any possibility of doubt. The woman, whom God made, was joined with the man, being very bone of his bones and flesh of his flesh, as we see in Adam's exuberant expression that follows:

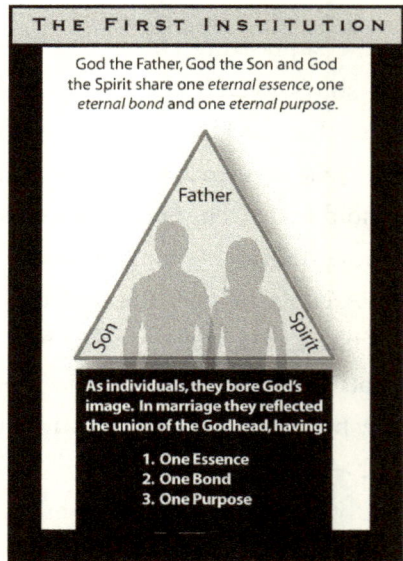

THE FIRST INSTITUTION

God the Father, God the Son and God the Spirit share one *eternal essence*, one *eternal bond* and one *eternal purpose*.

Father

Son

Spirit

As individuals, they bore God's image. In marriage they reflected the union of the Godhead, having:

1. One Essence
2. One Bond
3. One Purpose

Genesis 2:23-24

This is now bone of my bones,
And flesh of my flesh;
She shall be called Woman,
Because she was taken out of Man.
For this cause a man shall leave his father and his mother, and shall cleave to his wife; and they shall become one flesh.

There are many details offered in this text, however we will begin our study by considering one central truth about God's creation of marriage: the nature of their *unity*. Verse 24 informs us that the first husband, and the first wife, became *one flesh* in their marriage union.

The word employed here, denoting their oneness in the flesh, is the same Hebrew word used in the first great commandment in Deuteronomy 6:4 where God is described as one (*'eḥāḏ*) LORD.[49] Such *oneness* emphasizes not just singularity *per se*, but unity. The connotative relevance of this word, as it applies to the Godhead, is this: the Father, the Son, and the Spirit are perfectly unified having *one essence, one bond,* and *one purpose.*[50] By this unity we see that the man and the woman, who were created in *God's image*, were joined together in a manner which reflected *God's own unity*. As individuals they bore God's image and likeness, but also in their marriage union they reflected the unity of the Godhead, having *one essence, one bond,* and *one purpose.* They were still distinct persons and yet they became *one flesh by the ordination of God*; and the beauty and glory of this marriage union was derived from the beauty and glory of God Himself, for God the Father, God the Son, and God the Holy Spirit are perfectly unified; subsisting as three *distinct persons* while sharing the same *essence* of deity; having

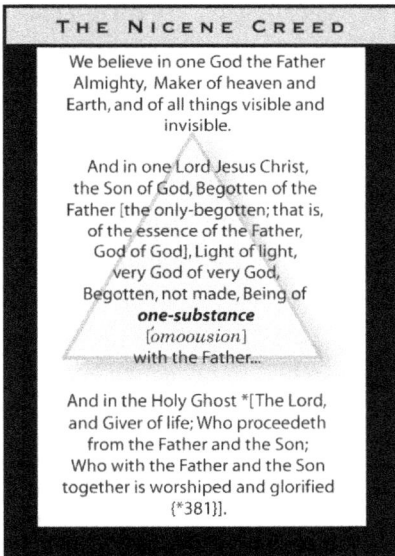

> **THE NICENE CREED**
>
> We believe in one God the Father Almighty, Maker of heaven and Earth, and of all things visible and invisible.
>
> And in one Lord Jesus Christ, the Son of God, Begotten of the Father [the only-begotten; that is, of the essence of the Father, God of God], Light of light, very God of very God, Begotten, not made, Being of **one-substance** [*omoousion*] with the Father...
>
> And in the Holy Ghost *[The Lord, and Giver of life; Who proceedeth from the Father and the Son; Who with the Father and the Son together is worshiped and glorified {*381}].

---

[49] H. *'ĕḥāḏ* – "one". This word can denote more than numerical one-ness, for it can speak of the unity of separate entities: Exod 26:6, 1; 36:13. Harris, Harris, Archer, Waltke, <u>Theological Wordbook</u>.

[50] John 10:30 "I and the Father are one." Such oneness expressed here may refer to all three realities of essence, bond and purpose (by implication): Because the Son was one essence with the father (John 8:58), having an eternal bond of love (John 17:24) this also meant that He could do no less than all that the Father willed (John 8:29). The great subject of the Trinity does exceed our discussion at this point. But, suffice it to say, that the reality of the Trinity's unity of essence, bond and purpose is in some wonderful way reflected in the union of Adam and his wife.

an eternal *bond* of relationship and having one shared *purpose* in keeping with the eternal counsel of God.

This point is crucial and will govern the thoughts of this chapter regarding the first institution of marriage. Marriage was created for a precious purpose: to reflect the image and glory of the Godhead through the unity and intimacy of the man and woman. It is a compelling thought to consider, that the marital union of Adam and his wife served the greater purpose of revealing God's own Triune nature. This observation is important for Christian couples of all generations, for it reminds us that all marital unions are to give glory to God in every aspect of life. With this principle in mind, let us consider the manner in which the first couple reflected the *essence, bond,* and *purpose* of the Godhead. By this careful examination we will learn about God's ultimate plan and purpose for all marriages:[51]

THE FIRST INSTITUTION
A UNIFIED ESSENCE:

By considering the nature of God's own unity, we can learn much about the unity of marriage. The glory and splendor of God's Tri-*unity* is revealed in the persons of the Father, Son, and Holy Spirit. In a wonderful and mysterious way, they each share the same essence (*or substance*)[52] of divinity in an undiminished, non-distinguishable

---

[51] Deuteronomy 6:4 "Hear, O Israel! The Lord is our God, the Lord is one!"

[52] The use of the term *essence* is in keeping with the early council of Nicea (325 AD). The sameness of the Father's, Son's and Spirit's substance (as God) was defended in accordance with Scripture. It was in this council that the *homo-ousian* (same substance) doctrine was defended by Athanasius against Arius. "The central point of the Nicene doctrine in the contest with Arianism is the identity of essence or the consubstantiality of the Son with the Father, and is expressed in this article of the (original) Nicene Creed: '[We believe] in one Lord Jesus Christ, the Son of God; who is begotten the only-begotten of the Father; that is, of the essence of the Father, God of God, and Light of Light, very God of very God, begotten, not made, being of one substance with the Father.'" Schaff, P., & Schaff, D. S., History of the Christian Church. Volume 3, Chapter IX, article 127 (Oak Harbor, WA: Logos Research Systems, Inc., 1997).

manner, for they are each *very God*.[53] This affirmation of the *co-equality* of all three members of the Trinity is a fundamental tenant of Christianity: the Father, Son, and Spirit are *absolutely equal in the essence of deity*. This crucial doctrine of *essential unity* has its parallel in the first man and woman who, together, were created *in God's image:* both were distinct *persons* and yet they were *essentially unified* (very human) as one flesh. *Therefore the woman shared the same fundamental essence (substance) of human nature as did the man such that Adam declared "This is now bone of my bones, and flesh of my flesh; She shall be called Woman, because she was taken out of Man."* Clearly, the man was *fully human* and the woman was *fully human* and, as such, they were drawn together as *one flesh* as husband and wife. This important truth must be kept at the forefront of our studies, especially when we embark on the discussions of role distinctions. It is a fundamental truth of Scripture that is often ignored in our modern society, that role distinctions between men and women do not, and cannot, diminish the *essential* equality of men and women. As members of the human race, *both are equal in value in the sight of God.*

We see this same truth affirmed within the New Covenant of Christ since both the man and the woman are deemed as members of the kingdom of Christ, and are of equal valuation before God as the *heirs of life.* This is why Peter reminded men that as they exercise leadership within their own homes, they must remember that marital role distinctions do not nullify our essential unity before God, therefore the woman is a *"fellow heir of the grace of life."*[54] But this is not the end of our discussion of the marriage union, for though there is an essential unity among men and women, this does not eliminate their separate personages, just as God's essential unity does not

---

[53] John 1:1-3, 1 Cor. 2:10-11.

[54] 1 Peter 3:7.

nullify the distinct persons of the Father, the Son, and the Holy Spirit.

THE FIRST INSTITUTION
A UNIFIED BOND:

The bond (or relationship) of the first man and woman was yet another manifestation of the divine image of God, who is one substance yet, as a Tri-*unity*, He subsists as three persons in an eternal, holy, and immutable relationship. Therefore there were no antecedent relationships or beings who existed before God, for the Lord alone is eternal. And when we consider the nature of this Trinitarian relationship, we must also admit that there is nothing lacking within the Godhead. Putting it in layman's terms: God has never suffered from boredom, loneliness, or any form of disunity![55] As the Father, Son, and Spirit abide together in their perpetual, relational unity, they subsist with absolute satisfaction being in need of nothing. This principle has been clearly pointed out in Jonathan Edwards own works:

> "...God is absolutely independent of us... we have nothing of our own, no stock from whence we can give to God; and that no part of His happiness originates from man."[56]

The Trinity's relational satisfaction and unity is indeed beautiful, mysterious, and truly awesome! The unity and relational bond within the Godhead is yet another dimension of God's image which was to be displayed through Adam and his wife. Throughout the Scriptures we see evidences of God's relational bond. The worthiness of this

---

[55] In our book of beginnings when we read that "In the beginning, God..." Before there were any angels, the glorious heavens, the earth or any created thing, God was thoroughly satisfied, in need of nothing.

[56] Jonathan Edwards, The Works of Jonathan Edwards vol. 1 (Hendrickson Publishers, Peabody, Massachusetts) p. 102.

subject could easily demand a book by itself,[57] however for the sake of brevity we will consider what the Apostle John wrote concerning the intimate and eternal communion between the Son and the Father. In the first chapter of his gospel, the Apostle John reveals a vastly beautiful and mysterious portrait of this eternal relationship:

John 1:1-3: 1 In the beginning was the Word, and the Word was **with God**, and the Word was God. 2 He was in the beginning **with God**.

John tells us (twice) that the eternal Son (the Word) *was with God the Father.* It is interesting to note that John uses the preposition *pros* rather than *para* or *meta*. These latter prepositions tend to represent a more general form of association, however context ultimately determines the nature of the relationship. But *pros* normally means *towards*, which represents a more intensive notion of communion.[58] For example, you could be sitting *with* or *beside* someone at a restaurant and perhaps never talk to them, especially if your back is to them, however, in an intimate dinner with a loved one you are positioned *towards them*, even face to face in private discourse. This is the picture that John gives us. The Son of God was not casually *with* the Father, but He was intimately *towards* the Father, residing in His bosom[59] in a personal and eternal love relationship.[60] Did the Father, Son, and Holy Spirit need to create us out of boredom or loneliness? May it never be supposed! God made us out of His own

---

[57] All Nations Under God, 2006 (The Armoury Ministries Publishing).

[58] "And the Word was face to face with God (*pros ton theon*). The meaning is that the Word existed in the closest possible fellowship with the father, and that he took supreme delight in this communion." William Hendriksen, New Testament Commentary, The Gospel of John (Baker Book House, Grand Rapids, Michigan), p. 70.

[59] John 1:18 No man has seen God at any time; the only begotten God, who is in the bosom of the Father, He has explained Him.

[60] John 17:24 "Father, I desire that they also, whom Thou hast given Me, be with Me where I am, in order that they may behold My glory, which Thou hast given Me; for Thou didst love Me before the foundation of the world."

good pleasure, not out of personal *need*.[61] What we can glean from the relational bond between the Father, Son, and Spirit is very important: as husband and wife, Adam and the woman were to reflect the glory of God's image through a relationship that expressed a similar satisfaction and intimacy. As a couple, *they were relationally sufficient.* As they were joined together in the inseparable bond of marriage, *in the Lord*, they had no other relational needs and therefore suffered no deficiencies. There was just *one man, one woman*, and *the Lord who joined them together*; it was all *very good*.[62]

Genesis 2:24 For this cause a man shall leave his father and his mother, and shall cleave to his wife; and they shall become one flesh.

This text reminds us of at least two fundamental principles regarding the *relationship* of marriage:

- **The Primacy of the Marriage Union:** The fundamental component of the family, by God's design, is the marriage union comprised of one man and one woman. This marriage relationship is of principal importance, even before the inclusion of children (Gen. 1:28). God has designed the marriage union to be a sufficient one such that, in Christ, a husband and wife should desire to leave their families and cleave to one another. This point should not be misused so as to conclude that married couples can live in isolation, or that they should treat their young as unimportant. This is certainly not the point at all. But the crucial principle that should emerge in our thinking is this: a man and his wife are sufficient as a married couple such that the adequacy of their union (in the Lord) should never be questioned. If they are unable to reproduce children, they are not *less married*. Neither will a couple experience a better marriage through the inclusion of children *per se*. God's ordained institution of marriage constitutes a union

---

[61] Eph. 1:5.

[62] Genesis 1:31

between one man and one woman, in the Lord, who have a loving relationship with one another.

- **The Purpose of Procreation:** When a marriage is blessed with children, the goal should not be to raise an assembly of home-bound children who live for the pleasure of their parents. Rather, the sons of men are called to leave their homes in order to establish new and independent marriage unions that will serve and worship the Creator. These new unions must *leave and cleave* in order to establish the primacy of God's first institution.

The unity of essence and bond, in the marriage union, is a reflection of the unity of God Who is *one essence,* and is eternally satisfied in the relational bond between the Father, Son, and Spirit. As patterned after God's own image, the marriage union itself is an intimate bond between one man and one woman who have been joined together in the unity of their *one essence* (one flesh). Therefore this relationship has a primacy over children, over one's parents or in-laws, and/or any other relationship within creation. Of course, this truth does not devalue those relations which reside outside of the scope of marriage, but it does herald the primacy of this unique institution. Additionally, marriage is a relational union that reminds us that we are not homosexual by God's design, nor are we animals in nature or practice. To the extent that men and women conduct themselves as such only demonstrates a depraved and willful departure from God's created design and holy will.[63] A married man and woman should remember that their ultimate sufficiency, as a family, is found in God who brought them together, and not in any other person or thing within creation.

---

[63] Romans 1:18-32

THE FIRST INSTITUTION
A UNIFIED PURPOSE:

Another way in which marriage reflects God's glory is found in the *unity of purpose* that is established in such a union. As individuals, and as a couple, Adam and his wife bore the image of God in every aspect of their being, to include a unity of purpose as husband and wife. Thus, when we speak of such unity of purpose, we refer to the domain of responsibilities and duties that the first couple possessed through the revealed will of God. Here again, we see that the very concept of a *unity of purpose* is an imitation of the Godhead; for the Father, the Son, and the Holy Spirit work with immutable unity to a common end:

> **Romans 11:36** For from Him and through Him and to Him are all things. To Him be the glory forever. Amen.

The reader should remember that Romans 11:36 reveals, not just the will of the Father, but the will of the Son and of the Spirit. All that has come into being has come from God to the end that God would receive the glory forever, or as Jonathan Edwards has summarized:

> "What God says in His word, naturally leads us to suppose, that the way in which He makes Himself His end in His work or works, which He does for His own sake, is in making His glory His end."[64]

The Father, Son, and Holy Spirit each perform great works in order to accomplish one clear end: the glory of the Godhead. This is a beautiful portrait of God's unified desire and purpose. Like God Himself, the man and the wife were to subsist in total harmony and unity. And together, they had but one purpose within their marriage

---

[64] Edwards, <u>Works</u>, Vol. 1, Chapter 2, Section III. p.1.

union: to serve the Lord with joy and to glorify Him in all things.[65] They were given the abundance of a beautiful earth that was adorned with the grandeur of the vast heavens, and they *were* commanded to obey God in view of His creation ordinances:

> **Genesis 1:28-29:** 28 And God blessed them; and God said to them, "Be fruitful and multiply, and fill the earth, and subdue it; and rule over the fish of the sea and over the birds of the sky, and over every living thing that moves on the earth." 29 Then God said, "Behold, I have given you every plant yielding seed that is on the surface of all the earth, and every tree which has fruit yielding seed; it shall be food for you;"

The first family had a unity of purpose established by the ordained will of God. They were to do the following:

- To be fruitful and multiply.

- To fill the earth.

- To subdue the earth.

- To rule over the animal kingdom.

- To enjoy the fruit of all of the plants and trees in all of the earth (with the exception of the tree of the knowledge of good and evil, Gen. 2:17).

- They were to enjoy each other in their marital bond.

- In all these things, they were to worship the Lord and enjoy Him in every God-ordained way.

---

[65] Gen. 1:31, 2:18.

Thus, the man and the woman were *unified* because of God's harmonious will. However, this unity of purpose does not mean that there were no distinctions in their calling before God. Their duties were clearly not the same as we see that their obedience to God's commands were to be accomplished in light of their distinct roles (Gen. 2). This is perhaps most apparent, and clearly illustrated, in light of the command of procreation. Both were commanded to fulfill this command (unity of purpose), but who could dispute the distinctions of their roles in accomplishing such a purpose of God? The woman was endowed with an ability to carry the gift of a child in her womb, not the man. The woman was also endowed to provide the infant's earliest meals through her own breast milk, not the man. Such realities necessitate that the woman was equipped to be the bearer and nurturer of the fruit from her womb, while the man was given the task of harvesting the food from the Garden.

THE FIRST INSTITUTION
UNITY, AND THE DISTINCTION OF ROLES:

Our modern culture, which advocates the notion of absolute *equality* between men and women, aggressively derides this very simple principle which is so clearly illustrated in the created order. Many often complain that a distinction of calling and roles between men and women leads to the repression and cruel subjugation of women; however such thinking demonstrates the ignorance of God's own nature and character. Contrary to the popular opinion of our day, the man and the woman's distinct roles are yet another manifestation of the very image and glory of God. For example, the Father, the Son, and the Holy Spirit each labor in order to accomplish a unified purpose, yet they do so in very distinct ways. This truth is wonderfully revealed to us in Ephesians chapter 1 where the Apostle Paul gives a very clear explanation of how the Trinity moved in order to procure the redemption of Christ's bride. In what is a Trinitarian doxology, the Apostle explains to us just how the bride of Christ was secured and protected by the Father, the Son, and the Holy Spirit. Each member of the Trinity did their part, however, they accomplished the miracle of redemption through very distinct roles:

- **The Father's Election [Ephesians 1:3-5]:** In this first section of Ephesians chapter 1 Paul explains to us that God the Father blessed His people through the means of choosing them from before the foundation of the world. He therefore predestined us on no other grounds but the kind intention of His will alone. The purpose of this choice of His is that we should be to the praise of the glory of His grace.

- **The Son's Submission to the Father's Will [Ephesians 1:6-12]:** Next we see that the Father's will was to be secured by a unique purchase, afforded by the blood of His Beloved One, Jesus Christ. Paul says that "...in Him we have redemption[66] through His blood, the forgiveness of our trespasses, according to the riches of His grace..." (Eph. 1:7). The precious truth unveils the reality that Christ's shed blood purchased the forgiveness of those whom the Father chose before the foundation of the world. His sacrifice for us was an act of perfect obedience and submission to the Father's will (John 6:38-40).

- **The Spirit was Sent by the Will of the Father and of the Son [Ephesians 1:13-14]:** Paul concludes this Trinitarian doxology by describing the Spirit's ministry of securing and protecting those for whom Christ died. Through the gifts of His grace and faith (Ephesians 2:8), the believer is "sealed in Him with the Holy Spirit of promise who is given as a pledge of our inheritance, with a view to the redemption of God's own possession..." (Ephesians 1:13-14). Those whom the Father chose before the foundation of the world were lovingly redeemed through the shed blood of Jesus Christ and

---

[66] G. *apolytrōsis* – The word employed here denotes a ransom that is made in order to purchase the freedom of one who is considered a slave. This is more fully expanded in Ephesians chapter 2 when Paul more fully explains the nature of our slavery, being that we were dead in our trespasses and sins (Ephesians 2:1-3).

secured through the Spirit whom He sent. The purpose of God is clearly unified, accomplished through the distinctive roles of the Father, Son and Spirit. Our redemption has been established by the Father's loving election (to the praise of the glory of His grace[67]), through the Son's unspeakable sacrifice (to the praise of His glory[68]), and by the Spirit's sealing and pledge (to the praise of His glory[69]).

Additionally, creation itself shows us the unified purpose and distinctive roles of the Godhead:

> **Genesis 1:1-2:** 1 In the beginning God created the heavens and the earth. 2 And the earth was formless and void, and darkness was over the surface of the deep; and the Spirit of God was moving over the surface of the waters.

All creation had its beginnings by the will of the Father (Ps. 33:6), wrought by means of the Son (John 1:3, Col. 1:16) and mediated by the abiding presence of the Spirit (Gen. 1:2, Psalm 104:30). To say that the individual members of the Trinity had distinct roles in the act of creation in no way demotes them as persons. God is infinitely unified, but, each member of the Trinity operates in a way that bears distinctions. When Jesus said "My food is to do the will of Him who sent me, and to accomplish His work," He was not making a statement of personal inferiority to the Father. The Son submits to the Father's will, but recognizing such practical distinctions within the Godhead does not demote its members in the least bit: such an assumption would be *blasphemy.* In view of this, it is a gross error to think that the distinction of roles in marriage devalues either the man or the woman. By this we see that the image of God is reflected in the institution of the family. The marriage union has a unity of

---

[67] Eph. 1:6.

[68] Eph. 1:12.

[69] Eph. 1:14. See also Eph. 2:7 concerning the *purpose* of God in our redemption.

purpose in light of the will of God, but each member of that union labors according to the specific calling of God. To attempt to sustain a marriage union apart from God's ordained standard is to leave the Word of God open to the attacks of its opponents. The Apostle Paul very clearly reminds us that those who forsake the practical distinctions of the man and woman in marriage are committing the error of *blaspheming* God's Word:

> **Titus 2:4-5:** 4 ...young women [are to]... love their husbands, to love their children, 5 to be sensible, pure, workers at home, kind, being subject to their own husbands, that the word of God may not be dishonored.

The Apostolic language here is quite strong, reminding us that the church's Gospel testimony is not only revealed through what it *says*, but through what it *does*. What God created in the marriage union is special and wonderful and should not be trifled with. Cultural pressures in this world will, of course, continue to attack the essential/relational and practical unity of marriage, but the family of God must resist those pressures by going back to the standard of God's Word concerning marriage. Much is at stake in the Gospel testimony of the family; to deride God's created order is to give opportunity for the Word of God to be blasphemed: *literally.* [70]

THE FIRST INSTITUTION
A PORTRAIT OF GOD'S LOVE FOR HIS PEOPLE:

Having looked at the unity of *essence, bond, and purpose* in marriage, we will conclude this discussion by considering the important subject of *love*. Adam and his wife were created with a God-glorifying unity *so that* they could enjoy a loving intimacy with the Lord, and with one another. Therefore, discussions concerning marriage's *essence*, *bond*, and *purpose* do not exclude this subject of love, rather they

---

[70] Dishonored – Gr. *blasphemetai* – Literally, to blaspheme.

establish an important foundation for it. Because of this it should be observed that the intimate love that Adam and his wife were to enjoy was yet another reflection of God's own gory, for the love and affection that He has for His people is also clearly illustrated through the institution of marriage:

- **Jeremiah 31:32** [Of Israel] " ...I was a husband to them," declares the LORD.

- **Isaiah 61:10** I will rejoice greatly in the Lord, My soul will exult in my God; For He has clothed me with garments of salvation, He has wrapped me with a robe of righteousness, as a bridegroom decks himself with a garland, And as a bride adorns herself with her jewels.

- **Hosea 2:19-20:** 19 "I will betroth you to Me forever; Yes, I will betroth you to Me in righteousness and in justice, In lovingkindness and in compassion, 20 And I will betroth you to Me in faithfulness. Then you will know the Lord.

These Scriptures, among others,[71] show us that marriage is a *type* of the very relationship that the Lord has with His chosen people. This is the very truth that is clearly presented by the Apostle Paul in his letter to the Ephesians:

Ephesians 5:22-33: 22 Wives, be subject to your own husbands, as to the Lord. 23 For the husband is the head of the wife, as Christ also is the head of the church, He Himself being the Savior of the body. 24 But as the church is subject to Christ, so also the wives ought to be to their husbands in everything. 25 Husbands, love your wives, just as Christ also

---

[71] The entire book of Hosea is designed to show the unfailing love of God for His people despite their sin as expressed in chapter 3 and verse 1: Hosea 3:1 Then the Lord said to me, "Go again, love a woman who is loved by her husband, yet an adulteress, even as the Lord loves the sons of Israel, though they turn to other gods and love raisin cakes."

loved the church and gave Himself up for her; 26 that He might sanctify her, having cleansed her by the washing of water with the word, 27 that He might present to Himself the church in all her glory, having no spot or wrinkle or any such thing; but that she should be holy and blameless. 28 So husbands ought also to love their own wives as their own bodies. He who loves his own wife loves himself; 29 for no one ever hated his own flesh, but nourishes and cherishes it, just as Christ also does the church, 30 because we are members of His body. 31 For this cause a man shall leave his father and mother, and shall cleave to his wife; and the two shall become one flesh. 32 This mystery is great; but I am speaking with reference to Christ and the church. 33 Nevertheless let each individual among you also love his own wife even as himself; and let the wife see to it that she respect her husband.

Perhaps the most romantic truth in the entire Bible is this: Christ *loved the church and gave Himself up for her* out of the great bounty of His love for the Father and for His bride. Unlike the first Adam, who loved his bride in unrighteousness and ate the forbidden fruit, Christ loved His bride in perfect righteousness, and gave His life as a ransom for her so that in glory she will be presented to Him in the union of marriage, having no spot or wrinkle:

Revelation 19:7-9: 7 Let us rejoice and be glad and give the glory to Him, for the marriage of the Lamb has come and His bride has made herself ready. 8 And it was given to her to clothe herself in fine linen, bright and clean; for the fine linen is the righteous acts of the saints. 9 And he *said to me, "Write, 'Blessed are those who are invited to the marriage supper of the Lamb.'" And he *said to me, "These are true words of God."

Revelation 21:2, 9: 2 And I saw the holy city, new Jerusalem, coming down out of heaven from God, made ready as a bride adorned for her husband...9 And one of the seven angels who had the seven bowls full of the seven last plagues, came and spoke with me, saying, "Come here, I shall show you the bride, the wife of the Lamb."

The marriage of the Lamb and His bride (the redeemed of God) will be consummated in the glory of heaven, and this glorious love that God has for His redeemed in Christ will show forth the glory of God's grace, forever without end. This truth aids us in understanding the fact that a godly marriage is itself a gospel testimony to this lost world.

At its best, marriage is an example of the unity of God, His Triune nature and work, and His magnificent love. At its worst, it is a breeding-ground for blasphemy.[72]

---

[72] Titus 2:5 [younger women are to be]... sensible, pure, workers at home, kind, being subject to their own husbands, *that the word of God may not be dishonored.*

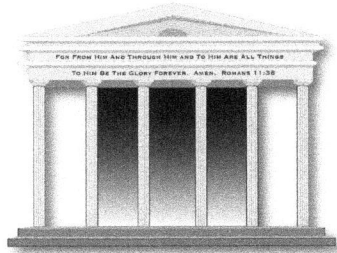

THE FIRST INSTITUTION

For From Him And Through Him and To Him Are All Things
To Him Be The Glory Forever. Amen. Romans 11:36

CHAPTER 2

THE SHAME OF

ADAM'S SIN

What took place in the Garden of Eden was beautiful, miraculous, and spectacular. All that God made was *very good* because it reflected His wisdom, power, goodness, and glory. Yet the story of Creation does not end here, rather it continues with the sad presentation of a most gruesome battle. The fact that this beautiful scene in the garden was quickly polluted by the forces of evil is yet another dark reminder that, in this vast universe of ours, planet earth is at the *dead center* of a cosmic war onto which all of the angels, elect and fallen, have their eyes locked. And with all of the displaced mass of stars and planets in the heavens, the affairs that take place upon this infinitesimally small ball of dust, that we call earth, is the *only important stage* whereby the forces of evil deliver their warfare. This is clearly evidenced when we simply turn the pages of Genesis from chapter 2 to 3. It is here that we see the Devil's schemes played out before our very eyes. In this significant chapter we see that Satan's attack against the first family was a kind of preview of the many ploys that would be launched against families of all generations. In any generation, marriages that fail do so by losing sight of the following two foundations of marriage.

- *First, there is the centrality of God in all things. No matter how complex a marriage may ever become, the worship of God must be the husband's and wife's daily priority and passion.*

- *Second, there must be a clear understanding of the God-ordained roles of both spouses as we have already depicted in the previous sections. The man is called to lead and the woman is called to be a helper to her husband. As in the particular case of Adam, his calling was uniquely oriented towards the protection of the garden through the prohibitive commandment, while he was to labor in the rest of the garden with great freedom. His calling was to lead and serve; her calling was to be a submissive helpmeet to him.*

Such were the very means of their worship to God, and it seems that as soon as these standards were instituted by the Lord they were polluted through the first *deception* and *transgression* as recorded in Genesis 3. The lessons of this difficult chapter will be foundational to the rest of this book, but for now, we begin our look at the core problems introduced into the first marriage.

THE FIRST DECEPTION AND TRANSGRESSION

Genesis chapter 3 begins with a very cunning, intelligent, and crafty being whose hatred for God is clearly evidenced through his hostile assault on God's crowning achievement in all of creation – the first institution of marriage. It is in Genesis 3 that we find the garden invaded by that hostile enemy of God who is identified as the serpent (*ophis*). A lengthy discussion could be secured here regarding the nature of Satan's appearance as a serpent, but this would detract us from the focus of our study on the family. It is sufficient to say that the serpent here is clearly Satan by the analogy of faith in the Biblical record:

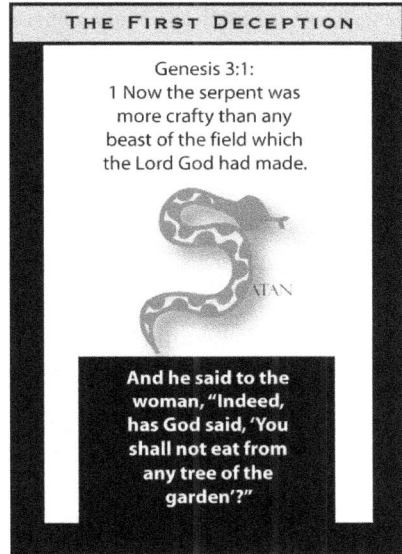

THE FIRST DECEPTION

Genesis 3:1:
1 Now the serpent was more crafty than any beast of the field which the Lord God had made.

And he said to the woman, "Indeed, has God said, 'You shall not eat from any tree of the garden'?"

- **Genesis 3:1** Now the serpent[73] was more crafty than any beast of the field which the Lord God had made.

---

[73] The LXX employs the Greek word *ophis* which is identical to the word employed in Rev. 12:9.

- **Revelation 12:9** And the great dragon was thrown down, the serpent of old who is called the devil and Satan, who deceives the whole world;

What takes place in Genesis chapters 1-3 is vast. The depth of the implications of these recorded events exceeds the scope of this study since we are focused on the topic of the family, therefore, not every detail can be meticulously covered; however, we will examine the key components of this important section. Let us consider the stage, and the participants of this massive tragedy that is about to take place:

- **Satan:** The serpent is given but one description in the Genesis narrative: "...the serpent was more crafty than any beast of the field." The word translated as *crafty* denotes one who is sound minded, prudent, and discerning. It is normally used of one who is endowed with wisdom from the Word of God as in the case of the qualified elder who is "sensible" (Titus 1:8).[74] Satan's craftiness is grounded in the very fact that he is very knowledgeable of God's Word and he has an intellect that enables him to abuse and malign that Word in a manner that can make a lie look like absolute truth.[75] As the most endowed defender of God's glory, Lucifer became filled with pride concerning his power, splendor, and wisdom (Ezek. 28:13-17); and in his condemnation he became the lowest of God's creations, being now the most skilled opponent of God: **Ezekiel 28:17** "Your heart was lifted up because of your beauty; You corrupted your wisdom by reason of your splendor. I cast you to the ground; I put you before kings, That they may see you." Through his fall, Satan's intellectual power did not vanish; rather it was corrupted by sin and has therefore been directed at the vain and maniacal effort of opposing the plan and program of God. Satan knows of the power and omniscience of God and yet, in his angelic insanity, he foolishly opposes the perfect plans of the

---

[74] LXX (*phonimotatos > phronimos*, sound or sober-minded).

[75] 2 Corinthians 11:14 And no wonder, for even Satan disguises himself as an angel of light.

immutable God. It should be clear that Satan opposes that which is most valuable according to the will of God such that he tried to tempt the incarnate Christ at the beginning of His ministry, and he deceived the woman in his frontal attack against the first family at their beginning.

- **The First Family:** Adam and his wife lived in the Garden of Eden; an unimaginably beautiful place, the greatest splendor of which was the very presence of God Himself. The garden was fully populated with a perpetual supply of splendor, delicious food, and the gloriously created animals that had been completely surveyed and named by Adam. Their orders were, principally, to enjoy the abundance of the garden, freely, as Adam labored by harvesting its abundance. They were to enjoy their relationship with one another as an act of worship to God. Thus, they were to serve God according to their respective callings in life: Adam in his servitude and leadership and his wife in her ministry of helps to him. What a portrait of God's goodness and grace. There was not one ounce of inadequacy in their life, no health issues, no deprivations…NO SIN. Adam had one prohibitive command that had been laid to his charge: to guard that one tree of the knowledge of good and evil. Could life be any more abundant and simple than this?

- **The Garden:** This Garden in Eden represented a small plot of land relative to the scale and size of the whole earth (Gen. 2:10-14). Relative to the solar system, our galaxy, and the vast Universe overall, it was less than microscopic, and yet in the wisdom of God's decree, a glorious plan of redemption was unfolding whereby the second person of the Triune God was at its center. Within this garden scene the greatest tragedy of the entire cosmos was about to occur and would lead to a climactic display of God's wisdom and glory, culminating in the heavenly union between the slain Lamb of God and His redeemed bride.[76] What will take place there in that

---

[76] Revelation 13:8 And all that dwell upon the earth shall worship him, whose names are not written in the book of life of the *Lamb slain from the foundation of the world.* [Italics mine].

minute Garden will affect every creature, star, planet, and element within the entire Universe.[77]

As we step through the events of the first deception, we must take our time and learn about the tactics of Satan; after all, the Apostle Paul says that we "are not ignorant of his [Satan's] schemes."[78] Now it is quite common to begin this discussion, concerning Satan's first deception, by examining *what Satan says*, but this would cause us to miss a more fundamental observation. Therefore, let us first examine *what it is that the serpent does:*

Gen. 3:1a ...he said to the woman...

Our first crucial observation here is to note *to whom* the serpent speaks. Why is this important? Consider for a moment our careful examination of the first couple's ordained responsibilities. It was Adam, not the woman, who was entrusted with the responsibilities of the ministry of the Word and the ministry of the garden. As his helper the woman was to be an aid to her husband but she could not rightfully be his substitute for such a ministry and calling. Thus, Satan's first deception is exposed, not by *what* he said, *but to whom he said it*. The serpent bypassed the man and went immediately to the woman[79] with his well-crafted question:

Gen. 3:1b Indeed, has God said, "You shall not eat from any tree of the garden?"

---

[77] 2 Peter 3:7 But the present heavens and earth by His word are being reserved for fire, kept for the day of judgment and destruction of ungodly men.

[78] 2 Cor. 2:11.

[79] Whitefield clearly summarizes the serpent's tactics when he says: "'And he said unto the woman.' Here is an instance of his subtlety. He says unto the woman, the weaker vessel, and when she was alone from her husband, and therefore was more liable to be overcome..." Whitfield, The Seed of the Woman.

Satan began with a crafty and well-tooled question. Like a deceptive lawyer in a courtroom, Satan presented the woman with a false dilemma, that is, he raised a question which required more than a simple yes or no. Satan said, *indeed,* or perhaps more specifically: *"In reality, has God said,"* but then offered a modified quotation that emphasized, not their liberty in the garden, but their restriction.[80] It is important to observe that Satan was not merely asking the woman for a yes or no answer, nor was he calling for a simple recitation of God's command, instead he was luring her into the process of making *an interpretation of God's Word and His motives.*[81] By offering his own twisted version of the Lord's meaning, Satan supplied a connotation of negativity in order to influence the woman, and through this deception she stepped out on her own in order to engage in a confrontation that was not hers. Through her severe mishandling of God's Word, she and the serpent both drew closer to the very tree that Adam *alone* was commanded to protect:

Genesis 3:2-4: 2 And the woman said to the serpent, "From the fruit of the trees of the garden we may eat; 3 but from the fruit of the tree which is in the middle of the garden, God has said, 'You shall not eat from it or touch it, lest you die.'" 4 And the serpent said to the woman, "You surely shall not die!"

It is important to note that the woman inserted a strange element of optimism in her response, and this can be easily missed through a

---

[80] Morris, Genesis Record, p. 110.

[81] "The Hebrew may, indeed, bear the meaning, 'hath God said, ye shall not eat of *every* tree?' but from the context, and especially the conjunction, it is obvious that the meaning is, 'ye shall not eat of *any* tree." The serpent calls God by the name of *Elohim* alone, and the woman does the same. In this more general and indefinite name the personality of the living God is obscured. To attain his end, the tempter felt it necessary to change the living personal God into a merely general *numen divinum,* and to exaggerate the prohibition, in the hope of exciting in the woman's mind partly distrust of God Himself, and partly a doubt as to the truth of His word." C.F. Keil and F. Delitzsch, Commentary on the Old Testament (William B. Eerdmans Publishing Company, Grand Rapids Michigan, 1991), p. 94.

casual reading of the text. God promised that death would *surely* occur in the event that they would eat the fruit of the forbidden tree. In this command the translators supplied the word *surely* in order to convey the Hebraic construction found in Genesis 2:17. What the woman did to that expression, regarding the certainty of death, is as follows: she modified the verbal form of the words - *surely die* - while adding an element of uncertainty. Here is a comparison of God's command to that of the woman's and serpent's versions:

ANATOMY OF THE FIRST DECEPTION		
God's Command *(Gen 2:17)*	"...you *shall surely die*..." (*môṯ tamôṯ*)	*Certain* *Death*
Woman's Version *(Gen. 3:3)*	"...lest you die..." (*pen_ṯᵉmuṯûn*)	*Possible* *Death*
Satan's Version *(Gen. 3:4)*	"...you *surely shall <u>not</u> die*..." (*l'ŏ môṯ tamôṯ*[82])	*Impossibility* *Of Death*

God had said "*...you shall surely die...*" (*môṯ tamôṯ*[83]) – an indicative statement that leaves us with no uncertainty. However the woman's response ("*...lest you die...*" - *pen*[84]_*ṯᵉmuṯûn*[85]) shows that she was just

---

[82] Qal infinitive absolute with the addition of the *objective* negative particle. Satan correctly quotes God's command (unlike the woman), but then he negates it with the objective negative particle denoting a *certain* denial, thus the original idea of a certain (indicative) future, intense death is *objectively* denied by Satan.

[83] *Qal infinitive absolute*: The infinitive normally increases the sense of certainty of outcome, i.e., you will *most surely* die. Such an infinitive normally "emphasizes not the meaning denoted by the verb's root but the force of the verb in context. When the verb makes an assertion, whatever its aspect, the notion of certainty is reinforced by the infinitive." Bruce K. Waltke, M. O'Connor, An Introduction to Biblical Hebrew Syntax (Eisenbrauns, Winona Lake, Indiana, 1990), p. 584.

[84] Here we have the Hebrew telic particle *p̄en* translated as *lest* in Gen. 3:3 and *might* in Gen. 3:22 "Then the Lord God said, 'Behold, the man has become like one of Us, knowing good and evil; and now, he *might* stretch out his hand, and *take* [*p̄en-yiślaḵ*] also from the tree of life, and eat, and live forever'" (NASB 1995 Updated, italics mine). The concept in both texts corresponds to the idea of a *possible future event*, rather than a certainty: "lest, so that not, i.e., a marker of a negative purpose, implying some apprehension or worry of a possible future event."

a few steps away from an outright denial of the penal consequences of defying God's commandment, for she adjusted the sense of certainty found in God's original instruction. This shift from certainty was then advanced further by Satan's outright denial of God's original command to Adam. John Calvin, in his commentary on the book of Genesis, is very helpful on this point:

> "...In proclaiming the punishment, she begins to give way, by inserting the adverb 'perhaps' when God has certainly pronounced, 'Ye shall die the death.' For although with the Hebrews *pen* does not always imply doubt, yet, since it is generally taken in this sense, I willingly embrace the opinion that the woman was beginning to waver. Certainly, she had not death so immediately before her eyes, should she become disobedient to God, as she ought to have had. She clearly proves that her perception of the true danger of death was distant and cold."[86]

How true it is that the transition from truth to heresy often comes in the form of incremental change. Like the little leaven that leavens the whole lump,[87] the woman's incremental error gave way to the satanic upheaval of truth. What is interesting here is that Satan, unlike the woman, correctly repeated the emphatic nature of God's command, but with that insidious denial included [surely shall *not*]. This emphatic aspect of God's warning is conveyed by the word *surely* and is contained in Satan's and God's statement, but is missing from the woman's statement *via* her deceived accommodation, and by this adjustment she accommodated Satan by softening the divine threat of judgment. In his sermon *The Seed of the Woman and the Seed of*

J. Swanson, <u>Dictionary of Biblical Languages with Semantic Domains : Hebrew Old Testament</u>, (Electronic Edition, Oak Harbor: Logos Research Systems, Inc.), (HGK7153).

[85] The Qal infinitive absolute is reduced to a simple infinitive and combined with the use of the telec particle (normally used to speak of possible future events): In total, this is not *what God said*.

[86] Calvin, <u>Commentaries</u>, Vol. I. p. 149.

[87] Matthew 16:6 And Jesus said to them, "Watch out and beware of the leaven of the Pharisees and Sadducees."

the Serpent, George Whitefield unfolds, with clarity, the events that led to the first deception:

"The former part of the answer was good, 'We may eat of the fruit of the trees of the garden, God has not forbid us eating of every tree of the garden. No; we may eat of the fruit of the trees in the garden (and, it should seem, even of the tree of life, which was as a sacrament to man in the state of innocence) there is only one tree in the midst of the garden, of which God hath said, ye shall not eat of it, neither shall ye touch it, lest ye die.' Here she begins to warp, and sin begins to conceive in her heart. Already she has contracted some of the serpent's poison, by talking with him, which she ought not to have done at all. For she might easily suppose, that it could be no good being that could put such a question unto her, and insinuate such dishonorable thoughts of God. She should therefore have fled from him, and not stood to have parleyed with him at all. Immediately the ill effects of it appear, she begins to soften the divine threatening. God had said, 'the day thou eatest thereof, thou shalt surely die;' or, dying thou shalt die. But Eve says, 'Ye shall not eat of it, neither shall ye touch it, lest ye die.' We may be assured we are fallen into, and

THE FIRST DECEPTION

Genesis 3:1-6

...ye surely shall not die.

lest ye die...

You shall surely die...

Genesis 3:3:
"...of the fruit of the tree which is in the midst of the garden, God hath said, Ye shall not eat of it, neither shall ye touch it, lest ye die."

begin to fall by temptations, when we begin to think God will not be as good as his word, in respect to the execution of his threatenings denounced against sin. Satan knew this, and therefore artfully 'Said unto the woman, (ver. 4) Ye shall not surely die,' in an insinuating manner, 'Ye shall not surely die. Surely; God will not be so cruel as to damn you only for eating an apple, it cannot be.' Alas! How many does Satan lead captive at his will, by flattering them, that they shall not surely die; that hell torments will not be eternal; that God is all mercy; that he therefore will not punish a few years sin with an eternity of misery? But Eve found God as good as his word; and so will all they who go on in sin, under a false hope that they shall not surely die."[88]

It is clear to see that the woman's thoughts were too quickly formed after the image of the serpent. In his final act of deception, Satan guided the woman into the belief that God was keeping the first family from something much better. He (Satan) overtly denied the sufficiency of God's provision, thereby making the forbidden fruit an even greater point of attraction to the woman:

> **Genesis 3:5-6:** 5 For God knows that in the day you eat from it your eyes will be opened, and you will be like God, knowing good and evil. 6 When the woman saw that the tree was good for food, and that it was a delight to the eyes, and that the tree was desirable to make one wise, she took from its fruit and ate; and she gave also to her husband with her, and he ate" ...13 Then the Lord God said to the woman, "What is this you have done?" And the woman said, "The serpent deceived me, and I ate."

The lessons unveiled in these texts are not a mere abstraction, bearing no practical value, instead, this sad narrative is foundational for our understanding of the ordained roles of men and women; and in particular, they render a dark preview of what can be expected when men and women fail to uphold their calling before the Lord. Thus, these horrific events in the garden provide an all-important warning to the children of God. Yes, both the man and the woman ate, but their reasons for eating were very different as the Apostle Paul clearly explained in 1 Timothy 2:11-14:

> **1 Timothy 2:11-14:** 11 Let a woman quietly receive instruction with entire submissiveness. 12 But I do not allow a woman to teach or exercise authority over a man, but to remain quiet. 13 For it was Adam who was

---

[88] Whitefield, G., Selected Sermons of George Whitefield, The Seed of the Woman, and the Seed of the Serpent (Oak Harbor, WA: Logos Research Systems, Inc., 1999).

first created, and then Eve. 14 And it was not Adam who was deceived, but the woman being quite deceived, fell into transgression.

As noted earlier, Paul's instructions to Timothy concerning the roles of men and women were not based upon a cultural argument; instead, they were based upon the historical facts of the creation account and the fall.[89] The Apostle's point is simple and is vastly applicable for men, women, and the institution of marriage: *Men are to exercise leadership in the church, and in the home, through the ministry of the Word, just as Adam was ordained to do with his stewardship within the garden.* A more careful examination of 1 Timothy 2:11-14 reveals this quite clearly, after all, the first basis of male leadership is established by Paul through the first couple's created order: *Adam was first created and then Eve* (this important detail was already considered in Chapter 1, *The Glory of God's Creation: The First Man, Ministry and Commandment).* The second reason supplied is no less important: it was the woman who fell into transgression *as a result of her deception,* but Adam fell *without deception.* Specifically, Paul clearly explains that the woman was *quite deceived* and then fell into transgression. In this expression - *quite deceived* - the translators have supplied a word that shows the detail of the text in the Greek. Instead of using the common word *deceive* (*apataō*), Paul used an *intensified* form of it (*exapataō*), denoting thorough; even extensive deception. Such intensification points us to the fact that the woman's deception was not simple, but was massive in proportion. Paul's contrast between the man and the woman is quite clear. Something took place within her in the face of satanic deception when she, on her own, did battle with the serpent and as a result she accommodated the serpent's deception which led to lustful desires[90] and final apostasy. Adam failed to guard[91] that

---

[89] H. Wayne House, Bibliotheca Sacra 145 (January 1988): p. 317.

[90] The relationship between deception, lustful enticement and transgression is clearly laid out in the first chapter of James. There were those in James' audience who were deceived in their

which was entrusted to him, while the woman, in her independence, fell into deception.

The tragedy of Genesis 3 carries with it many important lessons for our discussion of marriage. One of the greatest lessons that must be learned is that men must conduct themselves *as men* in the manner in which God created them: to be godly leaders for their families and in the local church. The other important lesson is that women are to receive the instruction and leadership of men (1 Timothy 2:12-14), whether in the home or in the church. In Chapter 3, *Restoring the Genesis 2 Marriage*, we will carefully consider the *application of these principles* as they relate to husbands and wives; but for now it is essential that we press on in our examination of the consequences that came when Adam and his wife stepped outside of their God-ordained roles. If we study well, we will learn a great deal from their failure.

THE FIRST DECEPTION AND TRANSGRESSION ILLUSTRATED:

The errors of Genesis 3 are highly instructive, for they teach us about the importance of leadership and submission, not only in marriage,

---

thinking such that their theology was corrupted, thinking that God causes us to perform evil. Such deceptive excuse making was leading some to sin without a sense of personal responsibility: James 1:13-17 13 Let no one say when he is tempted, "I am being tempted by God"; for God cannot be tempted by evil, and He Himself does not tempt anyone.14 But each one is tempted when he is carried away and enticed by his own lust.15 Then when lust has conceived, it gives birth to sin; and when sin is accomplished, it brings forth death.16 Do not be deceived, my beloved brethren.

[91] "St. Paul (1 Tim. 2:14) affirms that "Adam was not deceived [by Satan], but the woman being deceived by him fell into the transgression (*en parabasei gegone*). This implies that Adam did not believe the tempter's assertion that a good would follow the eating of the forbidden fruit and that death would not be the consequence. According to St. Paul, Adam was seduced by his affection for Eve rather than deceived by the lie of Satan. He fell with his eyes wide open to the fact that if he ate he would die. But in loving his wife more than God, he 'worshipped and served the creature instead of the Creator' and like Eve set up a different final end from the true one." Shedd, Dogmatic Theology, p. 554.

but also in all aspects of life. In fact the Apostle Paul used the errors of Genesis 3 in order to reprove and instruct the troubled church at Corinth. In the case of the Corinthians, their problems were extensive beyond measure, and yet their every error could be traced back to one root problem: like the woman in the garden, they had become *quite deceived*. One of the greatest problems at Corinth was that many of its leaders were resisting the leadership and authority of the Apostle Paul, therefore the divine revelation that was entrusted to Paul was being ignored, and even refused by many within Corinth. Because of this they were trying to function as a church outside of the authority of Christ Himself who spoke through Paul. Like Adam's wife, the Corinthian church was demonstrating the same propensity towards autonomy and deception. God's provision of leadership and protection had been presented to them through Paul, but many in their ranks stood aloof to Paul's leadership. In light of their deception Paul was horrified to hear about their eagerness to embrace false teachers and doctrine, and this is why Paul used the woman's error in Genesis 3 as an illustration for the Corinthian church. By this comparison we see the church's susceptibility to error:

> **2 Corinthians 11:2-4**: 2 For I am jealous for you with a godly jealousy; for I betrothed you to one husband, that to Christ I might present you as a pure virgin. 3 But I am afraid, lest as the serpent deceived Eve by his craftiness, your minds should be led astray from the simplicity and purity of devotion to Christ. 4 For if one comes and preaches another Jesus whom we have not preached, or you receive a different spirit which you have not received, or a different gospel which you have not accepted, you bear this beautifully.

Paul's jealous desire for the Corinthians was this: that they would be a faithful bride to Christ by submitting to His headship by means of His authoritative message and messengers (messengers like that of

Paul who was an Apostle of Christ).[92] As a direct representative of Christ Paul's jealousy is understandable, for there were those at Corinth who readily denied Paul's authority (2 Corinthians 11:5-11) and thereby they were drawing many away from Christ's headship as it was mediated through the Apostle. Paul likens their deception to the error of Genesis 3 by saying: *"But I am afraid, lest as the serpent deceived Eve by his craftiness, your minds should be led astray from the simplicity and purity of devotion to Christ."* Paul's comparison is very important. Eve's mind was corrupted with the crafty error of Satan[93] such that she *accommodated* him in his false teaching, leading to sinful desire and transgression. In a similar manner, Paul was concerned that the minds of the Corinthians would be *led astray* by the craftiness of Satan.[94] Through this comparison with the Genesis 3 account of the fall, it becomes quite evident that the Corinthians' weakness was that of *accommodation* and *tolerance*. Rather than refusing evil doctrine the moment it appeared, they *bore it beautifully* and were thereby becoming *corrupted*. The meaning of the expression - *you bear it beautifully* - is very significant since it gives us insight into the nature of the deception found within the woman in Genesis 3. When Paul said that the Corinthians *bore* error beautifully, he thus indicated that they accepted *as valid or true*[95] the precepts of the evil one and were therefore *receiving instruction with an open and attentive mind*.[96] Therefore, the Corinthian church was willing *to listen to* and even *engage in discourse* with evil men who

---

[92] 1 Corinthians 1:1.

[93] "Eve doubted God's goodness; she disbelieved his threatening; she aspired after forbidden knowledge." Charles Hodge, Systematic theology.Vol. 2 (Thomas Nelson and Sons, New York, 1872) p. 128.

[94] The words led astray represent the Greek word *ptharē*, which speaks of something that has become corrupted or destroyed: Genesis 6:11 Now the earth was corrupt [*epthare*] in the sight of God, and the earth was filled with violence.

[95] Swanson, Dictionary of Biblical Languages: Hebrew Old Testament, p. 462.

[96] Kittel, Gerhard, Geoffrey William Bromiley, and Gerhard Friedrich, Theological Dictionary of the New Testament.Vol. 1, ed. (Grand Rapids, MI, 1964-c1976), p. 359.

should have been *refuted and rejected*[97] by godly leadership. What the Corinthian church needed was to subject itself to the headship of Christ whose example of facing evil leaves us with little doubt that those who have the charge to lead with the Word must refute those who contradict the truth,[98] just as our Lord did when He was tempted in the wilderness three times by the Devil. He did not chat with Satan about the particular meaning of the Words of Scripture; He did not bear beautifully, or with patience discuss, the Devil's false interpretation of Psalm 91. Instead, our Lord gave us the model for Godly leadership in that He soundly refuted the Devil three times without giving any opportunity to discuss differences. William Shedd is right when he said:

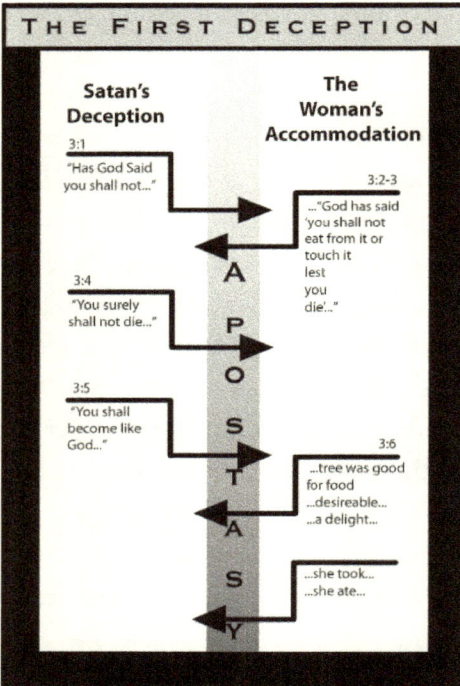

THE FIRST DECEPTION

Satan's Deception

The Woman's Accommodation

3:1
"Has God Said you shall not..."

3:2-3
..."God has said 'you shall not eat from it or touch it lest you die'..."

3:4
"You surely shall not die..."

3:5
"You shall become like God..."

3:6
...tree was good for food ...desireable... ...a delight...

...she took... ...she ate...

APOSTASY

"The woman alone entered into the discussion with Satan of a subject that ought not to have been discussed at all."[99]

Like Adam's wife, the Corinthian church was guilty of accommodating error and was therefore drowning in deception, while attempting to engage in spiritual warfare apart from Apostolic truth and authority. The bride of Christ at Corinth, in all her susceptibility to

---

[97] Titus 1:9-10 9 holding fast the faithful word which is in accordance with the teaching, that he may be able both to exhort in sound doctrine and to refute those who contradict. 10 For there are many rebellious men, empty talkers and deceivers, especially those of the circumcision.

[98] Titus 1:5-10, 2:15; 1 Timothy 5:21-23; 2 Timothy 4:1-3.

[99] William G. T. Shedd, Dogmatic Theology, Third Edition (P&R Publishing, Phillipsburg, New Jersey), p. 554.

error, stood alone in her battle against the satanic attack and was failing miserably. Like the church overall, Adam's helper was created to depend upon godly leadership and protection, but on her own she was all the more susceptible to error.[100] Consider the reflections of Augustine on the nature of the first couple's temptation:

> "...he [Satan] chose the serpent because, being slippery, and moving in tortuous windings, it was suitable for his purpose. And this animal being subdued to his wicked ends by the presence and superior force of his angelic nature, he abused as his instrument, and first tried his deceit upon the woman, making his assault upon the weaker part of that human alliance, that he might gradually gain the whole, and not supposing that the man would readily give ear to him, or be deceived, but that he might yield to the error of the woman."[101]

Augustine's observations give us a clear affirmation of the nature of the deception and error of Genesis 3. Adam's wife was not created to lead, but to accommodate and help her husband. However, her calling before God was quickly corrupted when she accommodated the authority of another, the father of all lies.[102] Although she was the first to transgress, it was not by her sin that all of mankind fell. Both sinned indeed: the woman ate in deception as a result of her corrupted accommodation of Satan, but our federal head ate with his eyes wide open (without deception) and thereby all of humanity was

---

[100] Paul's description of these events in 1 Timothy 2:11-14 helps us to understand the differences between men and women and therefore their distinctive roles: "Eve can lend support for the instructions to Christian women in general in vv 11–12. If these requirements are to be met, it is difficult to avoid the conclusion that Paul cites Eve's failure as exemplary and perhaps causative of the nature of women in general and that this susceptibility to deception bars them from engaging in public teaching." Douglas Moo, Trinity Journal 1, (Spring 1980): 70.

[101] Aurelius Augustinus (Augustine of Hippo), The City of God, (William Benton, Publisher: Encyclopedia Britannica, Inc.), p. 386.

[102] Chyrsostom is very forthright regarding the problem at hand when he says: "The woman taught once, and ruined all" 47. Hom. IX on 1 Tim 2:11–14, NPNF, XIII. 436.

plunged into ruin.[103] Let us conclude this section by reviewing some of the crucial truths learned from this portion of our study:

- In Adam's case, the duty of guarding the garden with the prohibitive commandment of God could not be delegated to any other, for it was Adam alone who was entrusted with this responsibility (Genesis 3:17). The ordained role of the man, as a leader, did not end with the fall, but continues to this day even though it was corrupted by sin.

- The woman was created to be Adam's helper and through this she was to accommodate his needs by submitting to his leadership. She was not placed in the garden to serve and guard it, nor was she entrusted with the headship responsibilities associated with God's commandment. Therefore, her attempt to handle her husband's unique stewardship was clearly revealed through her mishandling of God's Word.

- The deception/transgression narrative of Genesis chapter 3 also leaves us with many unanswered questions; nevertheless we still must assert that which is clearly presented in the texts of the O.T. and the N.T. What is most clear from this fateful event is that both men and women must take their God-ordained calling seriously. Men must embrace their responsibility of leadership with all seriousness and passion; and women must understand that their calling to receive leadership is a wonderful and noble one. Beautiful in the sight of God is the woman who has a gentle and submissive spirit. This is the spirit of a godly helper who delights in the goodness of the Lord's will.

Our differing roles as men and women do not denote a difference in *personal value or intelligence*, however they do point out a difference

---

[103] Augustine's summary is helpful here: "For not without significance did the apostle say, 'And Adam was not deceived, but the woman being deceived was in the transgression'; but he speaks thus, because the woman accepted as true what the serpent told her, but the man could not bear to be severed from his only companion, even though this involved a partnership in sin. He was not on this account less culpable, but sinned with his eyes open. And so the apostle does not say, 'He did not sin,' but, 'He was not deceived.'" Augustine, City of God, pp. 386-87.

in *service and calling*. We must remember that we can learn a great deal from our first parents, especially when we are reminded that Satan's tactics, along with mankind's acts of weakness, are clearly repeated throughout human history. Therefore, the Christian who is equipped with such wisdom from the Scriptures *will not be ignorant of Satan's schemes*.

THE FIRST CONDEMNATION

The tragedy of Genesis chapter 3 reads like an incident report for a violent traffic accident. What took place there happened quickly, unexpectedly, and produced nothing but horrific results. Yet the violence of Adam's iniquity exceeds all of the cumulative disasters of human history for this simple reason: it was Adam who transgressed as *our federal head*:

THE FIRST CONDEMNATION

Then *to Adam*, the Lord said - "Because you have listened to the voice of your wife, and have eaten from the tree about which I commanded *you*..."

"Cursed is the ground because of you... By the sweat of your face you will eat bread, till you return to the ground, because from it you were taken; for you are dust, and to dust you shall return."

Romans 5:12, 14: 12 Therefore, just as through one man sin entered into the world, and death through sin, and so death spread to all men, because all sinned— 14 Nevertheless death reigned from Adam until Moses, even over those who had not sinned in the likeness of the offense of Adam, who is a type of Him who was to come.

Nowhere in Scripture do we find the woman depicted as the means of universal sin and condemnation. The woman failed as Adam's helper, but Adam failed as the leader and head of humanity. The fact that Adam's sin brought about the corruption and condemnation of the whole human race is an essential doctrine of Christianity, and it is one that has import in our every aspect of life - *for all have sinned and fall short of God's glory*.[104] More will be said about the impact of universal sin later (Chapter 2, *The Shame of Adam's Sin: The First Child*), but for now we need to consider what ultimately happened to Adam and his wife as a result of sin:

- **A Changed Essence:** Before sin, Adam and his wife shared an essential unity such that they were both equals as sinless humans. But after the fall, their unity of essence included the corruption of sin: Adam was a sinful human and so was the woman, thus, the image of God in them became marred by the pollution of indwelling sin. They still shared the full essence of their humanity; however, their human nature became corrupted.

- **A Changed Bond:** In their innocence, they were designed to bear God's image through their relationship to Him and to one another, but as a result of sin, they experienced a serious transformation such that their mutual relationship and practice would never be the same. Through sin they were separated from God and would therefore experience division between one another. Because of their sin, God gave Adam and his wife over to the

THE FIRST CONDEMNATION

Adam and his wife still bore the image of God, however, that image had become marred by indwelling sin. They were still morally responsible to serve and honor the Lord, and yet sin had created a barrier between themselves and God

As individuals, they had indwelling sin and corruption. In marriage their sin had infected:

1. Their Essence
2. Their Bond
3. Their Purpose

consequences of their transgression and therefore the struggles that they would face as a married couple became prototypical for all marriages of all generations. Their relationship to one another became a matter of intense conflict and struggle.

---

[104] Rom. 3:23.

- **A Changed Relationship to God's Purpose:** God's sovereign and eternal decree never changes, as He the Lord changes not.[105] However, what did change was the first couple's ability to fulfill God's call to worship Him. The requirements of God's Word did not go away when sin entered the world, therefore because of indwelling sin, their status with God and His Word was that of enmity. As a consequence of their fall, they were unable to serve God and one another as they had before.

After Adam ate the forbidden fruit, there was an invisible death of the first couple that was made visible by their actions. First, their eyes were opened and they had an awareness of their nudity. Clearly, their original innocence was instantly corrupted:

Genesis 3:7-8: 7 Then the eyes of both of them were opened, and they knew that they were naked; and they sewed fig leaves together and made themselves loin coverings. 8 And they heard the sound of the Lord God walking in the garden in the cool of the day, and the man and his wife hid themselves from the presence of the Lord God among the trees of the garden.

This stands in stark contrast to their nakedness in innocence: Genesis 2:25 *"And the man and his wife were both naked and were not ashamed."* Before, in their innocence, they were without shame. Now, in their sin, they were both ashamed and made for themselves loin coverings. We also see the evidence of their spiritual death by means of their attempt to hide themselves from the presence of the omnipresent, omniscient God. In all of this it is evident that their acts of lunacy reflect, not the image of God, but the very image and likeness of the Devil who opposes the will of God. The very trees that were given for their pleasure and sustenance became the benign instruments of their sinful attempt to run away from the all-seeing God:

---

[105] Malachi 3:6, 1 Samuel 15:29 "And also the Glory of Israel will not lie or change His mind; for He is not a man that He should change His mind."

Genesis 3:9-13: 9 Then the Lord God called to the man, and said to him, "Where are you?" 10 And he said, "I heard the sound of Thee in the garden, and I was afraid because I was naked; so I hid myself."11 And He said, "Who told you that you were naked? Have you eaten from the tree of which I commanded you not to eat?" 12 And the man said, "The woman whom Thou gavest to be with me, she gave me from the tree, and I ate." 13 Then the Lord God said to the woman, "What is this you have done?" And the woman said, "The serpent deceived me, and I ate."

In every step of the way, the fallen first-couple demonstrated that a very serious death had occurred. Though they walked about with *physical life*, they became *spiritually dead* in their trespasses and sins (Eph. 2:1-3). In Genesis 3:9-13 it is clear that the Lord was guiding Adam with questions designed to point out and uncover his transgression. It is within the span of this question and answer session that we see the same patterns of sin that have plagued mankind throughout the generations. Like a defective template, the first couple serves as a corrupted archetype of every marital problem traceable throughout the span of history. Let us therefore learn, antithetically, from our first parents:

- **Denial of God:** By attempting to flee from the presence of God, Adam and his wife revealed the main ingredient to any marital problem: forsaking the very center and foundation of any marriage – God Himself.

- **Denial of Responsibility:** The man denied the responsibility of His role as the leader and blamed God for the woman's transgression and temptation. From this we learn, antithetically, that one of the first principles of leadership is to accept responsibility for one's own actions and household. Adam had failed to be an active leader and then dispensed blame in his sin. His error here is threefold: 1. He failed to accept responsibility for his own actions; 2. He blamed his wife for his sin, a burden that she cannot bear and 3. Adam blamed God, who can never be blamed nor accused for our fleshly temptations and sins.[106] Ultimately, his reasoning was clearly defective for no sin can ever be covered by another sin; the woman's sin found no solution through Adam's transgression.

- **Denial of Culpability:** As the carousel of blame continued to spin, the woman then cast blame on the serpent saying "the serpent deceived me and I ate." The fact that the deceptive serpent was present in the garden offers no excuse for sin, by itself. The more fundamental problem that the woman now avoids is that she, in the weakness of her autonomy, was deceived, tempted, and consequently *she* transgressed. Thus, as sinners, we must accept the reality of our culpability for sin.

A very fundamental point of marital counseling is in order here, one that will be expanded upon later in the sections to follow - no matter how complex a couple's problems may ever be, there are three simple principles that must always be maintained in light of the primal transgressions of our first parents: *1. Make the worship of God the center of your devotion and practice, both individually and as a couple; 2. Men – Sacrificially love and lead your homes in godliness and by means of the Word of God alone. Do not forsake or deny your role as the leader, either blaming your wife or God for the problems in your own home; 3. Women, pursue godliness in light of your God-ordained role and calling, being thankful for your calling, while not attempting to step away from it.* Nothing that has been said here is at all original or new, however nearly all of these principles are fiercely opposed in our modern culture. We will, of course, reinforce these

---

[106] James 1:13-15: 13 Let no one say when he is tempted, "I am tempted by God"; for God cannot be tempted by evil, nor does He Himself tempt anyone.14 But each one is tempted when he is drawn away by his own desires and enticed.15 Then, when desire has conceived, it gives birth to sin; and sin, when it is full-grown, brings forth death.

aforementioned principles throughout the remainder of the book, but for now we must return to the narrative of God's condemnation, moving ahead to the Lord's indictment against the woman and the man:

> **Genesis 3:16** To the woman He said, "I will greatly multiply your pain in childbirth, in pain you shall bring forth children; yet your desire shall be for your husband, and he shall rule over you."

The Lord's condemnation of the woman explains how she would experience the consequences of sin, both passively and actively. *Passively*, she would endure certain pain in childbirth. This is made clear through the use of the same verbal form found in Gen. 2:17 ("…you shall *surely* die"), and thus God declared that the woman's pain in childbirth will [surely] be multiplied. *Actively*, the woman would experience a change in her relationship with her husband stemming from her own fallen condition:

> **Genesis 3:16** Yet your *desire* shall be for your husband…

This Hebrew word translated *desire* (*teśuḵă*) speaks of the concept of stretching out after something so as to acquire it.[107] We need not go far in order to see a parallel use of this word. In fact, we can consult the next chapter (Genesis 4) for a helpful parallel to the judgment narrative in Genesis 3:

---

[107] The normal sense of the word here is to desire something. Such a craving could be positive or negative depending on the context. It would seem quite clear that in light of the corruption of their relationship and the overall context of the judgment narrative that the woman's desire would be similar to the usage in Genesis 4:7 – a desire which seeks to subvert or resist the man's authority: "a desire to dominate, or just be independent of the man" Swanson, <u>Dictionary of Biblical Languages: Hebrew Old Testament</u>, (HGK9592).

Genesis 4:7 (God speaking to Cain): If you do well, will not your countenance be lifted up? And if you do not do well, sin is crouching at the door; and...

...its *desire* is for you, but you must *master (rule over)*[108] it.

Genesis 3:16 (God speaking to the woman): Yet...

...your *desire* shall be for your husband, And he *shall rule over* you.

Genesis 4:7 gives us a very clear parallel to the lexical and grammatical construct of our verse in question (Gen. 3:16). The picture given to us regarding Cain and his sin is that of a contest or battle. In order for Cain's countenance to be lifted up, he must battle against, or rule over, his sin.[109] This portrait of Cain's battle against sin illustrates the conflict that will naturally arise from the woman's relationship with her husband. The woman, in her fallen nature, will tend to desire, covet, and compete with the leadership and authority of the man. In view of this, it would appear that the Lord's judgment against the woman was given in proportion with her transgression. Remember that the woman acted alone in order to seek and attain that which was forbidden (the fruit of the tree of the knowledge of good and evil). Here, in the judgment narrative, God gave the woman over to the corruption of her original desire: to seek the leadership role of the man. Her consuming desire would therefore be to subvert her husband, thus creating a power struggle for authority in the home. The man's response, because of his fallen nature, would become that of an indifferent and even unloving rule. This is not necessarily a conclusion drawn from the word *rule* since the concepts of *rule* and *authority* do not necessarily denote sin; however, the implicit concept points to a leadership that is corrupted by sin. This

---

[108] The very word translated as *rule* in Gen. 3:16 is used here in Gen. 4:7: *māśāl*.

[109] Galatians 5:17 For the flesh sets its desire against the Spirit, and the Spirit against the flesh; for these are in opposition to one another, so that you may not do the things that you please.

is why we see in Scripture that men are repeatedly instructed in the matter of giving a loving, caring, and compassionate leadership: one that is characterized by Christ-like sacrifice and affection (Eph. 5:22-33, Col. 3:19). Consider this excellent summary of the first couple's sinful state:

"'And he shall rule over thee.' Created for the man, the woman was made subordinate to him from the very first; but the supremacy of the man was not intended to become a despotic rule, crushing the woman into a slave, which has been the rule in ancient and modern Heathenism, and even in Mahometanism also, - a rule which was first softened by the sin-destroying grace of the Gospel, and changed into a form more in harmony with the original relation, viz. That of a rule on the one hand, and subordination on the other, which have their roots in mutual esteem and love."[110]

God's judgment of the man then follows:

Genesis 3:17-18: 17 Then to Adam He said, "Because you have listened to the voice of your wife, and have eaten from the tree about which I commanded you, saying, 'You shall not eat from it'; Cursed is the ground because of you; In toil you shall eat of it all the days of your life. 18 "Both thorns and thistles it shall grow for you; And you shall eat the plants of the field;

Notice carefully the nature of God's indictment of Adam - *it is twofold*: 1. He (Adam) listened to the voice of his wife and 2. He ate from the tree of which he alone received the prohibition "'you shall not eat from it." Together, these infractions form one transgression, but their delineation is important. Adam's responsibility was to lead by God's authority alone. His leadership cues were therefore to come from God and no one else. But we see that Adam's first error led to the second, for his choice to partner himself with the independent

---

[110] Keil and F. Delitzsch, <u>Commentary on the Old Testament</u> p. 103.

choices of his wife led him to the path of destruction when he ate the forbidden fruit. As a result of this, Adam's precious privilege of work became plagued with toil, hardship, and vanity *all the days of his life;* and along with this, his privilege of protecting the garden with the sword of the Word of God was forever removed. In his place a cherubim, possessing a flaming sword, stood in guardianship over the garden (v. 24). Both the man and the woman were ex-communicated from the beautiful Garden and cast out into the world in order to seek their daily provisions. Their lives were resultantly characterized by trials, hardship, and difficulty. The disturbing events of their transgression and condemnation leave us with three important conclusions at this point:

- **Their Corrupted Essence:** The man and the woman both shared the same sinful humanity as one another. They still bore the image of God, however, that image became grossly mangled by sin. In the future their progeny would reflect their same sinful patterns of behavior. Their body, soul, and spirit was polluted by sin, and they (at this point) were left in a state of hopelessness due to their essential corruption.

- **Their Conflicted Bond of Marriage:** Adam and his wife were no less married than before their transgression, however, their marital union would suffer great relational trauma in light of the fall. The first of all relationships to consider was their relationship with God. In their new state of spiritual corruption they were at enmity with God and would therefore have conflict with one another. Because of this, Adam and his wife could no longer love and care for each other as the Lord had originally designed.

- **Their Conflicted Purpose:** Adam and his wife's fall did not revoke their fundamental roles. While Adam lost the governorship of the garden itself, he was still required to serve God as a leader; and he was also called to labor, but now he would do so by the sweat of his brow. Adam's ability and desire to care for his wife, protect her, and nurture her would face the continual challenges wrought by his indwelling sin. As well, the woman was still called to be Adam's helper, and yet this ordained role of hers would also be maligned through indwelling sin.

Mankind's condemnation is a difficult truth, but it is a necessary one that we all must face. Most people in our world have never been told the truth about why our world is filled with disease, death, warfare, and corruption, but the Scriptures give us a very clear reason for it all such that we know that every tear, heartache, death, divorce, and all acts of wickedness find their beginnings in the corrupt root of Adam's sin.

We therefore leave this chapter on a very dark and difficult note; yet amidst the stark reality of mankind's sin and condemnation we see that the Lord, in His boundless grace and mercy, provided a beautiful gem of hope amidst it all.

THE FIRST PROMISE

One can only imagine the gravity of this moment as experienced by the first man and woman. Their marriage, their future offspring, and the whole world had been mutilated and corrupted by Adam's sin. Yet despite the darkness of this moment, Adam did something that was very interesting. As the ordained head and leader of his family, Adam chose to rename his wife in a manner that conveyed his hope and trust in the Lord:

Genesis 3:20 Now the man called his wife's name Eve, because she was the mother of all the living.

THE FIRST PROMISE

Genesis 3:15: And I will put enmity
Between you and the woman,
And between your seed and her seed;
He shall bruise you on the head,
And you shall bruise him on the heel."

1 John 3:8
For this purpose
the Son of God was manifested,
that He might destroy the works
of the devil.

The name *Eve* means *life*, which is an appropriate name for the *mother of all the living*.[111] The basis for Adam's choice of the name Eve should be quite evident, especially when we consider the condemnation narrative delivered to the Serpent:

Genesis 3:15 And I will put enmity between you and the woman, And between your seed and her seed; He shall bruise you on the head, And you shall bruise him on the heel.

When God delivered His indictment against the serpent, He nested a very key promise regarding a special seed, born of a woman, who would ultimately *crush* Satan's head. This first promise in Scripture is wonderfully clarified in the New Covenant of Christ:

1 John 3:8: ...to this end was the Son of God manifested, that he might destroy the works of the devil.

1 John 3:8 reminds us that there is only one person who will exact the final judgment against the serpent: The Lord Jesus.[112] It is Christ who

---

[111] The LXX employs the Greek word *zōē* for the Hebrew word *ḥăwā* denoting that Eve was renamed in view of the living seed which would eventually be born through her womb.

[112] "This spiritual seed culminated in Christ, in whom the Adamitic family terminated, henceforward to be renewed by Christ as the second Adam, and restored by Him to its original exaltation and likeness to God. In this sense Christ is the seed of the woman, who tramples Satan under His feet, not as an individual, but as the head both of the posterity of the woman which kept the promise and maintained the conflict with the old serpent before His advent, and also of all those who are gathered out of all nations, are united to Him by faith, and formed into one body of which He is the head (Rom. 16:20)." Keil and Delitzsch, <u>Commentary</u> p. 102.

was born of a woman, who alone will execute the final crushing blow to Satan when He returns.[113] By this we are reminded that amidst the depressing realities forecast in Genesis 3, there was given a bright ray of hope provided by the Lord who promised to judge the serpent in the end. God did provide a living seed *through a woman,* and this seed will condemn the Devil forever without end. This promise of the seed of God was not only entrusted to Adam, but it was also passed on to subsequent generations through the patriarch Abraham, as it is written through the Apostle Paul:

Galatians 3:16 Now the promises were spoken to Abraham and to his seed. He does not say, "And to seeds," as referring to many, but rather to one, "And to your seed," that is, Christ.

From Adam to Abraham, God's divine promise of the coming Redeemer was faithfully revealed. Adam and his wife originally received this promise of the coming seed, but only after they fell in sin; and it was to be the basis of their redemptive hope. However, prior to their fall in sin, the divine revelation that God gave to them was a lawful one, and by this their worship of God was based upon their obedience to that law. Because of their state of grace they were able to serve God by means of the law; but after the fall, their worship of God was no longer predicated on the observance of the law, but upon faith in God's promised Redeemer;[114] and the indirect means of this promise was the *life giving womb of the woman.* At the time, the promise given was quite veiled and general. What our first family did not know was that God's provision of Christ would come many generations later; however, their sole focus was to persevere in the will of God by continuing the posterity of the woman with the hope

---

[113] Rev. 20.

[114] Hebrews 11:13 All these [OT saints] died in faith, without receiving the promises, but having seen them and having welcomed them from a distance, and having confessed that they were strangers and exiles on the earth.

that what would proceed from her womb would eventually be used of God to fulfill the promise of Gen. 3:15. Thus, the redemptive promises that were entrusted to them *were centered in what God would provide through the process of childbearing as they continued in faith, being fruitful, multiplying, and filling the earth.*[115] Therefore, Adam called his wife Eve because he realized that their hope was centered on the life that would come forth through her.[116] God's promise was also a great mystery, for it contained many unanswered questions,[117] but through faith in God and His promises they possessed *an assurance of things hoped for and a conviction of the things which were not yet seen.*[118]

Before they were sent out of the Garden, God gave them one more disclosure regarding their dire need, as well as God's sole ability to provide for them. Fortunately, the message of Genesis 3 is not just about God's judgment against Adam's sin; rather there are wonderful previews of mercy and grace that further underscore God's promise of hope in Genesis 3:15. We see this in the closing verses in Genesis 3 whereby the first couple, before being evicted from the garden, received a wonderful provision from the Lord:

---

[115] 1 Timothy 2:15: 15 "Nevertheless she will be saved in childbearing if they continue in faith, love, and holiness, with self-control." Matthew Henry indicates that Paul's concluding instructions in 1 Timothy 2:15 established an important principle for all women of all generations when he says: "...it is a word of comfort (v. 15) that those who continue in sobriety shall be saved in child-bearing, or with child-bearing—the Messiah, who was born of a woman, should break the serpent's head (Gen. 3:15); or the sentence which they are under for sin shall be no bar to their acceptance with Christ, if they continue in faith, and charity, and holiness, with sobriety." Matthew M. Henry, Matthew Henry's commentary on the whole Bible Complete and unabridged in one volume (Peabody: Hendrickson), (1 Ti 2:15).

[116] "It was through the power of divine grace that Adam believed the promise with regard to the woman's seed, and manifested his faith in the name which he gave to his wife." Keil and Delitzsch, Commentary, p. 106.

[117] Eph. 1:7-8, 3:4-5 4 (...by which, when you read, you may understand my knowledge in the mystery of Christ),5 which in other ages was not made known to the sons of men, as it has now been revealed by the Spirit to His holy apostles and prophets:.

[118] Hebrews 11:1.

Genesis 3:21 And the Lord God made garments of skin for Adam and his wife, and clothed them.

When considering Genesis 3:21 it is important to remember that before the fall Adam and his wife were naked *without shame.* However, after the fall they were aware of their nudity and were ashamed in the self-consciousness of their own sin. As well, it is important to recall what they had attempted to do with their shameful nudity *by their own theological ingenuity:*

Genesis 3:7 Then the eyes of both of them were opened, and they knew that they were naked; and they sewed fig leaves together and made themselves loin coverings.

It should be clear that what happened in Genesis 3:21 gave the first couple a clear picture about the inability of man, as well as the unquestioned sufficiency of God's provision. *God made garments for them* and then *He clothed them Himself.* This is such a short and succinct verse, and yet it presents a treasury of truth which typifies the ultimate need of the whole human race.[119] Adam and Eve's need for atonement, in light of their sin, was threefold:

- **Atonement Supplied by God:** Their shameful condition does require a covering, but only God can make it.

- **Atonement Procured by Sacrifice:** What they require for a covering was a garment of skin, procured through the shedding of blood.

---

[119] "They learned, in type, that an 'atonement' (or 'covering') could only be provided by God and through the shedding of blood on the altar." Morris, <u>Genesis Record</u>, p. 130.

- **Atonement Applied by God:** Once these garments of skin were made, God Himself adorned them.

Just as they were given Biblical revelation about the coming Christ in Gen. 3:15, so too did they receive a type respecting their need for a blood sacrifice to cover their sin. Moses did not give us the details about what animal God used in order to provide a *garment of skin*, how He killed it or shed its blood. All that we can draw from this precious verse is that God had provided a very simple illustration for them regarding their spiritual need and His coming provision. By this we have a very clear preview of the One who would shed His blood in order to cover the sin and shame of His people.

With this provision of God, we have a primitive foundation of worship established for the first family regarding God's redemptive protection and covering. From Adam to John the Baptist, the message of God's first promise has always been the very centerpiece of revelation:

Hebrews 1:1-2: 1 God, after He spoke long ago to the fathers in the prophets in many portions and in many ways, 2 in these last days has spoken to us in His Son, whom He appointed heir of all things, through whom also He made the world.

The Lord revealed to His people the truth concerning His Son *in many portions and in many ways*, but He first established the promise of Christ with Adam and his wife Eve. The prototypical sacrifice that God made in the garden, on their behalf, previewed what God would do for them in Christ. It is this sacrificial type that would be later reflected in the acceptable sacrifices of Abel,[120] Job, Noah, and Abraham, and it would be more completely established with the sacrificial system entrusted to the nation of Israel. By all of

---

[120] Heb. 11:4.

this, we are reminded that the promise of Christ was to be the hope of every generation. The importance of this particular section underscores what will follow in the coming chapters: *that Christ alone is the center of our lives and of our worship.* For now, as we proceed in the Genesis narrative, we find an important event that takes place between Adam and Eve. This event will provide crucial lessons for our discussion concerning children and parenting...

...Adam and his wife had a child and his name was Cain.

THE FIRST CHILD

...and Cain killed Abel (Genesis 4:8).

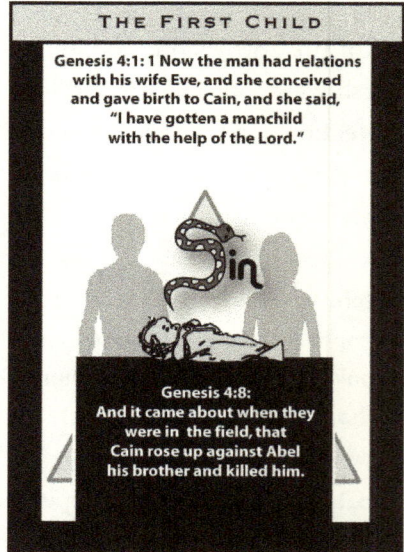

THE FIRST CHILD

Genesis 4:1: 1 Now the man had relations with his wife Eve, and she conceived and gave birth to Cain, and she said, "I have gotten a manchild with the help of the Lord."

Sin

Genesis 4:8:
And it came about when they were in the field, that Cain rose up against Abel his brother and killed him.

What more could be said about the nature of Adam's progeny? It seems counter-intuitive to suggest that a child, who is called a gift of the Lord,[121] is also a naturally born sinner and potential killer, but it is true. The violence of Abel's murder serves as a stark contrast to that first moment when Adam and Eve joyfully received their first fruit of the womb. A precious little child, born in their likeness, given to them by God just as Eve had celebrated:

> **Genesis 4:1** Now the man had relations with his wife Eve, and she conceived and gave birth to Cain, and she said, "I have gotten a manchild with the help of the Lord."

---

[121] Psalm 127:3 Behold, children are a gift of the Lord; the fruit of the womb is a reward.

How quickly was the depravity of mankind illustrated for Adam and his wife through their first child, and how clearly were the consequences of their own sin displayed when their precious first born mutilated the life of their second son, Abel. Sadly, the story of mankind's corruption does not end there. Genesis chapters 4 and 5 take us through the dismal journey of the first family's genealogy whereby we find repeated acts of jealousy, hatred, murder, arrogance, boasting, sexual immorality, stealing etc. In fact, all of the children of Adam and Eve lived and sinned in the *image and likeness* of their parents. This is clearly evidenced in Genesis chapter 5, which unveils the details of the first family's genealogy after Cain and Abel:

> **Genesis 5:1-3:** 1 This is the book of the generations of Adam. In the day when God created man, He made him in the likeness of God. 2 He created them male and female, and He blessed them and named them Man in the day when they were created. 3 When Adam had lived one hundred and thirty years, he became the father of a son in his own likeness, according to his image, and named him Seth.

Man was originally made in God's image *with perfection*; however the descendents of Adam and Eve are all born in the *likeness* and *image* of their sin and corruption. The inescapable truth is that all the descendents of Adam and Eve enter the world having the same corruption of sin as their parents. We see this truth illustrated very clearly in the sixth chapter of Genesis where we have a brief summary given regarding Adam and Eve's continued posterity:

> **Genesis 6:5** Then the Lord saw that the wickedness of man was great on the earth, and that every intent of the thoughts of his heart was only evil continually.

Genesis 6:5 gives us an amazing and emphatic statement regarding the depth of man's sinful condition. This verse tells us, with no shortage of detail, that the children of men will never rise above the condition as stated in Genesis 6:5 – that *every intent* of the thoughts of their heart would be *only evil, continually.* This is no pretty picture. This clearly states that man's heart, mind, and his every intent and thought is corrupted with the influences of sin and that there is nothing that man can say or do that can be deemed as acceptable in the presence of the holy God who rendered this verdict. While it is true that not all men evidence this depravity equally *on the outside*, yet all men are neuthetically and spiritually depraved to the core,[122] worthy to be drowned in a deluge and committed to hell forever. As for Noah, he was a man graced by God and preserved from the destruction of the flood, and yet he too was a sinner in need of God's salvation since he was cut out of the same Adamic fabric.[123]

From Adam to Noah, and to the present day, the indictment of mankind has continued with no change, just as we see in Paul's indictment of all humanity - both Jew and Gentile:

Romans 3:9-18: 9 What then? Are we better than they? Not at all; for we have already charged that both Jews and Greeks are all under sin; 10 as it is written, "THERE IS NONE RIGHTEOUS, NOT EVEN ONE;
11 THERE IS NONE WHO UNDERSTANDS,
THERE IS NONE WHO SEEKS FOR GOD;

---

[122] Hodge clearly summarizes Adamic corruption: "The state therefore to which Adam was reduced by his disobedience, so far as his subjective condition is concerned, was analogous to that of the fallen angels. He was entirely and absolutely ruined. It is said that no man becomes thoroughly depraved by one transgression. In one sense this is true. But one transgression by incurring the wrath and curse of God and the loss of fellowship with Him, as effectually involves spiritual death, as one perforation of the heart causes the death of the body; or one puncture of the eyes involves us in perpetual darkness." Hodge, <u>Systematic Theology</u>, p. 128.

[123] Genesis 8:21 ...the Lord said to Himself, "I will never again curse the ground on account of man, for the intent of man's heart is evil from his youth; and I will never again destroy every living thing, as I have done.

12 ALL HAVE TURNED ASIDE, TOGETHER THEY HAVE BECOME USELESS;

THERE IS NONE WHO DOES GOOD,

THERE IS NOT EVEN ONE."

13 "THEIR THROAT IS AN OPEN GRAVE,

WITH THEIR TONGUES THEY KEEP DECEIVING," "THE POISON OF ASPS IS UNDER THEIR LIPS";

14 "WHOSE MOUTH IS FULL OF CURSING AND BITTERNESS"; 15 "THEIR FEET ARE SWIFT TO SHED BLOOD, 16 DESTRUCTION AND MISERY ARE IN THEIR PATHS, 17 AND THE PATH OF PEACE HAVE THEY NOT KNOWN." 18 "THERE IS NO FEAR OF GOD BEFORE THEIR EYES."

None, no one, not even one does good. All have sinned! The systemic nature of man's depravity is one of the most repeated doctrines in Scripture. It is a sad report to consider, but it is necessary in order to understand man's true need. Man is not *mostly depraved*, he is *totally depraved* and this is the case from *his youth*:

> **Genesis 8:21** ...the Lord said to Himself, "I will never again curse the ground on account of man, for the intent of man's heart is evil from his youth; and I will never again destroy every living thing, as I have done."

The Scriptures are extremely clear on this difficult subject, that men are sinners from birth. Not being holy ourselves, we cannot fully comprehend our own sinfulness, nor can we fully appreciate the corruption that is found in those cute and cuddly little children that we love to hold and admire. However the Scriptures remind us that, while they do not have the physical strength nor the intellectual ability to evidence it yet, it is still the case that children come into this world as natural born sinners:

- **Psalm 58:3** The wicked are estranged from the womb; These who speak lies go astray from birth.

- **Psalm 51:5** Behold, I was brought forth in iniquity, and in sin my mother conceived me.

This repeats the diagnosis of man as found in Genesis 8:21, that the intent of man's heart is evil *from his youth*. Charles Hodge correctly observed the implications of man's depravity since his youth:

"When we look on a new-born infant we know that whatever may be uncertain in its future, it is absolutely, inevitably certain that, should it live, it will sin."[124]

But many in our world have believed that, contrary to the teaching of Scripture, children are born in a natural state of purity and innocence. There have even been some who have taught this, suggesting that this is the testimony of Scripture as well, but their arguments normally come from extra-Biblical reasoning rather than from exegesis. Such thoughts most likely come from the observation of children in their state of *ignorance* and *pre-maturity*, however, give that angry, screaming baby the strength of a sumo wrestler and suddenly their apparent innocence will be perceived rather differently! No matter what our experimental perceptions may be, the Word of God tells us plainly that the children of Adam and Eve are all plagued with a sinful, condemnable nature, and that their only hope is in Christ who alone can save them.

Having established this reality of original guilt and sin, we must understand how to act on such truth. It is one thing to acknowledge the sinfulness of children, but it is another to understand the implications of this truth. While it is true that children are naturally sinful, this does not mean that they have the same ability to sin as adults. At the earliest stages of youth children have neither the intellectual or physical capacity to sin as only adults possess. This

---

[124]Hodge, <u>Systematic theology</u>, p. 229.

does not mean that children are without the defilement of sin. In fact, in their underdeveloped state, children do have a higher level of naïveté which governs their habits of sin. The Bible refers to this naïveté as foolishness, and while it is true that such foolishness is common among men of all ages, it is especially evident in the young. It is for this reason that Children are highly prone to behave foolishly due to the foolishness of their own heart, or even as the result of the evil and foolish influences that surround them. Repeatedly, children are referred to as being foolish and are therefore lacking the wisdom and moral fortitude to do that which is right. Again, while it is true that all men are by nature foolish, the naïveté of the child renders a foolishness which is of a special character. The Old Testament employs as many as ten words to speak of foolishness,[125] however, there are two words that are used most frequently to speak of the foolishness of children. While their meanings are quite similar, and their nuances can be fairly broad, there are important distinctions among these words that should be noted. Below is a generalized presentation of these two Hebrew words in question:

- **Foolishness (Moral Corruption):** (*'ewiyl*) – Pronounced: eweel, speaks of a foolishness that is natural, relating to the primitive constitution of fallen, corrupted man.[126] The emphasis here is focused more upon the source of foolishness and the propensity to make foolish decisions.[127] **Proverbs 22:15** Foolishness (*'ewiyl*) is bound up in the heart of a child. **Proverbs 15:5** A fool (*'ewiyl*) rejects his father's discipline, But he who regards reproof is prudent.

---

[125] William Williamson, <u>Wilson's Old Testament Word Studies</u> (Hendrickson Publishers, Peabody Massachusetts), pp. 173-174.

[126] Harris, Harris, Archer, and Waltke. <u>Theological Wordbook</u>, Article 44e.

[127] Ibid., article 1011e.

- **Foolishness (Confidence):** (*k̲esel*) – This frequently used Hebrew word often speaks of the outward actions which constitute one who is foolish. This is often manifested by the act of being very trusting, open minded, and willing to follow another. The word can be used in a variety of ways since its focus is upon the notion of trust. Conceptually, this could be a good thing, or a bad thing, depending on what the individual is trusting. [**Self-Confidence**] **Psalm 49:10,13: 10** ...The stupid and the senseless alike perish, And leave their wealth to others...13 This is the way of those who are foolish (*k̲esel*), And of those after them who approve their words. [Selah]. [**God-Confidence**] **Proverbs 3:26** ... the Lord will be your confidence (*b̲iyk̲eselek̲ā*).[128]

Of the several words in the Old Testament used to speak of foolishness, these two dominate the book of Proverbs. Their importance is obvious in light of the fact that the book of Proverbs is the principal book of wisdom dealing with children and child training. As we enter into the discussion concerning child training, these lexical concepts will become very helpful and important. If parents do not understand the nature of their children, and their propensity to do foolish things, then they will often become frustrated and unnecessarily provoked by their children's behavior. Those who become angry in their parenting can be greater fools than their children! Children are not little angels, they are children, which simply means that they are merely *underdeveloped* descendents of Adam and Eve. They are not without spiritual corruption because they are children who are begotten in our *image and likeness*.[129] The Word of God clearly teaches us that children have a compositional foolishness in their hearts that, while still underdeveloped in their

---

[128] It may be that Paul employed this notion of having an open minded trust (*kesel*) with the Lord in his address to the Corinthian church? His ironic approach may have incorporated this idea: 1 Corinthians 4:10 We are *fools* for Christ's sake, but you are prudent in Christ; we are weak, but you are strong; you are distinguished, but we are without honor. [Italics mine].

[129] Genesis 5:3.

infancy, will develop in time as it has been the case with all of the descendents of Adam and Eve. The popular philosophy of today (that has been around for generations) is that these "innocent" children should be allowed to develop and grow in their own way while following their own desires, thoughts, and wisdom. This worldly philosophy is raising up a new generation of grown children who will epitomize foolishness and corruption:

> **2 Timothy 3:1-5:** 1 But realize this, that in the last days difficult times will come. 2 For men will be lovers of self, lovers of money, boastful, arrogant, revilers, disobedient to parents, ungrateful, unholy, 3 unloving, irreconcilable, malicious gossips, without self-control, brutal, haters of good, 4 treacherous, reckless, conceited, lovers of pleasure rather than lovers of God; 5 holding to a form of godliness, although they have denied its power; and avoid such men as these.

How true it is that the wages of sin are death! The Biblical point made in this section is that *all* of Adam's descendents are procreated in the image and likeness of his corruption and sin. Their need is not mere morality, good manners, or church attendance; their need is identical to the needs of all mankind – *they need to be born again.* They need new hearts that beat the lifeblood of faith in the promised seed, Jesus Christ, who alone can crush Satan and provide the needed sacrifice on their behalf. Therefore, the priority of parents must be to train up their children with a pedagogy that will lead them to Christ through the message of the Gospel. To do this, parents must give priority to their own central calling in life, which is the worship of God.

For From Him And Through Him And To Him Are All Things
To Him Be The Glory Forever. Amen. Romans 11:36

THE FIRST INSTITUTION

CHAPTER 3

RESTORING THE GENESIS 2

MARRIAGE

Any attempt to restore a marriage back to God's standards without first consulting the foundation of Holy Writ is a fool's errand. Like the self-styled mechanic who attempts to repair his car without a single glance at his repair manual, so too is the couple who tries to "fix" their marriage without first consulting the very Scriptures that clearly explain to us the manner in which God made the institution of marriage. This is precisely why we began

> ## THE FIRST INSTITUTION
>
> **Matthew 19:4-6**
> "Have you not read, that He who created them from the beginning made them male and female, and said, 'For this cause a man shall leave his father and mother, and shall cleave to his wife; and the two shall become one flesh'?"
>
> "Consequently they are no longer two, but one flesh..."

with the first of all books, the book of Genesis. It is in this book that we have presented to us the very bedrock principles for the institution of marriage, both in its purest form before the fall, and then in its corrupted form after the fall. The theology of Genesis chapters 1-3 will prove to be essential to us as we proceed in our discussion of the practical aspects of marriage and parenting, therefore, let us briefly review the events that took place in the garden:

- *The man was created first and was entrusted with the unique responsibility of serving and guarding the garden by means of the Word of God. He was created to be the leader and head of his wife.*

- *The woman was uniquely created having been drawn out of the man's side. She was his special companion and wife who would be his loving helper.*

- *In their original condition they were pure, without the defilement of sin. Their calling in life, as individuals and as a married couple, was to manifest the glory of God as beings created in His image. The*

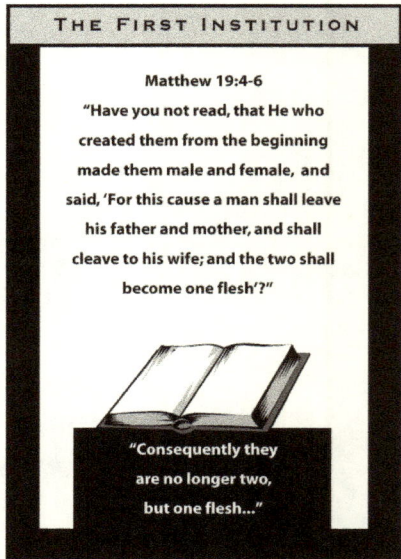

special institution of marriage, in which they were joined together, was designed to display the glory of the Godhead through the unity of the man and the woman. Together, they shared a unity of essence, bond, and purpose in a way which reflected the very image of God Himself.

- *However, they both transgressed God's law by different means. The woman transgressed through her independent action of eating the forbidden fruit, in deception. The man transgressed through his confederacy with the woman whereby he ate the forbidden fruit, without deception.*

- *Though both transgressed, it was only by means of the man's sin that all have sinned and fall short of the glory of God. Adam failed as the federal head and leader of the human race.*

After the fall, the man still remained as the ordained head and leader of his family, while his wife was still ordained to help him as his loving companion. However, their indwelling sin would ultimately pollute all aspects of their lives and their every relationship, ultimately because of their sinful enmity with God. What was true for Adam and Eve has been true for every generation of their descendents, and this will remain so until the Lord returns. Fathers are sinful; wives are sinful; and their children are...sinful. Because of reigning sin, families are powerless to mend their own ways. Their enmity with God is often manifested by a multitude of sins to include: marital conflict or neglect; career worship; materialism; divorce; the neglect, abuse or perhaps the idolatrous adoration of children; or any other assortment of typical sins that are so common in our modern culture. But though our world is filled with such corruption, there is indeed a greater hope! The great hope of God, which was first communicated to Adam and Eve in the promised seed, has been fully realized in the person of Jesus Christ, God's only Son in the flesh:

John 1:1-3,14: 1 In the beginning was the Word, and the Word was with God, and the Word was God. 2 He was in the beginning with God. 3 All things came into being by Him, and apart from Him nothing came into being that has come into being... 14 And the Word became flesh, and dwelt among us, and we beheld His glory, glory as of the only begotten from the Father, full of grace and truth.

John 1:10-13: 10 He was in the world, and the world was made through Him, and the world did not know Him. 11 He came to His own, and those who were His own did not receive Him. 12 But as many as received Him, to them He gave the right to become children of God, even to those who believe in His name, 13 who were born not of blood, nor of the will of the flesh, nor of the will of man, but of God.

The eternal Son of God came to earth, became a man, was rejected by men and was crucified on a cross as a substitute for sinners. However death could not keep the Lord of life[130] in the grave. On the third day after His crucifixion Christ rose again from the dead and is now seated at the right hand of the Father in eternal glory. Christ is the only hope for mankind, since He is the only Savior of the world.[131] Without Christ there is no hope,[132] but in Christ, there is all hope. Thus, He is the only basis of hope for anyone, past, present, and future. Without Christ there is no reconciliation with God the Father, nor can there be any *genuine* reconciliation of any other relationships in this world. Such Christ-less living is often characterized by enmities, strife, jealousy, outbursts of anger, disputes, dissensions, factions, drunkenness, carousing, immorality, impurity, sensuality, man-centered morality, along with a list of other

---

[130] John 1:4.

[131] John 4:42, 1 John 4:14.

[132] Ephesians 2:12 remember that you were at that time separate from Christ, excluded from the commonwealth of Israel, and strangers to the covenants of promise, having no hope and without God in the world.

deeds of the flesh (Galatians 5:19-21). But in those homes where Christ abides, there you will find the progressive increase of the fruit of the Spirit:

Galatians 5:22-23: 22 But the fruit of the Spirit is love, joy, peace, patience, kindness, goodness, faithfulness, 23 gentleness, self-control; against such things there is no law.

THE FIRST PROMISE

2 Corinthians 5:17:
Therefore if anyone is in Christ,
he is a new creature;
the old things passed away;
behold, new things have come.

The corruption and division brought on by sin has only one solution - Christ who was crucified for our sin. Only in Christ can the bond and purpose of marriage be restored, and only in Him are we new creations.

THE SPIRIT-FILLED FAMILY

The Christ-centered family is not perfect in practice, but is like a growing and budding tree that brings forth fruit in due season. Families who subject themselves to the Word of God, and the Spirit's leading, will *progressively* yield the fruit of godliness. With this in mind it is crucial to remember that the process of raising a family for the glory of God is not a mechanistic one. It cannot be reduced to a mere set of formulas which, if ritualistically obeyed, will guarantee a God-honoring outcome.[133] Unregenerate families may adopt a series of rules and regulations that may give them the occasional

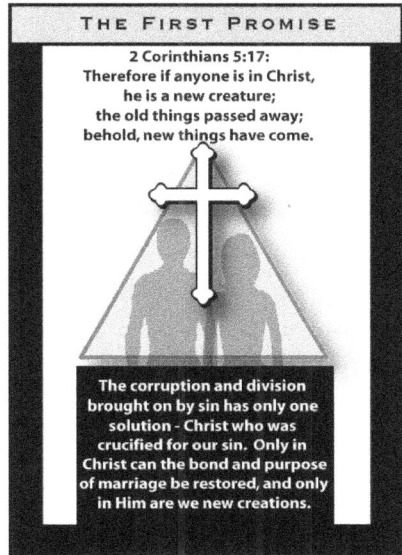

---

[133] The ultimate goal of the parent is not the external obedience of children, but rather their spiritual regeneration which will in turn beget a genuine obedience from the heart. While the process of Biblical child training does give the parent genuine hope (Proverbs 19:18), it still does not give an absolute guarantee that one's offspring will be born again. Some confusion has been spawned over this very issue as some have taught that the faithful parent is even *guaranteed* a particular outcome for their efforts. J. Richard Fugate in his book *What The Bible Says About Child Training* p. 2, has advanced this form of thinking, though perhaps unwittingly, when he says: "Parents who utilize this system [Biblical child training] consistently from the time their children are very young have God's guarantee of success." Such teaching has the potential to foster a spirit of presumption and even pride if parents believe that it is by their doing (ultimately) that their children are "successful."

appearance of godliness, but this is not genuine Christianity. John chapter 3 gives us a very clear example of this. It is in this section of Scripture that we see the Lord encountering a certain Pharisee by the name of Nicodemus: a powerful member of the Sanhedrin and chief teacher of Israel.[134] From his youth, he was most likely trained in the Scriptures in the manner described by Philo:

"Since the Jews esteem their laws as divine revelations, and are instructed in the knowledge of them from their earliest youth, they bear the image of the law in their souls. They are taught, so to speak, from their swaddling-clothes by their parents, teachers, and those who bring them up, even before instruction in the sacred laws and the unwritten customs, to believe in God the one Father and Creator of the world."[135]

While there should be no doubt that Nicodemus had experienced the rigors of regular instruction from his youth, he sadly did not know God.[136] This is the very reason why Christ explained to Nicodemus that he needed to be born again:

John 3:3,6,7: 3 Jesus answered and said to him, "Truly, truly, I say to you, unless one is born again, he cannot see the kingdom of God.".…6 "That which is born of the flesh is flesh, and that which is born of the Spirit is spirit. 7 "Do not marvel that I said to you, 'You must be born again'"

---

[134] In his gospel, John reminds us that Nicodemus was a Pharisee and a ruler of the Jews, indicating that he was a member of the powerful council of the Sanhedrin which had many judiciary powers and responsibilities. As a Pharisee, he was probably the chief instructor of the Scriptures to the council, thus Christ referred to him as *the teacher of [the] Israel* [the repeated article is called the article of *par excellence* denoting uniqueness of identity]. John 3:1,10 1 Now there was a man of the Pharisees, named Nicodemus, a ruler of the Jews; 10 Jesus answered and said to him, "Are you the teacher of Israel, and do not understand these things?"

[135] Emil Schürer, A History of The Jewish People, Second Division, Vol II (Hendrickson Publishers, 1995), p. 48, citing Philo, "Legat. ad Cajum," 31, Mang. ii. 577.

[136] John 3:1-7

Nicodemus was very much like those religious leaders who searched the Scriptures diligently (even from youth), but who did so without a genuine faith in God.[137] The lesson of Nicodemus is a powerfully important one and should serve as a clear warning for all who name the name of Christ: like a parrot that learns to replicate the sounds of the human voice, so too can men and women parrot religion as a mere mechanism, but the Lord calls us to be born again (literally: *be born from above*).[138] Men are not converted by the ritual of memorizing laws, rather they are changed when God transforms them with a new heart.[139] When a sinner is born from above, trusting Christ as his Savior, he is eternally forgiven of his sin and thus he experiences true peace with God rather than enmity and condemnation.[140] Therefore, the father, mother, and children who have been transformed through faith in the Lord Jesus Christ have a special calling in life as a family of God's own possession. This calling is that which transcends an external and heartless exercise. The family of God is called by the grace of God *to become* more like the person of Jesus Christ through a genuine imitation of Him, wrought by means of the inner workings of the Holy Spirit:

Ephesians 5:1-2: 1 Therefore be imitators of God, as beloved children; 2 and walk in love, just as Christ also loved you, and gave Himself up for us, an offering and a sacrifice to God as a fragrant aroma.

---

[137] John 5:39-42: 39 "You search the Scriptures, because you think that in them you have eternal life; and it is these that bear witness of Me; 40 and you are unwilling to come to Me, that you may have life. 41 "I do not receive glory from men; 42 but I know you, that you do not have the love of God in yourselves.

[138] The translation of the word *anōthen* as *again* in John 3:3 & 7 is of course adequate in that it denotes a new birth, however the word is frequently use by our Lord regarding that which is *from above*: John 3:31, 19:11, 23; Matt. 27:51, Mark 15:38. This thought [being born from above] is consistent with the overall thought expressed concerning the need for regeneration from the Spirit who is from heaven above. In either case, it must be understood that Christ instructs Nicodemus that he had yet to experience this spiritual transformation.

[139] Ezekiel 36:25-27.

[140] Romans 8:1-17.

This initial command of Paul's (Ephesians 5:1) must not be missed, for he instructs us *to be* [or literally *to become* (*ginesthe*)] imitators of Christ as beloved children. The implication of Paul's instruction here is profound. Christians are called to more than just an occasional mimicry of Christ; rather they are to become imitators of Christ *as a way of life*. As children imitate their parents, so too are the children of God to imitate Christ in their daily lives as children of light who appear as lights in this world:

> **Ephesians 5:8** for you were formerly darkness, but now you are light in the Lord; walk as children of light

The family that has trusted Christ as their Lord and Savior has a great responsibility in this life, for not only are they members of God's coming kingdom, but they are the King's citizens here on earth as His representatives. And as citizens and representatives of God, the family of God is called to walk in a manner worthy of the calling by which they have been called in order to display the beauty of God's mercy and grace, along with the glory of His Tri-unity.[141] This means that the natural tendency that husbands and wives have towards conflict with the Lord, and each other, will progressively be defeated in their lives as they are brought into greater conformity with the will of God through the ministry of the Spirit. This process of spiritual growth is often referred to as *the progressive sanctification of the believer* and ultimately enters into that important subject of *the perseverance of the Saints.* In His sovereign work of grace, the Lord not only saves His people from the condemnation of Hell, but He is also faithful to continue His work of grace in them such that they will continue in a life of increasing growth and godliness.[142] This marks the very centerpiece of spiritual battle in this world: there are those

---

[141] Ephesians 4:1-3.

[142] Philippians 1:6, 2:12-16.

who are the friends of this world, and are therefore at enmity with God;[143] but there are also those who desire to live godly in Christ Jesus who will face adversity in this life for their faith.[144] It is a fight indeed, but it is the good fight of faith which will endure amidst God's remnant until He returns for His people.[145]

Many generations have come and gone since the days of the first couple and there have been many different battles over the centuries, but the battle lines have not changed in any way. The spiritual war still rages on and therefore the need for spiritual vigilance remains high. The great challenge for the family of God continues to be found in the daily combat of life, where the pursuit of holy living stands in direct opposition to a fallen world-order that constantly opposes the Lord and His Word. It is to this front-line struggle of daily living that we now turn our attention. In order for the family of God to be spiritually successful, there must be a regular commitment to apply the theology of marriage to daily life. How crucial it is that husbands and wives embrace their God ordained roles within marriage remembering that they, in light of mankind's fallen nature, will have to face the conflicts and enmity which characterize all unions between the sons and daughters of Adam and Eve. The tendencies of marital conflict have already been clarified for us:

- *The Wife's Tendency to Resist the Man's Leadership: Genesis 3:16 "Your desire (ṭešuḳá)[146] shall be for your husband..." As discussed before, the tendency of the woman would be to attempt to act independently of the husband, even defying his leadership role.*

---

[143] James 4:4 You adulteresses, do you not know that friendship with the world is hostility toward God? Therefore whoever wishes to be a friend of the world makes himself an enemy of God.

[144] 2 Timothy 3:12 And indeed, all who desire to live godly in Christ Jesus will be persecuted.

[145] 2 Timothy 4:7-8.

[146] See chapter 2, The First Condemnation.

- *The Man's Tendency to be Indifferent in His Leadership:* Genesis 3:16 *"...and he will rule over you."* The concept of the man ruling is emphasized by the preposition/pronoun construct: over you *[bākē].*[147] *The natural man's rule would be characterized by a loveless indifference. By contrast, Abraham was instructed to command his family: not with indifference, but rather in love for the Lord and for his family.*

The complexities of sin in marriage can be quite extensive and exhausting, however no matter how complex marital problems may ever become it is always important to remember that Genesis 3:16 supplies us with the very root of most problems in marriages today, and throughout history. However, against these fleshly tendencies, the wife is to serve the Lord through her joyful submission and reverence rendered to her husband, in the Lord. As well, the husband must lead his home as the one who has been appointed to serve and guard his household as a loving shepherd. His leadership is crucial, for without it his wife may flounder and his children will most likely wander into the paths of rebellion. The husband must *act like the man* that God has called him to be, without wavering or compromise. For better or for worse, the husband's impact on the family will be evident in all cases. A family that is not led well by the father will become a haven for fleshly attitudes and activities; a home like this is subject to division and rebellion. Ultimately, such a leaderless home is like that difficult church at Corinth which Paul frequently exhorted to amend their ways. One of the Apostle's most decisive calls for spiritual vigilance came at the end of 1 Corinthians. His final exhortation to the leadership of that church serves as a

---

[147] In the LXX the words *sou kuriesei* are employed to denote the exercise of leadership that the man will have with respect to the woman. Peter reminds us that Sarah called Abraham *kurion* as an example to women who obey their husbands. Leadership and authoritative rule in the home is not the problem; what is problematic is the nature in which such rule is exercised by men.

reminder, to any leader, that the responsibility of leadership carries with it the necessity of spiritual vigilance - like that of a soldier:

> **1 Corinthians 16:13** Be on the alert, stand firm in the faith, act like men, be strong.

Paul's exhortation should serve as a strong jolt to any man who flounders in apathy, whether in marriage, or in any other context. Paul's corrective is not only needful for the church, but also for the modern family which, like the contemporary church in America, has become like the church at Corinth: sleepy, faithless, impotent, fleshly, and *systemically feminized*. Paul's command to the leadership of Corinth to *act like men* [*andrizesthe*][148] was a clear battle cry to those who had fallen asleep at their post. The leaders at Corinth needed to rise up as soldiers and *be on the alert, to stand firm,*[149] *and act like men.* In fact, these instructions reflect the very battle commands given to Joshua:

> **Joshua 1:9** Have I not commanded you? Be strong and courageous![150] Do not tremble or be dismayed, for the Lord your God is with you wherever you go.

In all of these texts, we are reminded that men fail the most when they flee from the front lines of their ordained role as leader in the home; but if the American family is to reclaim Biblical ground, then men must stand firm in the battle of life, *being strong and courageous in the strength of the Lord.* The need for male leadership in our

---

[148] G. *andrizesthe* – Someone who is courageous, bold or manly. Swanson, J. (1997). Dictionary of Biblical Languages with Semantic Domains : Greek (New Testament) (electronic ed.). Oak Harbor: Logos Research Systems, Inc.

[149] A common military expression given to front line soldiers of the Roman army. Soldiers were to maintain a strong front line by *standing firm* or *holding the line* rather than fleeing to the rear. This tactic of the Roman army was one of the keys to the success of the Romans in battle.

[150] LXX – *ischue kai andrizou* – literally, be strong and and manly [act like a man].

nation may be at an all-time high. Our secular culture derides the standards of the first institution of marriage with alarming eagerness. To the extent that families in America are faltering, it is because of an utter lack of *spiritual conversion* in our land, and consequently - *a lack of godly male leadership.* Apart from the Spirit's work in men and women, such decay is to be expected. Yet, despite this cultural context, it is essential that the man of God fully embrace his privilege and duty as the family's spiritual leader. He must be careful to embrace the clear teaching of Scripture in order to provide a leadership to his home that will honor the Lord. His calling, along with the calling of his wife, must be clearly established by Scripture if true revival is to take place in this land of ours.

It is at this point that we need to move to those discussions that will help us consider the practical application of the very doctrines that we have studied. To do so we will consult the text of Ephesians 5:22 – 6:4 in order to consider what a Spirit-filled family actually looks like. Of course, we will examine other texts as well (especially when we enter the discussion of children and child training), but Ephesians 5:22-6:4 will give us an important roadmap for the family. When we first considered this section of Scripture, we noted that physical marriage is not an end, but a means to the greater end of reflecting God's glorious image and His unique love for His people. This truth aids us in understanding the fact that a godly marriage is itself a witness and testimony of the Triune God in this lost world. At its best, marriage is an example of the unity of God, His Triune nature, His work, and His magnificent love. At its worst it is a breeding ground for blasphemy.[151] When the individual members of a family pursue their God-ordained roles, they give testimony to the wisdom and glory of the God.

---

[151] Titus 2:5.

Let's now examine our roadmap of Ephesians 5:22-6:4:

THE FIRST INSTITUTION

Matthew 19:6
"What therefore God has joined together, let no man separate."

Revelation 19:7
"Let us rejoice and be glad and give the glory to Him, for the marriage of the Lamb has come and His bride has made herself ready."

Ephesians 5:22-6:4 – 22 Wives, be subject to your own husbands, as to the Lord. 23 For the husband is the head of the wife, as Christ also is the head of the church, He Himself being the Savior of the body. 24 But as the church is subject to Christ, so also the wives ought to be to their husbands in everything. 25 Husbands, love your wives, just as Christ also loved the church and gave Himself up for her; 26 that He might sanctify her, having cleansed her by the washing of water with the word, 27 that He might present to Himself the church in all her glory, having no spot or wrinkle or any such thing; but that she should be holy and blameless. 28 So husbands ought also to love their own wives as their own bodies. He who loves his own wife loves himself; 29 for no one ever hated his own flesh, but nourishes and cherishes it, just as Christ also does the church, 30 because we are members of His body. 31 For this cause a man shall leave his father and mother, and shall cleave to his wife; and the two shall become one flesh. 32 This mystery is great; but I am speaking with reference to Christ and the church. 33 Nevertheless let each individual among you also love his own wife even as himself; and let the wife see to it that she respect her husband. 6:1 Children, obey your parents in the Lord, for this is right. 2 Honor your father and mother (which is the first commandment with a promise), 3 that it may be well with you, and that you may live long on the earth.4 And, fathers, do not provoke your children to anger; but bring them up in the discipline and instruction of the Lord.

Before we examine the particular instructions given to husbands, wives, and children, we must first consider the important context in which this text lies. Ephesians 5:22-6:4 is actually an advancement of

Paul's five commands to Christians (Eph. 5:15-18) concerning how they are to live as children of light: children who seek to do that which is pleasing to the Lord (Eph. 5:8-10). These commands, which are antecedent to this section on the family, are contextually crucial. Paul tells the Ephesian believers that in order to walk as children of light they must be *watchful (5:15), wise (5:17a), discerning (5:17b), sober (5:18a) and spiritual (be filled with the Holy Spirit, 5:18b).* Paul then describes what Spirit filled living actually looks like:

> **Ephesians 5:19-21:** 19 speaking to one another in psalms and hymns and spiritual songs, singing and making melody with your heart to the Lord; 20 always giving thanks for all things in the name of our Lord Jesus Christ to God, even the Father; 21 and be subject to one another in the fear of Christ.

Our day and age has seen much erroneous teaching regarding the true ministry of the Holy Spirit. Ecstatic experiences, visions, extra-Biblical revelations, and even so-called fallible prophecy adorn the pulpits of many in our day and age. Such preachers advance a confusing message concerning the Spirit's ministry; however, by contrast, we see that the Apostle Paul gives us a very clear description of what the Spirit-filled children of light actually look like. Paul indicates that those who are genuinely *filled with the Spirit* will engage in *godly encouragement with the brethren* (speaking to one another in psalms and hymns and spiritual songs, v. 18); *God-centered praise* (singing and making melody with your heart to the Lord, v. 19); *thanksgiving* (always giving thanks for all things, v. 20) and *servitude of the brethren* (be subject to one another in the fear of Christ, v. 21). When Paul gives us this fourth description of a Spirit filled life, he in essence reminds us of the important example of Christ to all the children of God:

Mark 10:45 For even the Son of Man did not come to be served, but to serve, and to give His life a ransom for many.

Mutual servitude is as fundamental to the Christian life as eating is to our daily existence. Paul's use of the reciprocal pronoun in Eph. 5:21 reminds us that we have an obligation to be servants to all members of the body of Christ, beneath the authority of the church's head - Jesus Christ. Thus, when the body of Christ assembles, its individual members should be more concerned about the needs of others over and above their own (Phil. 2:3-4). Such a mutual servitude is a beautiful manifestation of the Spirit of God and is essential to its overall health and vitality. However, such concepts of service do not nullify the clear Biblical standards of leadership and submission in the church and family.[152] The brethren are to be subject to one another as the servants of Christ, however, that subjection does not eliminate the truth regarding the unique leadership of pastors/teachers within a local church (Ephesians 4:11);[153] nor does it ignore the husband's special leadership in the home. For this reason Paul declares:

Wives, be subject[154] to your own husbands, as to the Lord. For the husband is the head of the wife, as Christ also is the head of the church, He Himself being the Savior of the body.

---

[152] While it is true that the family of God holds priority over fleshly relationships (Matt. 12:48-50), this does not mean that the institution of marriage is nullified or eliminated in the church. This was a misconception in the early church, a matter that Paul addressed to the Corinthian church (1 Corinthians 7:3-5, 27). Marriage is not unspiritual, demeaning nor inferior. Though Paul preferred the benefits of singleness for various reasons (1 Cor. 7:7-8, 26), he in no way denigrated the institution of marriage. More than this, Paul explains to us how it is that the marriage union is in fact a type of the loving union of Christ and the church – this is the overall point of Ephesians 5:22-33.

[153] Hebrews 13:17 Obey those who rule over you, and be submissive, for they watch out for your souls, as those who must give account. Let them do so with joy and not with grief, for that would be unprofitable for you.

[154] The lack of a verb or verbal in verse 22 is understandable in light of the context. The elliptical sense here is that wives are to subject themselves to the community of the brethren (v.

Paul's entire argument in this section flows from his command to be filled with the Holy Spirit (Ephesians 5:18). Hence, we see in the overall presentation of Ephesians 5:22-6:4 that the family being described is a *spiritual family.* Such a spiritual family is one that possesses three simple ingredients:

- *The husband/father exercises his position of leadership in a manner that reflects the loving leadership of Jesus Christ unto his wife and children;*

- *The wife/mother submits to her own husband's leadership just as the church submits to Christ.*

- *Children are called to honor and obey their parents as they are nurtured with discipline and instruction, in the Lord (Ephesians 6:1-4).*

In its highest form, Ephesians 5:22-6:4 shows us the spiritual family in action, living as children of light in a dark world.[155] With this contextual framework of our text in question, we can knowledgeably proceed with our analysis of the spiritual practices of the husband, wife, and children.

These roles and priorities of the family will not simply happen by nature, for our *fallen nature* resists the ways of God. Therefore husbands and wives must be active in their pursuit of godliness. As we continue on our Ephesians 5:22-6:4 pathway, we will begin with a

---

21), after observing the higher priority of *subjecting themselves* to their *own* husbands. Paul makes it very clear that his discussion of mutual subjection within the body of Christ in no way eradicates the distinctive leadership of husbands with respect to their wives.

[155] Ephesians 5:8-11 8 for you were formerly darkness, but now you are light in the Lord; walk as children of light 9 (for the fruit of the light consists in all goodness and righteousness and truth), 10 trying to learn what is pleasing to the Lord. 11 And do not participate in the unfruitful deeds of darkness, but instead even expose them;

careful examination of the important *actions of the spirit filled husband.*

THE SPIRIT-FILLED HUSBAND

The Apostle's description of true spirituality gives us an important platform for Ephesians 5:22-6:4: In patterning his life after Christ, the husband understands that his servitude to his family will be predicated upon a godly leadership; for Christ, who was the greatest leader of all, was also the greatest servant of all (as stated earlier Mark 10:45). It is crucial to understand that Christ's service to the church did not eradicate His office as leader,

THE SPIRIT-FILLED HUSBAND

Ephesians 5:31:
a man shall leave his father and mother, and shall cleave to his wife; and the two shall become one flesh.

Ephesians 5:25:
Husbands, love your wives, even as Christ also loved the church, and gave himself up for her;

rather it confirmed it.[156] Much confusion has been unnecessarily concocted from such a principle, but the example of Christ is quite clear. As Christ is the head and leader of the church, so is the man the head and leader of his home. Such a man is to *serve* God as Abraham did by *commanding* his household in the Lord. This is Paul's clear point to be sure, that a man serves his wife and children *by sacrificially leading them.* Paul gives us two clear descriptions of the man's leadership: *first*, the man is the head of his home by the calling of God, and *second*, he explains to men how they are to lead their homes with a Christ-imitating passion. His emphasis of teaching is focused upon the latter subject (Christ-imitating passion), however, before we enter into that study we should first consider the

---

[156] Eph. 1:18-23, Colossians 1:18, Rev. 5:7-14.

117

concept of the man's position of headship. Paul shows us the quality of the man's headship through the principal verb found in verse 23 where Paul says, "...the husband *is* the head of the wife, as Christ also is head of the church." This simple statement ratifies the very basis for the wife's submission to the husband. The fact that the husband *is* the head of his wife reflects the created order established by God in the institution of marriage. Paul offers no conditions to these facts. Using an indicative verb (the verb of reality), Paul describes the husband in terms of his God-ordained role: he *is* the head. The concept of headship here (*kephale)* denotes primacy and leadership as illustrated earlier in Ephesians 4:15 "...but speaking the truth in love, we are to grow up in all aspects into Him, who is the head, even Christ." Thus, for the husband, such a position of leadership cannot be changed except by death or divorce.[157] Beyond such extreme circumstances as these, the man *is* the head of his wife and household. Even in Peter's exhortation to women, we see a reminder that the man's position *remains unchanged*, even if he is disobedient to the Word:

> ***1 Peter 3:1-2**: 1 In the same way, you wives, be submissive to your own husbands so that even if any of them are disobedient to the word, they may be won without a word by the behavior of their wives, 2 as they observe your chaste and respectful behavior.*

The principle of male headship must not be underestimated here, especially since there are many who offer circumstantial excuses for avoiding such headship. Some men, being quite deceived, will be convinced that they are exempt from this standard simply because they do not believe that they are well suited to be the leader in their home, however his faulty thinking does not change the *fact* that, by virtue of the bond of marriage, all men are the ordained heads and leaders of their wives and families. However, even though men are

---

[157] Romans 7:2, 1 Cor. 7:39, Matt. 19:9.

positionally ordained to be the heads of their households, this does not mean that they fulfill such an office perfectly. In view of this, we are reminded of that important truth gleaned from the *first condemnation*: in the weakness of his flesh, the man's rule will tend towards a rule of indifference, for he (Adam) was inclined to rule *over* his wife. The fact that Adam was to rule his family was a part of God's good and holy will, however, through indwelling sin his headship would be infected with the corruption of sinful indifference. The preposition *over* gives such an implication concerning the nature of Adam's defection as a leader. Similar language in the Old and New Testaments reflects this concept of indifferent leadership as in the case of Korah's complaint against Moses, Christ's description of Gentile rulers, and Peter's exhortation to elders:[158]

> *1 Peter 5:2-3:* *2 shepherd the flock of God among you, exercising oversight not under compulsion, but voluntarily, according to the will of God; and not for sordid gain, but with eagerness; 3 nor yet as lording it over those allotted to your charge, but proving to be examples to the flock.*

It is important to clarify that the concept of exercising rule over another is not necessarily sinful,[159] for God is a great King *over all the earth*.[160] But as it relates to the discussion concerning *man as a fallen being*, it is often the case that such language indicates a kind of rule which lacks care, concern, compassion, and love. History is unfortunately filled with examples of men who have abused their God-given authority, either through a harsh dictatorship, or by

---

[158] *Korah's charge against Moses:* Numbers 16:13 "Is it not enough that you have brought us up out of a land flowing with milk and honey to have us die in the wilderness, but you would also lord it over us?" *Christ's description of the harsh rule of the Gentile leaders:* Matthew 20:25 But Jesus called them to Himself, and said, "You know that the rulers of the Gentiles lord it over them, and their great men exercise authority over them.

[159] Hebrews 13:17 Obey your leaders, and submit to them; for they keep watch over your souls, as those who will give an account. Let them do this with joy and not with grief, for this would be unprofitable for you.

[160] Psalm 47:2.

means of careless neglect. In either extreme, *the heart of the issue is the sin of indifference*. This, therefore, establishes the principal battleground for the redeemed husband: it is the battle of the Spirit against the flesh in the inner man.[161] Men must understand that *godly* leadership does not come *naturally*, but *spiritually* by the work of God's grace in him. There was only One who was ever a *natural born leader*,[162] and it is He who was born as the King of all kings and the Lord of all lords: the Lord Jesus Christ. All others who wish to lead with a godly leadership must follow after the pattern of King Jesus who exercises a leadership that is filled with love, compassion, and great care for His bride – *the very antithesis of indifference*.

This then leads us to the second quality of the man's headship. Paul does not simply leave us with the mere fact of the man's position as head, rather he describes how the Spirit-filled man is called to serve passionately in this role. To do this, Paul supplies us with four descriptions of Christ's passion for the church, and through this he gives husbands the reigning example of godly leadership. Christ's perfect example therefore instructs men regarding how they are to resist their sinful indifference through four Christ-like passions: *1. Passionate Love (v. 25a); 2. Passionate Protection (v. 25b); 3. Passionate Leadership (vs. 26-27); and 4. Passionate Care (vs. 28-32).* These examples are enumerated and expanded below:

1. THE HUSBAND'S PASSIONATE LOVE

Ephesians 5:25 "Husbands, love your wives, just as *Christ also loved the church* and gave Himself up for her." Paul wastes no time in getting to the foundation of a spiritual marriage: Ephesians 5:25a

---

[161] Galatians 5:17

[162] Isaiah 9:6 For a child will be born to us, a son will be given to us; And the government will rest on His shoulders; And His name will be called Wonderful Counselor, Mighty God,Eternal Father, Prince of Peace.

"Husbands, *love your wives, just as Christ also loved the church.*" Immediately we see that the spiritual husband is to look to the example of Christ's love for the church, rather than to the standards of the world. What Paul was teaching the believers at Ephesus was a truth that clearly transcended the culture's understanding of love, because the first century concepts of love in marriage were readily plagued by the false deities of both the Greeks and the Romans. For example the Greek god *Erōs,* along with the Roman counterpart *Cupid,* represented a kind of romantic love that sought personal satisfaction as the highest priority.[163] Such self-centered thoughts about love and romance were very popular and were considered as an integral part of divine worship. In Roman secular ideology a man was considered to be successful in life if he accomplished all that he desired in life, including the matter of personal pleasure in marriage. Being philosophically driven by their mythologies, the secular culture saw marriage as an opportunity for self satisfaction, mediated and supported by the gods as depicted in this ancient wedding poem to the god of weddings, Hymenaeus: "Live well, newlyweds, *and spend your youth in constant lovemaking.*"[164] The secular understanding of love was therefore focused on the natural enjoyment and pleasure of the man and wife, and the gods were seen as facilitators of this pursuit of personal pleasure. But contrary to the false definitions and deities of love in his day, Paul pointed beyond the earthly realm to Christ Himself as our example of love: *Husbands, love your wives, just as Christ also loved the church.* It is this love of Christ that is the master gem out of which all of the jewels of His mercy and compassion are fashioned; and the husband who walks in the Spirit will indeed manifest such love towards his wife, understanding that

---

[163] Altar to an Unknown Love, 2011 (The Armoury Ministries).

[164] Jo-Ann Shelton, As The Romans Did, A Source Book in Roman Social History (Oxford University Press, New York), p. 43.

love is the Spirit's first fruit in the life of a believer.[165] The husband's standard for love is Christ Himself, but in what sense does Christ love His bride? What are the characteristics of this love about which Paul speaks? Well, it is often explained that this is the love of sacrifice and service, which is certainly true, however there is more to this concept of love than that of *sacrificial love*. It is wonderfully true that Christ's sacrifice was indeed the outcome of His love for the church, and that *agape* love does often speak of service as well as the act of seeking out the good of the one who is loved; but it can also speak of a love that flows from one's own desire and good pleasure. It is often tempting to limit Paul's meaning of love in this passage by a mere lexical analysis of the word *agape,* however, the analogy of Scripture points us to a more multifaceted connotation with respect to Christ's actual love for the church. For example, the introductory chapters of Ephesians teach us that Christ's love for the church cannot be characterized by servitude alone, for His love is far more extensive than this. Christ's multifaceted love included a special desire for the elect, whom the Father gave to Him before the foundation of the world (Ephesians 1:1-14). This very idea regarding Christ's unique love and desire for His bride certainly expands our thoughts about the nature of His love; but there is even a more fundamental concept of love in the example of Christ where we see that He loved the church as an outflow of His eternal love *for, and from,* God the Father:

- *Christ desired that the world would know of His love for the Father: John 14:31 but that the world may know that I love the Father, and as the Father gave Me commandment, even so I do.*

- *Christ expressed His love for the Father through His obedience to His will: John 6:38-39 – 38 For I have come down from heaven,*

---

[165] Galatians 5:22 But the fruit of the Spirit is love, joy, peace, patience, kindness, goodness, faithfulness.

not to do My own will, but the will of Him who sent Me. 39 And this is the will of Him who sent Me, that of all that He has given Me I lose nothing, but raise it up on the last day.

- **Christ desired that His disciples would know of the Father's special love for the Son: John 10:17** *For this reason the Father loves Me, because I lay down My life that I may take it again.*

We learn from these verses that Christ's love for the Father was antecedent to His love for the church. A careful study of the Scriptures reveals the fact that there are many facets to the gem of Christ's love; however, His principal love for the Father stands at the forefront of all other manifestations of His affections. Thus, as a result of His eternal love for the Father we see that the Son expended Himself in order to do the Father's perfect will. As well, those whom the Father chose before the foundation of the world[166] were given to the Son so that He might redeem them according to the Father's merciful plan. Therefore the elect of God are precious to Christ because the Father gave them to the Son,[167] and because the Son gave Himself as a sacrifice for their redemption and justification. This example of Christ gives us the greatest standard of measurement for love within the marriage union: *the spiritual man loves his wife as an outflow of his love for God, and therefore, the Lord is his passionate priority before any other.*[168] This presents the very teaching of the Lord Jesus concerning all worshippers, whether married or not:

Mark 12:28-31 – 28 And one of the scribes came and heard them arguing, and recognizing that He had answered them well, asked Him, "What commandment is the foremost of all?" 29 Jesus answered, "The foremost is, 'Hear, O Israel! The Lord our God is one Lord; 30 and you

---

[166] Ephesians 1:4.

[167] John 6:38-40.

[168] John 2:13-17.

shall love the Lord your God with all your heart, and with all your soul, and with all your mind, and with all your strength.' 31 "The second is this, 'You shall love your neighbor as yourself.' There is no other commandment greater than these."

The union of marriage is to be understood with this priority of love – the husband is not to place his wife above all, rather the Lord is his highest priority. Such a priority does not demean the wife nor lessen the quality of love that the husband has for her. On the contrary, this is the highest quality of love that he can offer to her – *the godly love of Christ*. The implications of this concept of love are vast and, consequently, the imitation of Christ takes on some wonderful connotations with such an observation. As Christ cherished the church as a gift from the Father, so too is the spiritual man to love his bride as a gift from God. In imitating Christ, the spiritual husband will grow in his desire, compassion, and faithfulness towards his wife in view of the surpassing goodness and grace of the One who gave her. The true believer holds dearly to the endowments of the Lord because of his deep love for the Giver Himself:

> **James 1:17** Every good thing bestowed and every perfect gift is from above, coming down from the Father of lights, with whom there is no variation, or shifting shadow.

By this we see that the Spirit-filled man has a passionate desire for his wife because she is a wonderful and special gift from God Himself.[169] Because of this, the husband's valuation of His wife is not based upon her performance, physical beauty, or skill at cooking; rather it is based upon this key truth: Proverbs 18:22 "He who finds a wife finds a good thing, And obtains favor from the Lord." The spiritual husband is to love his wife in a multifaceted way, but his love for her must be God-centered such that he cherishes her *in the Lord*.

---

[169] Gen. 2:23.

I should also remind the reader that these aforementioned truths do not diminish the reality of the husband's personal desire for his wife, for the Lord Jesus Christ loved the church as His bride with a genuine desire *for her*. As discussed earlier in chapter 1 *The Glory of God's Creation (The First Institution)*, marriage is a type of God's own relationship with His chosen people. The nuptial language that is employed in this sense is common in the Bible, as in Isaiah 62:5 "For as a young man marries a virgin, so your sons will marry you; and as the bridegroom rejoices over the bride, so your God will rejoice[170] over you." Note the clarity of the comparison: *"As the bridegroom rejoices over the bride*, so your God will rejoice over you." God compares His desire for his elect to that of a husband's desire for his wife. This thought is not only presented in the O.T., but we also see that the consummation of the union of the Lord with His people is established through a future, heavenly wedding: Revelation 19:7 "Let us rejoice and be glad and give the glory to Him, for the marriage of the Lamb has come and His bride has made herself ready." In addition to these texts, we see that the strong desire of a husband for his wife is likened to the fiery passions of God Himself: Song of Solomon 8:6 "Put me like a seal over your heart, like a seal on your arm. For love [*agape*] is as strong as death, jealousy is as severe as Sheol; its flashes are flashes of fire, the very flame of the Lord." The Lord is passionate about His people, and marriage reflects this very love and desire. The Lord is not flippant with this choice, but is earnest in His commitment to His people such that He has an abiding affection for them.[171] In reflecting on this it should be noted that a spirit-filled man, who loves his wife, will have a strong desire for her *like the very flame of the Lord*. For every husband his bride is a gift from God Almighty (as the church is to Christ) and so he must prize her in light of the One who gave her. This is the attitude which

---

[170] H. *sus* – denoting deep affection, love or joy for another.

[171] Deuteronomy 7:7-9.

is patterned after Adam when the Lord brought the woman to him[172] and Adam recognized what a prize she was in light of God's creation and provision. In view of these principles, a man's fidelity to his wife is a manifestation of his own devotion to God:

> **Proverbs 5:15-19** 15 Drink water from your own cistern, And fresh water from your own well. 16 Should your springs be dispersed abroad, Streams of water in the streets? 17 Let them be yours alone, And not for strangers with you. 18 Let your fountain be blessed, And rejoice in the wife of your youth. 19 As a loving hind and a graceful doe, Let her breasts satisfy you at all times; Be exhilarated always with her love."

A husband who is being led by the Spirit of God will learn to cherish and desire his wife *in the Lord*. His love for her will be at its best when it mirrors Christ's love for the church the most:

- *Christ loved the Father and therefore He loved the church because she was a unique gift from Him.*

- *Christ loved the church despite herself and thus His love transcended her gross imperfections (Romans 5:8).*

Christ's example of love is a necessary foundation for any man who desires to love his wife *in the Lord*. As a special gift from God, his wife will become more cherished to him as the years pass. A romance such as this transcends the temporal and sexual aspects of passion and desire. As he becomes more like Christ, he will find himself prizing his wife as Christ does the church to the extent that he will gladly sacrifice himself for her safety and purity. This is true love: a love and desire that manifests itself in godly servitude – for Christ loved the church *and gave Himself up for her.*

---

[172] Gen. 2:22.

2. THE HUSBAND'S PASSIONATE PROTECTION

Ephesians 5:25 "Husbands, love your wives, just as Christ also loved the church and *gave Himself up for her*." Christ's love for His Father and the church was manifested in the greatest manner possible: by the humility of His incarnation and death on the cross. When the apostle declares that Christ loved the church and *gave Himself up for her (Eph. 5:25)*, he teaches us very clearly that the Lord's love was genuine, unique, and rooted in great humility. The depth of His affections, measured by the severity of His actions, show that His is a deep and abiding love. His love for the Father and for the church was so compelling that He made the greatest sacrifice that could ever be made, by humbling Himself to the extent of becoming a man and dying on a cross as a substitute for His bride. John 15:13 says - "Greater love has no one than this, that one lay down his life for his friends." In order to redeem His bride, Christ became a man and thus shared the same substance of humanity with His bride, yet without sin. In all of this, we see a stark contrast between Adam and Christ: the first Adam, who was one flesh with his wife, failed utterly and brought condemnation to all. But the last Adam, who emptied Himself by being made in the likeness of men, shared the essence of our humanity (without corruption) and laid down His life as our sacrificial substitute. Here is the fruit of genuine love: the humble sacrificing of self *for the protection, safety, and benefit of another*. It is necessary to point out that the sacrifice of Christ for the church was more than a moral example. It was a genuine act of love that was utterly necessary for the salvation of those whom the Father chose before the foundation of the world. There is no greater story of manliness and chivalry in all of human history. He is the spiritual husband's greatest hero and example. Christ's God-centered motive and sacrificial love is the standard and goal for any man who would love his wife *in Christ*. As the spiritual man grows in his understanding that his wife is a gift to him from God, he will cherish his bride with nobility and protect her with greater vigilance and passionate love. It is this concept of valuation that is crucial: Romans 5:7-8 "...one will hardly die for a righteous man; though perhaps for the good man someone would dare even to die. But God demonstrates His own love toward us, in that while we were yet sinners, Christ died for us." Christ's self sacrifice was established by the Father's sovereign choice[173] and not by the loveliness of the one for whom the sacrifice was made. If love has a condition here, it is the condition of the Father's gift of the elect, given to His Son, rather than our worthiness to be loved by Him. Without taking the analogy too far here, we can apply this principle of love to the husband and his wife. When a man is joined together to a woman in marriage, he accepts his bride as God's will for his life. Once that union is established, the husband receives his bride as God's provision and thus his love for her should be based upon *that condition alone. Such a love that is conditioned solely upon God's will is unconditional with respect to the wife.* Christ did not lay down His life because we were worthy of His sacrifice. By extension, if love had to be given based upon the worthiness of the recipient, then all marriages would tumble and fall very quickly. We can be glad that the church's worthiness was not the condition for Christ's love; after all, we were blemished beyond recognition, horribly mangled by indwelling sin. But Christ, who passionately loved the Father, immersed His elect bride in His own blood that she should be holy, blameless, and beautiful in the sight of the Father.

In all of this we see the husband's true standard of *self-sacrifice.* The husband who truly loves his wife (*to the praise of God's glory*) will passionately expend himself for her. Her body, soul, and spirit will be his serious concern. Even with children in mind (Ephesians 6:1-3), the husband's first priority is to care for his wife. This does not mean

---

[173] Eph. 1:3-7.

that the husband is the wife's errand-boy (so to speak) fetching whatever the wife desires. This is a common error seen throughout history and is a frequent one of the modern age. Christ is certainly not the church's cosmological genie, granting any wish offered up by the church. Rather, our Lord gives the church what she *actually* *needs* for her sanctification and growth, which is Paul's next point in Ephesians 5.

3. THE HUSBAND'S PASSIONATE LEADERSHIP

Ephesians 5:25-27: "...Christ also loved the church and gave Himself up for her...*that He might sanctify her, having cleansed her by the washing of water with the word, that He might present to Himself the church in all her glory, having no spot or wrinkle or any such thing; but that she should be holy and blameless.*" Christ's genuine passion for the church led Him to do all that was necessary for her safety, protection, and benefit. Looking to the Father's will, the Son labored to present His bride in such a manner that she would be *holy and blameless before Him* (Ephesians 1:4). This He did by His shed blood, through which the sinner is justified by faith in Christ.[174] But there is yet another principle presented in this text which deals with the Lord's *leadership* of the church. Not only did Christ sacrifice Himself for her, but He also cleansed her *by the washing of water with the Word;* and this He did before and after His crucifixion:

- *Before His crucifixion, Christ guarded His disciples in the truth (John 17:12) through His faithful ministry to them as Teacher and Lord.*

---

[174] Romans 5:1 Therefore having been justified by faith, we have peace with God through our Lord Jesus Christ.

- *After His resurrection Christ sent the Holy Spirit to His bride so that she would be sanctified in the Word of God: "...when He, the Spirit of truth, comes, He will guide you into all the truth; for He will not speak on His own initiative, but whatever He hears, He will speak; and He will disclose to you what is to come. He shall glorify Me; for He shall take of Mine, and shall disclose it to you" (John 16:12-14). Now that the Spirit has been given, Christ's bride is faithfully and continually cleansed by the washing of water with the Word.*

Christ's desire for His bride has always been that she would be sanctified throughout the course of her existence upon the earth, by means of the Word of God; and that she would be finally presented in glory having no spot or wrinkle, but that she would be holy and blameless.[175] Here is a precious and important example for husbands. The man's passion for leadership must be grounded by these Christ-like priorities. His wife's holiness, sanctification, purity, and godliness must be his chief goal of husbandry. Here is the unavoidable calling of the man – *spiritual leadership in his home.* The man of God who genuinely loves his wife will spiritually lead her, understanding that she was created to depend on that leadership as the weaker vessel:

1 **Peter 3:7** You husbands likewise, live with your wives in an understanding way, as with a weaker vessel, since she is a woman; and grant her honor as a fellow heir of the grace of life, so that your prayers may not be hindered.

The Spirit of God, through the Apostle Peter, warns the husband about the dangers of treating his wife in such a manner that ignores her frailty as a woman, as well as her equality in Christ. As to the former thought, we ought to remember that while it is true that all the sons and daughters of Adam and Eve have their weaknesses,

---

[175] John 17:17, Eph. 5:26.

Peter says that it is the woman who is *the weaker vessel (asthenēs)*.[176] This term, in its broadest sense, speaks of a person who is in a state of helplessness and therefore dependency. To assume that Peter has in mind here a *physical* dependency/weakness only, requires that we bypass the broader context of the Apostle's presentation. Remember that he had previously called upon women to consider the example of Sarah, whose dependency upon Abraham led her, not to fear, but to boldness through her ultimate dependency upon Almighty God:

> **1 Peter 3:5-6:** 5 For in this way in former times the holy women also, who hoped in God, used to adorn themselves, being submissive to their own husbands. 6 Thus Sarah obeyed Abraham, calling him lord, and you have become her children if you do what is right without being frightened by any fear.

Peter's mention of the woman's *frailty* consists of much more than her physical stature and stamina. In context, Peter is also speaking of the emotional frailty that attends the wife's calling of dependency and submission. Calvin comments well on this important connection:

> "The weakness of the sex causes women to be suspicious and timid, and therefore morose; for they fear lest by their subjection, they should be more reproachfully treated. It was this that Peter seems to have had in view in forbidding them to be disturbed by any fear, as though he had said, 'Willingly submit to the authority of your husbands, nor let fear prevent your obedience, as though your condition would be worse, were you to obey.' The words may be more general, 'Let them not raise up commotions at home.' For as they are liable to be frightened, they often

---

[176] "...pertaining to a state of helplessness in view of circumstances." Louw, J. P., & Nida, E. A. (1996, c1989). Greek-English lexicon of the New Testament : Based on semantic domains (electronic ed. of the 2nd edition.) (1:242). New York: United Bible societies.

make much of a little thing, and thus disturb themselves and the family."[177]

These principles bring us, once again, to the calling of the first family. Adam was to lead his wife, and she was to help him in a manner that would best facilitate his role as head. Therefore, the wife's most immediate provision of leadership comes from her husband and she is therefore called to depend upon that leadership as God's provision. As well, the woman is to pursue her husband's leadership, even seeking it out with a spirit of investigation and inquiry:

> **1 Corinthians 14:35** And if they desire to learn anything, let them ask their own husbands at home; for it is improper for a woman to speak in church.

The woman's dependency upon her husband must never occasion pride and arrogance within the man. The wife's submission and dependency does not mean that she is a lesser person at all, rather, the godly husband is to treat his wife with compassion and thereby become all the more desirous to aid and support her in view of her role. This is why Peter then instructs men to value (or honor) their wives (*timē*). She *is* a weaker vessel, *but* she is also a fellow heir of the grace of life. Her nature as a helper does not make her inferior by any means. The man is the head of his wife and he is therefore to be her protector and defender, and this he does by means of the cleansing water of the Word; just as Adam was to *protect* the garden with the commandment of God. In genuine love he is to show her great humility and compassion while he renders such leadership. His love for her will be manifested in various ways, to include his own self-sacrifice for her protection and sanctification, just as Christ did for the church.

---

[177] Calvin, <u>Commentaries</u>, Vol. XXII. p. 98.

From creation to the fall, and even to the present, it is quite evident that the struggles of men and women are essentially the same throughout human history. In terms of our common sin, men tend to forsake their leadership roles, while women tend to ignore or even subvert the man's headship. Should we pretend that these battles are not real, then we will fail every time. Because of this, it is necessary that men and women remember the primal failures of the first couple. In particular, how the woman and the man capitulated to Satan's deception is significant for our understanding of their failures. We are reminded that it was the woman, not the man, who was deceived. This again is the reason that is set forth by the Apostle concerning the distinctions of roles among men and women. As Adam's helper, the woman was created in such a manner that she was to depend upon Adam's leadership as he serviced the garden and guarded it through the instrumentality of God's Word. But in her independent actions, she was susceptible to deception as is clearly evidenced in her transgression in Genesis 3. The fact that the woman is called the weaker vessel, and that the man is the ordained head and leader, is crucial. In light of these truths, it is necessary that the wife depend upon her husband's leadership for her protection because even though he is an imperfect vessel, he is still the Lord's provision for her. If a man, upon reviewing these truths, resolves to become arrogant in his thinking then he has missed the whole point regarding these distinctions. These distinctions do not measure out to standards of supremacy or inferiority, but they are differences ordained by God for His greater glory.[178]

We should be careful not to carry Paul's portrait in Ephesians 5:25-27 beyond its intended purpose. The husband is not Christ Himself, nor is he the Holy Spirit. The husband, in his passionate self-sacrifice and

---

[178] See Chapter 1, The First Institution.

leadership, cannot save his wife[179] nor can he sanctify her as only Christ and the Holy Spirit can. However, such a reminder should not cause us to retreat from Paul's clear point: the man is called to be the leader and shepherd of his home in such a way that reflects the loving ministry of Christ and the Holy Spirit. His is a pedagogical ministry (in the Word) to his wife and children. His leadership will bring blessings to his family, just as Abraham would bless his family by commanding his children and his household after him by means of God's Word (Gen. 18:15). His leadership, like Christ's, is grounded in truth, compassion, and love.

4. THE HUSBAND'S PASSIONATE CARE

Ephesians 5:28-32: *"...husbands ought also to love their own wives as their own bodies...just as Christ also does for the Church."* As Christ's passion for the church continues to this day, through His daily care for her, so too should the spirit-filled husband care for his wife. The Apostle's continued discussion concerning the husband's love for his wife is now summarized with the principle of Christ's continued care for His people:

> **Ephesians 5:28-32:** 28 So husbands ought also to love their own wives as their own bodies. He who loves his own wife loves himself; 29 for no one ever hated his own flesh, but nourishes and cherishes it, just as Christ also does the church, 30 because we are members of His body. 31 For this cause a man shall leave his father and mother, and shall cleave to his wife; and the two shall become one flesh. 32 This mystery is great; but I am speaking with reference to Christ and the church.

In these final verses Paul brings us to the heart of Christ's care and compassion for the church. The Lord rescued his church in her state

---

[179] 1 Corinthians 7:16 For how do you know, O wife, whether you will save your husband? Or how do you know, O husband, whether you will save your wife?

of weakness,[180] and He continues to supply her needs as she is dependent upon Him for everything.[181] As Christ loved the church in this way, so must the husband care for his bride. As quickly as one might put on a jacket when cold, or eat a meal when hungry, so too will the man who loves his wife expend himself for her genuine needs. Her body, soul, and spirit will be his genuine and continual concern. This principle of passionate care is perhaps best understood in light of the man's responsibility to work and thereby provide for his wife and children. This principle of the man's work, rendered on behalf of his wife, was established at the very beginning of our study in Genesis 2, and it continues to this day even though a man's labor will be plagued with hardship.

2 Thessalonians 3:7-12: 7 For you yourselves know how you ought to follow our example, because we did not act in an undisciplined manner among you, 8 nor did we eat anyone's bread without paying for it, but with labor and hardship we kept working night and day so that we might not be a burden to any of you; 9 not because we do not have the right to this, but in order to offer ourselves as a model for you, that you might follow our example. 10 For even when we were with you, we used to give you this order: if anyone will not work, neither let him eat. 11 For we hear that some among you are leading an undisciplined life, doing no work at all, but acting like busybodies. 12 Now such persons we command and exhort in the Lord Jesus Christ to work in quiet fashion and eat their own bread.

1 Timothy 5:8 But if anyone does not provide for his own, and especially for those of his household, he has denied the faith, and is worse than an unbeliever.

---

[180] Romans 5:6 "For while we were still helpless [*asthenōn*], at the right time Christ died for the ungodly." The word helpless [*asthenōn > asthenēn*] is the same term that Peter used to speak of the wife as being the weaker/dependent vessel. It should therefore be no wonder that Paul spoke of Christ's bride as the weaker vessel [*asthenōn*], such that His sacrifice supplied what was necessary for her protection and redemption.

[181] John 15:5.

This priority of work is crucial for any man who seeks to love his wife as Christ loved the church. His desire for her must include this duty of providing for her practical needs. Work is the man's means of giving to his household first as well as to others in need:

> **Ephesians 4:28** ...let him labor, performing with his own hands what is good, in order that he may have something to share with him who has need.

It must be said that work is not an end, but a means to the greater end of worshipping God and giving joyfully - to the Lord, to one's family, and to others who have need. A man of God will never make his career his chief end in life. No amount of money can replace the godly care and shepherding ministry that a father is to give to his family. The acquisition of material things for them, while crucial, should not be emphasized beyond what is necessary. Work is an ordained *means* of worship, but it is never to be the *object* of worship. Again, this principle must not be missed here: employment is a means by which a man upholds a godly ministry to his family. It is a part of his ministry of passionate care for his wife and children.

The Apostle Paul then concludes his important discussion concerning husbands by offering a summary statement that leaves us where he began: Ephesians 5:33 "Nevertheless let every one of you in particular so love his wife even as himself; and the wife see that she reverence her husband."[182] Paul's concluding thought here reverts back to the conduct of wives, only now he advances the thought slightly by addressing the nature of the wife's loving attitude towards her husband, which we will address in the next section on wives.

---

[182] The Holy Bible : King James Version. Oak Harbor, WA: Logos Research Systems, Inc., 1995.

THE SPIRIT-FILLED HUSBAND
A FINAL APPLICATION

For the spirit-filled husband, Christ alone provides the valid measure for true manliness and godly leadership. Leadership that is patterned after the Savior will yield genuine peace, joy, and growth for the family of God. Productive relations within the family, which build up and edify, require constant vigilance and labor in the Spirit, however, conflict in marriage requires little effort at all. Like an automobile with poor alignment, all that is required to veer off course is the removal of the driver's hands from the steering wheel. Some men may fail to lead their homes because they have allowed themselves to become infected by the popular culture; or perhaps others have simply never been taught the principles of godly leadership. But the Christian husband who desires to do the will of God will surely seek to apply the truths of Scripture in order to progress in his imitation of Christ in the home as well as in all aspects of life. Such a response to Scripture is a fruitful evidence of new life in Christ. Remember, the godly husband is *a man who has new life in Christ and is led by the Holy Spirit*. A man may, for a season, behave like a spirit-filled husband but such showmanship is not what the apostle calls for in Ephesians 5. As Jesus declared to Nicodemus: *"...you must be born again."* If you have never truly recognized your sin, as well as your need for the Savior, then all of the aforementioned instructions will have no bearing or reality in your life. Without Christ; without the transformation of a new heart given by the Spirit of God, you are powerless to render any change in your own life or in the life of your family. Call upon the Lord to forgive you of your sin, placing your faith in the Son of God who died in order to save those who believe in Him. You cannot hope to be like Christ if Christ is not your Lord and Savior. Only the truly redeemed husband will look to the pattern of Christ-likeness, not only by the instructions found in Ephesians 5, but especially by looking to the full counsel of God's Word. Consider the following examples of Christ's godly ministry to the church throughout the Scriptures, and as you do, consider how Christ above all is the husband's example for godly leadership in the home as well as in all contexts of life:

Christ, the Teacher: In Ephesians 4 the Apostle Paul explains that Christ sacrificed Himself in order to give the gifts of the apostles, prophets, evangelists, and pastors-teachers for the building up of the body of Christ to full maturity (Ephesians 4:7-13). This, coupled with the truth that Christ washed His bride with the water of the Word (Ephesians 5:26), is a clear reminder to men that an essential imitation of Christ will include a continual ministry of the Word in the home. The man who loves his wife (as Christ loved the church) will be actively engaged in the process of guiding and instructing her in the Scriptures. Unlike the first Adam, who failed to guard his stewardship with the commandment of God, the Last Adam[183] (Jesus Christ) stands as the consummate example of a loving husband who faithfully guards His bride with the pure and cleansing Word of God. The Savior's example of such guardianship is repeatedly seen in the Gospels through His supply of teaching and reproof. In this ministry of the Word, there were occasions when He taught regardless of the circumstances surrounding Him. On the other hand there were times when He taught specific lessons that were a response to an event, debate, or even a question. When we consider the multifaceted nature of Christ's teaching ministry, we are reminded of the importance of a man's readiness to instruct, or correct, in season and out of season.[184] Such a man as this will be one who is apt to teach his family *when he sits in his house, when he walks by the way, when he lies down or when he rises up.*[185] This is the portrait of Christ who

---

[183] Romans 5:14 Nevertheless death reigned from Adam until Moses, even over those who had not sinned in the likeness of the offense of Adam, who is a type of Him who was to come.

[184] 2 Timothy 4:2

[185] Deuteronomy 6:7

continually showered His people in the truth of God, in keeping with His prayers for them.[186]

- *The example of Christ must remind men to delve into the Scriptures regularly; knowing that you are not only feeding yourself spiritually, but what you take in will become profitable to your wife and children in many ways.*

- *Men must be committed to providing regular times of family worship so that the Scriptures may be taught in the home, proactively (regularly). But the husband must also seize opportunities, as they arise, whereby he offers instruction through conversations in the home, or in response to specific conflicts. He must be ready in season and out of season, always being ready to provide spiritual food for his household.*

- *The man of God must understand that his teaching ministry is indelibly linked to his life and conduct. It is not enough for a man to speak about truth, he must seek to live it in day-to-day life if he is to be effective as a teacher in his home.*

Christ, the Shepherd: The Lord calls Himself the Good Shepherd who lays down His life for the sheep (John 10:11), and therefore, His sheep hear his voice and they follow Him (John 10:27). The picture that the Lord supplies in John 10 is that of a tender, caring shepherd who knows his sheep and calls them out by name (John 10:3). It is a picture of tenderness, intimacy, and continual care. In like manner, the father's ministry in the home ought to reflect such tenderness, care, and communication like that of Christ. The Lord's example of shepherding care for His disciples is indeed instructive, for how often do we see the disciples engaged in infighting (Luke 22:24), offering worthless speculations (John 9:1-2), resisting His authority (Matt

---

[186] John 17:17 "Sanctify them in the truth; Thy word is truth."

16:22), or being guilty of having little faith in His authority (Matthew 6:30, 8:26, 16:8, 17:20). And yet despite this we see that the Lord never neglected His ministry to them and He never left them as orphans. His constant care and communication with them was a perfect expression of love, and by this we should note that sheep can only learn the voice of their shepherd if he speaks to them. This the Lord did throughout His faithful ministry here on earth. This principle of communication is crucial for a husband who seeks to lead and nurture his wife. A man who communicates with his wife, and prays for her regularly, will foster a stronger relationship with her in the Lord. Though problems will arise, such communication will minimize the relational conflicts that so often crop up in marriages. The best way to allow for conflict and relational degradation is for men to neglect faithful communication with their wives. Alternately, regular communication is a clear mark of spiritual leadership, like that of the Lord Jesus Christ. The Lord knew, with perfection, how to pray for His disciples. Of course, He knew all things infallibly. But even though He knew their needs with perfection it is evident that the Savior regularly fellowshipped with them and conversed with them about all matters of life. In following Christ, a husband should seek to engage in fellowship and communication with his wife and children regularly. Unlike the Lord, the husband *must* communicate with his family in order to learn about their genuine needs, for the simple reason that he is not omniscient.[187] By this shepherding ministry, the praying husband can labor as the priest of his home with greater effectiveness as he brings the needs of his family to the throne of God's grace. Men are not always so conversant, and such habits of life are easier for some than others, but as the shepherd of your home you should be the greatest expert on earth regarding your family's spiritual and physical needs. Christ endured many things from His disciples, and yet He remained

---

[187] Matthew 6:8 "Therefore do not be like them; for your Father knows what you need, before you ask Him."

faithful as a shepherd to them. And though the disciples were at times exasperating, the Lord did not resort to pugnacity with them; rather He rebuked them in love and corrected them in a manner that was profitable. Fortunately for us, His words of correction and comfort continue in the NT epistles to the churches. The Lord loves all of His people, for He is and always will be their Good Shepherd. Consider the following thoughts and questions:

- *What are your tendencies when family problems arise? When you fail as a leader, do you tend to avoid conflict or do you resort to anger? Is communication easy for you, or is it more of an effort? How might you pattern your life after the shepherding care of Christ better?*

- *Do you speak your mind too freely and in a manner that is not profitable to your wife? There are times when a man should consider if or when he might speak to his wife about difficult matters (i.e., work, finances or family issues). After all, the Lord out of His compassion for His disciples sometimes withheld matters of which they were not prepared to hear.*[188]

- *How knowledgeable are you to pray for your family? What are their true needs? Let your prayer life then be filled with prayers and petitions on behalf of the flock of your family. Pray for them in the privacy of your quiet times; pray with them in your times of family worship and meals. This is your great privilege as the protector and priest of your home.*

Christ, the Devoted Bridegroom: Christ laid down His life for only one bride: *those whom the Father chose before the foundation of the world.* The doctrine of particular redemption teaches us many important truths, one of which is this lesson regarding the Lord's unique love for His people. The Lord did not set His unique love

---

[188] John 16:12 "I have many more things to say to you, but you cannot bear them now."

upon all without exception; rather He set His particular and special love upon His chosen bride. Christ's particular sacrifice for His bride is a beautiful example of how a husband ought to have a particular and singular love for his wife. As well, it should be remembered that Jesus Christ did not love the church out of mere duty or obligation. His love was not mechanical and passionless. Let it never be said that the husband's love for his wife is simply a matter of mere obligation or servitude. Christ loved the church with a passion and desire that was God-centered and that was genuinely focused upon His elect bride. As discussed earlier, the Lord delights in His people as the bridegroom does over his bride: *"...as the bridegroom rejoices over the bride, so your God will rejoice over you."* In like manner the husband who loves his wife does so with a great desire and joy for her. God has ordained in human marriage that a man and wife have such a desire for one another such that their physical and spiritual intimacy will be predicated on much more than mere duty. The important point here is this: *a man should let his heart and mind be filled with thoughts of his wife.* As the Scriptures declare: *"...let your fountain be blessed, and rejoice in the wife of your youth. As a loving hind and a graceful doe, let her breasts satisfy you at all times; be exhilarated always with her love."* (Proverbs 5:18-19). The husband should therefore remember that it is crucial that he be devoted to his wife in his heart and mind, desiring none other. The potential distractions in this world are myriad such that a temptation could come from the physical beauty, personality, or even piety of another woman. Whatever the source of temptation may be, the husband must understand that the root of the problem is the unfaithfulness and lust of his own heart.[189] He must guard his heart and mind in this world, knowing that the modern culture is filled with lewdness, promiscuity,

---

[189] James 1:13-15 13 Let no one say when he is tempted, "I am being tempted by God"; for God cannot be tempted by evil, and He Himself does not tempt anyone.14 But each one is tempted when he is carried away and enticed by his own lust.15 Then when lust has conceived, it gives birth to sin; and when sin is accomplished, it brings forth death.

immodesty, and pornography of every kind. Television shows, radio programs, billboard signs, newspapers, magazines, and internet websites are often infested with images that can tempt a man to sin in his heart. The images that can pollute one's mind are so commonplace that even a modern TV commercial can reveal enough temptation to entice a man to sin with his thoughts. But like our brother Joseph, we must flee at the first sight of temptation knowing that, as men, we should not toy with such dangerous interactions. We should not trust ourselves enough to flirt with such worldliness. The crimes of the heart may not be seen by others, but the Lord sees them all: Proverbs 5:20-21: "For why should you, my son, be exhilarated with an adulteress, and embrace the bosom of a foreigner? For the ways of a man are before the eyes of the Lord, and He watches all his paths." The husband should see to it that his physical and spiritual intimacy with his wife is not polluted with impure thoughts. Let us rejoice in Christ's singular devotion to His bride, for He laid down His life for her *and for her alone*. He did it, not merely out of duty, but out of a genuine love and desire that was set upon His own bride. By the imitation of Christ, let the man of God rejoice in the wife of his youth, being invigorated by her love.

Christ, the Servant: Christ's example as a servant stands as the absolute standard for any man who would seek to nurture and care for his wife. Every husband must be a leader in every capacity, such that he cares for and protects his wife and children in every way that he can. He is to lead his home in the Scriptures and in prayer. He is to lead by godly example through his own growth and sanctification. He is to be committed to the spiritual and physical nurturing of his wife and children, leading his family in regular family worship. As well, part of the husband's spiritual leadership in the home comes from his employment to provide for his family. As long as a man is capable of working, he is to give priority to the matter of providing for his own household. The Scriptures address this important subject frequently, and even Paul takes the importance of this matter so far as to indicate that the man who refuses to provide for his own family is "worse than an unbeliever." The seriousness of this discussion must be understood. In today's culture of materialism, it is too easy for families to over-extend themselves financially such that they require more than what the husband can provide through his salary. Life circumstances will vary from family to family, but it should be the goal of the husband to be the provider for his family, securing the freedom of his wife to labor in the home.

Christ, the Obedient Son: The Lord Himself declared: "My food is to do the will of Him who sent me and to accomplish His work." The obedience of Christ to the Father's will is a precious example that reaches into many significant facets of life. For example, when Christ was 12 we see that He continued in subjection to His parents, as unto His heavenly Father.[190] At the beginning of His ministry He subjected Himself to the baptism of John, in obedience to God the Father.[191] As well, He came to the temple for prayer out of His love and devotion to the Father (John 2:13-19, Matthew 21:12-17), and drove out those who had falsified the true worship of God by making His Father's house a house of merchandise. The Lord displayed a continual devotion to the Father through His obedience to Him, and through His pursuit of purity in worship. Though Christ was Himself perfectly holy and without need of anything, He willingly subjected Himself, in obedience, such that He learned obedience from the things which He suffered.[192] How precious is the example of Christ who demonstrated the importance of obedience to God and His authority. In our culture which seems to deride any form of authority, this is an especially important lesson that we must glean. While men are the leaders of their home, theirs is a leadership that

---

[190] Luke 2:51.

[191] Matthew 3:13-17.

[192] Hebrews 5:8.

must be under a greater authority, for Christ is the head of every man, and the man is the head of a woman, and God is the head of Christ.[193] The husband who desires that his wife follow his lead ought also to set an example of obedience by placing himself under God's authority in the daily practice of his life. This is the pattern of Christ's own leadership to His disciples, for He led them by way of example. The example that the husband/father sets in the home is crucial in this vein. His willingness to subject himself to the ordained authorities of the local church and even to civil government is, in itself, a significant testimony to his wife and children.

- What examples are you setting for you for wife who is called to submit to your leadership, though it is an imperfect leadership?

- What are your children learning from you as a father concerning your own responsiveness to the authorities in your life – to the church as well as to governing authorities?

Christ, the Great High Priest: Christ prayed for His church before His crucifixion (John 17) and He continues His ministry of intercession on our behalf as our Great High Priest in heaven. Christ prayed in His High Priestly prayer:

- For the fullness of our joy (John 17:13)

- For our preservation from evil (John 17:15)

- For our sanctification in God's Word (John 17:17)

- For our Gospel ministry in the world (John 17:18)

- For our unity and ultimate glorification in Christ (John 17:21)

---

[193] 1 Corinthians 11:3.

Christ offered up these petitions for us before His death, burial, and resurrection, and now in glory He always lives in order to make intercession for us.[194] Christ's devotion of love is clearly expressed by means of His continual intercession for His own bride. Here again is an important example for the Christian husband, for this ministry of prayer is central to his own priestly leadership in his home. Not only is the husband called to pray for his family, but as an imperfect man he must take heed unto his own life to ensure that his own sins are not impeding his priestly duties. Once again, we are reminded of Peter's instructions regarding the matter of sin and prayer:

> 1 Peter 3:7 You husbands likewise, live with your wives in an understanding way, as with a weaker vessel, since she is a woman; and grant her honor as a fellow heir of the grace of life, so that your prayers may not be hindered.

It is a remarkable and sobering thought to consider, that a man's prayers can be hindered through his sinful indifference towards his wife. A man's failure to treat his wife with compassion (protecting her as a weaker vessel) and his failure to treat her as his equal before the Lord (as a sister in Christ) can lead to the hindrance of the man's prayer life. Such a reality is stark and sobering. There is a sense in which a man's sin in the home can take on a spiraling effect, accelerating even more as the man steeps himself into greater sin. If it were not for God's grace in the life of the believing husband, this digression would find no end. But the sobering reality of this instruction must be embraced for all that it has to offer. It is crucial that men take regular inventory of their lives in order to see where fleshliness is being manifested. The deeds of the flesh (which are seeded in the fleshly thoughts of one's heart/mind) include adultery, fornication, uncleanness, lasciviousness, Idolatry, witchcraft, hatred, variance, emulations, wrath, strife, seditions, heresies, envying,

---

[194] Hebrews 7:25

drunkenness, and carousing (Galatians 5:19-21). Question: are there areas of your life that are characterized by such sin? Perhaps you have never committed adultery in the flesh, but have you admired and desired other women in any capacity? Confess it to God and ask for the Spirit's work in your life, that you would manifest His fruit, which is, love, joy, peace, patience, kindness, goodness, faithfulness, gentleness, and self-control. The spiritual husband must make it his first priority to seek the Lord daily in prayer, praying for the Spirit's filling, leadership, and guidance. Such a devotion to prayer is an imitation of Christ who intercedes perpetually on behalf of the church. While both the husband and wife have direct access to the Father through Christ indeed, it is still a significant leadership ministry of the husband to pray and petition on behalf of his wife and children. In order to uphold the purity of this priestly ministry, the man must take regular account of his own relationship with the Lord, his wife, and children to see if there be any shortcomings that must be surrendered and confessed to the Lord.

THE SPIRIT-FILLED WIFE

The role of the wife and mother in the home, society, and the world, should never be underestimated. Like the husband, the wife's effect and influence on the family can be wonderfully beneficial, or stupendously damaging, depending on her life and conduct. Just as the first woman's role was indispensably crucial in the garden, so is the role of the wife in the Christian home. In chapter 1 *The Glory of God's Creation* (*The First*

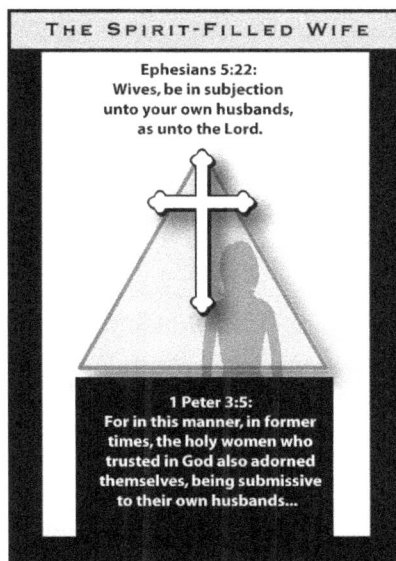

THE SPIRIT-FILLED WIFE

Ephesians 5:22:
Wives, be in subjection
unto your own husbands,
as unto the Lord.

1 Peter 3:5:
For in this manner, in former
times, the holy women who
trusted in God also adorned
themselves, being submissive
to their own husbands...

Woman), we examined the nature of the woman's calling and role when the Lord fashioned her from Adam's side. She was made to be his unique *companion as his wife* and she was to be his *helper* and aid. These ordained roles of the woman were not removed by the fall, but they were marred by sin. Like Adam, whose natural tendency of leadership was corrupted by the fall, so Eve was also corrupted and became, by nature, one who would naturally stray from her calling as *companion* and *helper*. It is therefore no surprise that the New Testament consistently instructs husbands and wives in a manner that directly corrects the fallen condition of marriage: the man is repeatedly exhorted to *love* his wife and the wife is repeatedly exhorted to be *submissive* and *respectful* to her husband.

In our analysis of Ephesians 5:22-33, we began our study with the role of the husband. Clearly, this choice was a matter of logical priority rather than textual order. Because of this, we must return to the beginning of Paul's instructions on the family so that we may consider the role and calling of women in the Christian home. In verses 22 Paul's first instruction is directed to wives as he qualifies the scope and extent of subjection within the body of Christ:

> **Ephesians 5:21-24:** 21 and be subject to one another in the fear of Christ. 22 Wives, be subject to your own husbands, as to the Lord. 23 For the husband is the head of the wife, as Christ also is the head of the church, He Himself being the Savior of the body. 24 But as the church is subject to Christ, so also the wives ought to be to their husbands in everything.

The significance of verse 22 is most obvious in light of the previous text. Men and women are subject to one another as servants beneath the Lord's authority, however this does not nullify the distinctions of servitude and authority found within the church and home, as already discussed. The Lord has created several structures of authority that must be recognized in our daily lives: the authority of leaders in the church (Ephesians 2:20, 4:11-12); the authority of parents regarding their children (Ephesians 6:1-3); and the authority of husbands with respect to their wives (Ephesians 5:22-33). These are important distinctions of authority that help us consider the distinguishable manner in which the saints of God are to serve one another in the fear of Christ. Additionally, Ephesians 5 is not the only text that addresses the relationship between wives and their husbands. Consider the commonality of the following, relevant texts:

- ***Ephesians 5:22*** *Wives, be subject to your own husbands...24 ...as the church is subject to Christ, so also the wives ought to be to their husbands...*

- ***Colossians 3:18*** *Wives, be subject to your husbands, as is fitting in the Lord.*

- ***1 Peter 3:1*** *In the same way, you wives, be submissive to your own husbands so that even if any of them are disobedient to the Word, they may be won without a word by the behavior of their wives.*

- ***Titus 2:5*** *[younger women are] to be sensible, pure, workers at home, kind, being subject to their own husbands, that the Word of God may not be dishonored.*

The consensus of Scripture is clearly laid out before us: *the pattern of holy living for wives is found in a relationship that is deeply rooted in a joyful and loving submission to their husbands, as to the Lord.* The husband is to mimic Christ's godly leadership and the wife is to follow the example of the church's submission to Christ. Paul's use of the word *be subject*[195] in Ephesians 5 is further qualified by his last instruction to wives in verse 33:

---

[195] The imperatival use of the word *submit* is found in Colossians 3:18, whereas in Ephesians 5:21-24 it is implied by virtue of the context. The church is commanded to respond in

Ephesians 5:33 Nevertheless let each individual among you also love his own wife even as himself; and let the wife see to it that she respect her husband.

Joined together, Paul's instruction to wives clearly mirrors the form of relationship which the church is to have with her husband, Jesus Christ: *submission and respect.* This analogy of Christ's headship is crucial for the husband just as the picture of the church's relationship to Christ is crucial for the wife. We should also note that it cannot be assumed that Paul was omitting the concept of a wife's love for her husband, after all, the injunctions of *submission* and *respect* are the very *acts of love* to which the Lord calls His people:

Deuteronomy 10:12-13*:* 12 Now, Israel, this is what the Lord your God wants you to do: respect the Lord your God, and do what he has told you to do. Love him. Serve the Lord your God with your whole being, 13 and obey the Lord's commands and laws that I am giving you today for your own good.[196]

How important it is to understand that these concepts of submission and respect are merely facets of the larger gem of godly love, and this is the Apostle's point to women in Ephesians 5:22-33. In a sense Paul is helping the Christian wife to see what genuine love actually looks like: *it looks exactly like the church as she lovingly submits to and reverences Christ.* From beginning to end, Paul points wives to the privileged calling of the church in order to instruct them regarding their God ordained calling in marriage. Within these injunctions of submission and reverence lies the implicit reminder of the woman's original calling in Genesis chapter 2:

---

obedience to Christ, not with heartless compulsion, but with joyful enthusiasm. See also, 1 John 5:3.

[196] The Holy Bible : New Century Version , containing the Old and New Testaments. 1991. Dallas, TX: Word Bibles.

Genesis 2:18 Then the Lord God said, "It is not good for the man to be alone; I will make him a helper suitable for him."

As discussed in chapter 1 *The Glory of God's Creation (The First Woman)*, the meaning of the word *helper* speaks of one who comes to the aid of another as a willing servant or helpmeet. It is quite clear that the woman's role as helper is sustained by the Apostle's instructions in Ephesians 5, however the difference is this: rather than emphasizing the *objective* duties of the wife (the works of her hands), he stresses what her *subjective* attitudes should be (the attitude of her heart). The wife is not to *help* her husband with a heartless devotion; rather, she is to be his *helpmeet* with loving humility, subjection, and reverence. This is the Apostle's crucial point. In light of this particular focus of Paul's address to wives, we will branch out and consult a number of additional passages in order to enlarge our study of the important role of the spiritual wife. Therefore, as we consider *The Spirit Filled Wife* in this section, we will take a careful look at the works of her hands as well as the attitudes of her heart. *What* the spiritual wife does in the home is no less important than *how* she does it before the Lord. As the husband's precious spouse and helpmeet, her *overall ministry* in the Christian home is indispensable.

Identical to the calling of the husband, the spirit-filled wife is to do all things for the good pleasure of the Lord Himself; after all, she is to be subject to her own husband *as to the Lord*. This final qualification, *as to the Lord*, gives us the heartbeat of the spirit-filled wife's ultimate goal in all her actions and attitudes: *she is a servant of Jesus Christ who serves Him with gladness.* Her sanctification in God's Word, her every prayer for her family, her every act of servitude in the home, in the local church, and in her community at large is to serve the greater purpose of giving glory to God in everything. Like her husband, she is to view her every action and attitude in life as an act of worship that is directed to the Lord Jesus Christ. From the monumental to the mundane, from the act of instructing her children the Scriptures to the preparation of a meal, *her every action is to be offered up to the glory of God.* Without a doubt, the ministry of the spirit-filled wife is incomprehensibly crucial. It is often an invisible ministry, the impact of which is clearly seen through the resultant fruit of her labors. We are often amazed at the resolute godliness of men like Samuel who, without compromise, judged Israel prior to the establishment of the monarchial era. Or Timothy who was Paul's own child in the faith and carried on the ministry of the Word in Paul's stead. By the grace of God, these men stand out in Scripture as being true champions of the faith, and yet we are reminded that their beginnings were formulated in the crucible of a godly home, where godly women like Hannah, Eunice, and Lois were faithfully serving the Lord. Thus, the visible ministries of these men began with the invisible ministries of women who worshipped the Lord with faithfulness!

However, in our modern era, the concept of a *housewife* is viewed as archaic, backwards, and is almost entirely shunned by the secular culture today. The feminist movement in America has changed the face of the family as well as the composition of the workforce at an alarming rate. By modern standards a woman is commonly said to be one who *works* only if she is employed outside of the home. When a housewife is asked the question: "Do you work?" the question typically connotes the thought of wage-based employment rather than work in the home. The underlying sources of these changes are many. In our modern era we have been surrounded with many materialistic philosophies regarding the proper employment of men and woman. For one to suggest that the woman's place is to work in the home, for the good of her children and as a help to her husband, is thought to be too archaic to consider seriously. Let me call your attention, once again, to the official statement from the *National*

Study of the Changing Workforce, but with the broader context of that statement:

> "The proportion of women and men in the wage and salaried workforce is now nearly equal (51% men and 49% women), and men have become far more accepting of women's participation in the workforce over the past 25 years. Two in five men, however, still think women's place is in the home. Over the past 25 years, women have achieved increasingly higher educational levels and steadily moved into managerial and professional occupations—such that today women employees are significantly better educated and significantly more likely to hold managerial and professional positions than men. However, women's annual earnings are still significantly less than men's earnings ($36,716 versus $52,908). Possible reasons for this persistent gender difference in earnings include women's greater likelihood of working part time and in administrative positions, as well as other factors explored in more detail in the full study. In addition, employees who have greater responsibility for care of their children—whether men or women—report lower earnings. *In dual-earner couples, there is a significant third job that has to be done at home—family work.*"[197]

As noted earlier, what is particularly telling in this report is the revelation that family life constitutes *the third job* of parents. The honesty of this statement clearly unveils the prevailing attitude of our wage-centered society. A woman's work is not said to be in the home, but is increasingly thought to be outside of the home, while the care of the family is given the last place in our dual-income culture. The sad conclusion revealed here is *that these secular priorities represent a complete upheaval of God's ordained plan for the family.*

This noble work of the godly wife is oftentimes demeaned in our modern culture as being useless, mundane, and unimportant.

---

[197] National Study of the Changing Workforce, 2002 [italics mine].

Mothers are indeed called to work, but it is crucial that the body of Christ comprehend what her true domain of employment should be. The Scriptures do not leave us in a lurch on this very important subject, for the role of the working mother is clearly laid out in the Word of God. When the Apostle Paul exhorted younger women to engage in the godly labor of being a wife, he clearly indicated how such work should be prioritized:

> **Titus 2:4-5***:* 4 ...encourage the young women to love their husbands, to love their children, 5 to be sensible, pure, workers at home, kind, being subject to their own husbands...

The mother's labor of love for her family is not her third, but her first *job.* As workers in the home, they are called to *love their husbands and to love their children* as their principal duty in the Lord. This labor of love in the home is to be done with *sensibility*, *purity*, and *kindness*. Such *love* for a husband and children is characterized by the form of love known as filial love which is conveyed in the text by the Greek word *phileō*. The significance of Paul's use of this word in Titus 2 is profound. In its root form, this love [*phileō*] speaks of the natural affection that one would have for a relative or close friend. It is no wonder that this word was commonly used to refer to the love of parents towards children, the affection of friends, and the love of spouses towards one another. The primitive concept here is that of *belonging to a particular group of people* and therefore it bears the distinction of being that form of love which seeks to benefit, protect, and preserve those who are the members of one's household or tribe.[198] This love of human affection therefore goes beyond mere feelings, but extends itself to the *works and actions* that would be necessary in order to benefit and preserve the well-being of others. Therefore, when Paul instructs young wives to *love* their husbands and children, he is not calling them to a static adoration but to the

---

[198] Kittel, Bromiley & Friedrich, <u>Theological Dictionary</u>, p. 113.

dutiful love that labors in order to enhance and strengthen the family overall. This affectionate love will therefore be filled with the *practical duties that normally attend a wife's relationship to her husband, her children, and even the home in which the family lives.* Additionally, the stated order of priorities in Titus 2 is particularly important: in the Lord, her first ministry is to her husband, then to her children, and then to her home/residence. The alteration of this order could quickly bring upheaval to any Christian home, for children are not to be given priority over the husband, and the home cannot be given greater priority over any member of the family. With this order of priority in mind, let us look more carefully at the spirit-filled wife's 1. *Love for her Husband,* 2. *Love for her Children and* 3. *Labor in the Home:*

1. A WIFE'S LOVE FOR HER HUSBAND

The godly wife's first act of worship in the home is to honor and submit to her husband. It may not seem intuitive to refer to this as an act of worship, or to refer to it as the primary work of the wife in her home, but it is the reality of her calling before God. As noted earlier, the wife is repeatedly instructed to submit to her own husband (Ephesians 5:22, 24; Colossians 3:18; Titus 2:5; 1 Peter 3:1) and to reverence him in the Lord (Ephesians 5:33). These repeated instructions in the N.T. remind us of the corrupted nature of men and women, for in Genesis chapter 3 the judgment of the man and the woman left the first marriage in a state where the man would rule with indifference and the wife would tend to subvert the authority of her husband.[199] The correctives of the N.T. are therefore quite clear: the husband is not to lead with cold indifference, but with love and compassion, while the wife is not to over-rule the authority of the husband, but to submit to his authority as to the Lord. This is indeed the godly wife's first crucial work in the home! Without it, her ability

---

[199] See chapter 2, The First Condemnation.

to flourish and grow as a wife and mother will always be hampered. The adverse affects which result from a woman's lack of submission is a subject that is frequented in the book of Proverbs:[200]

Proverbs 27:15 A constant dripping on a day of steady rain and a contentious woman are alike;

The contentious woman mentioned above is one whose presence is rather disturbing and irritating. The Hebrew is quite explicit: her tendency is to *contend* [H. *mā<u>d</u>ôn*] in a judicial or argumentative sense, as one might expect a layer to do, or even a king who has the authority to uphold legal rulings within his kingdom.[201] Such an attitude is the polar opposite of the woman whose labor is characterized by humility, gentleness, and tender submission. As the wife's labor increases in this area, her home will be less characterized by disturbing contention and more characterized by the beauty of the church as she submits to the Lord Jesus Christ.

Because this world is dominated by feministic ideology, the word submission can nearly be referred to as the "s" word, as though it were a derogatory concept. Rather than viewing submission as the wife's emulation of Christ in all His humility, the world views this attribute as being the product of religious oppression and abuse. In a culture that exalts self-esteem, self preservation, and individualism, the commands of submission and reverence will probably seem extra-terrestrial to many. Ultimately they are extra-terrestrial, for they come from the Lord of the heavens and the earth! Submission to authority in any context has become more of a philosophical oddity in our culture. For most in our world, self rule and autonomy are

---

[200] Proverbs 21:9, 19; 25:24.

[201] Harris, Harris, Archer, Waltke, <u>Theological Wordbook</u> p. 188, Article 426c. TWOT presents the word *mā<u>d</u>ôn* as being a strong synonym to *šā<u>p</u>aṭ* and *mišpāṭ*, the two most common words for law, commandment or judgment.

seen as strengths, while submission and humility constitute inferiority. But whether we are in subjection to a king, an employer, or (in the case of a wife) a husband, godly submission is the ultimate imitation of Christ whose own humility stands as the highest mountain-top over all others. With this in mind, it should seem quite obvious that it is necessary to examine the Biblical qualities of the wife's godly submission and reverence to her husband. To be sure, many cultures have made the role of the woman into that of a slave or a mere piece of property, but the Biblical mandate of godly submission knows nothing of this man-made error. In light of this, the danger that is presented to the church is one that revolves around the question of the importance of the wife's submission. In a culture that exalts a woman's independence, it is not surprising to find that the American wife can legally pursue her independence through separation, by invoking mandatory arrest laws,[202] and through no-fault divorce proceedings at online services like www.yourfriendlydivorce.com.[203] By secular/civil standards, a woman would not have to submit to her husband, ever, if she didn't want to. Her ability to invoke the protections of the law is so great in our culture that even a domestic argument could potentially end in the arrest of the husband. These realities place even greater pressure upon families and confuse the important priorities of the Word of God in relation to civil authority. Men and women are to obey governing authorities indeed, but we are not necessarily free to pursue legal channels at the expense of Biblical mandates. There is a great need to clarify the priorities of marriage amidst the cobwebs of

---

[202] In light of the Federal Violence Against Women Act of 1994, the principle of *mandatory arrest* has become the standard for domestic house calls made by police in most states.

[203] The demotion of the marriage covenant in our nation is further illustrated by the ease in which a married couple can renounce their union. Examples: www.ourdivorceagreement.com; www.selfdivorce.com and www.yourfriendlydivorce.com to name a few. These online services can process a divorce proceeding with a simple online payment and the completion of just a few forms.

157

secular culture and civil law. This is why we must be instructed by the text of Scripture above everything else.

Marriage is a fragile creation of God. In even the best of marriages, the husband is imperfect and so is the wife. Therefore, in light of the fragile nature of marriage, godly forbearance is most important for both partners. The husband, even at his best, will always fall short of the perfect leadership that Jesus Christ supplies for His church, but this reality does not nullify the importance and need of the wife's submission. In like manner, the wife is an imperfect helpmate, but such a reality does not grant the husband the license to forsake his covenant with his wife. The wife is to submit to the God-ordained means of leadership provided through her husband, and as the wife relates to her husband's leadership, it will be crucial that she embrace the full import of the Apostolic commands in Ephesians 5 (submission and reverence), knowing that she is placing herself beneath the leadership and protection of an *imperfect man*. But the wife can submit to her husband *without fear* just as Sarah did when she obeyed Abraham. In our earlier examination of 1 Peter chapter 3, we saw that the Apostle Peter presented the lesson of Sarah amidst the very important teaching regarding Christian humility. This broader context of humility is utterly crucial since it strengthens the Christian's attitude towards authority; therefore, this text merits a second visitation. Read carefully the context of Peter's presentation of the Christian's humility in Christ, noting carefully Peter's *explicit* and *implicit* references to submission, as noted in *bold* and *italics*, respectively:

1 Peter 2:13-3:18: 13 **Submit** yourselves for the Lord's sake to every human institution, whether to a king as the one in authority, 14 or to governors as sent by him for the punishment of evildoers and the praise of those who do right. 15 For such is the will of God that by doing right you may silence the ignorance of foolish men. 16 Act as free men, and do not use your freedom as a covering for evil, but use it as bondslaves of God. 17 Honor all men; love the brotherhood, fear God, honor the king. 18 **Servants, be submissive** to your masters with all respect, not only to those who are good and gentle, but also to those who are unreasonable. 19 For this finds favor, if for the sake of conscience toward God a man bears up under sorrows when suffering unjustly.20 For what credit is there if, when you sin and are harshly treated, you endure it with patience? *But if when you do what is right and suffer for it you patiently endure it, this finds favor with God. 21 For you have been called for this purpose, since Christ also suffered for you, leaving you an example for you to follow in His steps, 22 who committed no sin, nor was any deceit found in His mouth; 23 and while being reviled, He did not revile in return; while suffering, He uttered no threats, but kept entrusting Himself to Him who judges righteously; 24 and He Himself bore our sins in His body on the cross, that we might die to sin and live to righteousness; for by His wounds you were healed. 25 For you were continually straying like sheep, but now you have returned to the Shepherd and Guardian of your souls.* 3:1 In the same way, you **wives, be submissive** to your own husbands so that even if any of them are disobedient to the word, they may be won without a word by the behavior of their wives, 2 as they observe your chaste and respectful behavior. 3 And let not your adornment be merely external— braiding the hair, and wearing gold jewelry, or putting on dresses; 4 but let it be the hidden person of the heart, with the imperishable quality of a gentle and quiet spirit, which is precious in the sight of God. 5 For in this way in former times the holy women also, who hoped in God, used to adorn themselves, **being submissive** to their own husbands. 6 **Thus Sarah obeyed Abraham**, calling him lord, and you have become her children if you do what is right without being frightened by any fear. 7 You husbands likewise, live with your wives in an understanding way, as with a weaker vessel, since she is a woman; and grant her honor as a fellow heir of the grace of life, so that your prayers may not be hindered. 8 To sum up, let all be harmonious, sympathetic, brotherly, kindhearted, and humble in spirit; 9 not returning evil for evil, or insult for insult, but giving a blessing instead; for you were called for the very purpose that you might inherit a blessing. 10 For, "Let him who means to love life and see good days refrain his tongue from evil and his lips from speaking guile. 11

"And let him turn away from evil and do good; Let him seek peace and pursue it. 12 "For the eyes of the Lord are upon the righteous, And His ears attend to their prayer, But the face of the Lord is against those who do evil." 13 And who is there to harm you if you prove zealous for what is good? 14 But even if you should suffer for the sake of righteousness, you are blessed. And do not fear their intimidation, and do not be troubled, 15 but sanctify Christ as Lord in your hearts, always being ready to make a defense to everyone who asks you to give an account for the hope that is in you, yet with gentleness and reverence; 16 and keep a good conscience so that in the thing in which you are slandered, those who revile your good behavior in Christ may be put to shame. *17 For it is better, if God should will it so, that you suffer for doing what is right rather than for doing what is wrong. 18 For Christ also died for sins once for all, the just for the unjust, in order that He might bring us to God, having been put to death in the flesh, but made alive in the spirit;*

Peter's thematic development here is crucial. Four times in this section Peter speaks of the godly Christian's humble *submission* to authority [*hupotagēte*: 1 Peter 2:13, 18; 3:1, 5]. While these relationships are obviously different, they still require Christ-like submission. Thus, Peter calls all believers to pattern their lives after the submission of Christ, Who obeyed the Father's will [1 Peter 2:20-25] by subjecting Himself to godless rulers who ultimately crucified Him. This holy submission *resulted in His suffering for righteousness sake.* Submission, humility, gentleness, and reverence [1 Peter 3:15] are qualities that are heralded as the crucial Christ-like imitations that establish a godly testimony before men. Therefore, self sacrifice, rather than self-preservation, is the result of such humility and submission. When Peter enjoined wives to submit *in the same way,*[204] he was calling them to the same imitation of Christ that is needful of all believers, no matter what their context of life may be. Peter's

---

[204] G. *omoiōs* – In the same way or in like manner. "'In the same way' (*omoiōs*) implies that the paragraph is another in a series devoted to the subject of Christian submission." D. Edmond Hiebert, 1 Peter, (BMH BOOKS, Winona Lake, Indiana), p. 195.

160

audience at that time was most needful of these instructions in light of the fact that his epistle was most likely written during the 9th year of the reign of Emperor Nero. It would only be a year later that the Neronian persecution of the church would commence on a large scale. Prior to this (A.D. 64), the church had already become a cultural outcast and was often the object of rejection, ridicule, and scattered persecutions. It is for this reason that Peter spoke to his audience in terms of their being *distressed by various trials* such that their faith was being refined as they were *tested by fire.*[205] Therefore Peter's audience was in desperate need to be reminded of Christ's message of discipleship: *in this world, the way of the cross includes suffering.*[206] Concerning the harassment that the church experienced in the world, he instructed believers not *to fear their intimidation nor be troubled,* and if suffering should come, *let it be for righteousness sake.* It is in this broader context that he then instructs wives concerning their important ministry in the home: *in the same way, wives are to be submissive to their own husbands.* This instruction is in exact harmony with the parallel instruction to wives as found in Ephesians 5:22-33, Col 3:18 and Titus 2:5, with one qualification: like the godly servants mentioned in 1 Peter 2:18, who were to *be submissive* to the good and gentle masters as well as those who were unreasonable, wives are instructed to submit to their husbands whether they be godly or *if any of them are disobedient to the Word.* Only in Peter's epistle is the context qualified to include such a condition.[207] This important qualification reminds us that even in the case of a husband who is being disobedient to the Word, godly

---

[205] 1 Peter 1:1:6-7.

[206] Matthew 16:24-26.

[207] This subordinate *hina* clause (a clause that establishes a special condition or circumstance) is included by Peter in order to present a distinct possibility, for he says "*if any* are disobedient" (*hina kai ei tines apeithousin tō logō*). The statement corresponds in meaning to his instructions to servants: some will have good masters, others will be unreasonable – in either case, godly submission is the path in which the believer glorifies God.

submission is still the way of Christ. Matthew Henry gives us an important reminder on this subject:

> *"A cheerful subjection, and a loving, reverential respect, are duties which Christian women owe their husbands, whether they be good or bad; these were due from Eve to Adam before the fall, and are still required, though much more difficult now than they were before, Gen. 3:16; 1 Tim. 2:11."* [208]

Peter's point is quite clear: the wife's calling is to submit whether the husband is obedient to the Word or not. It is typically the case that commentators will offer an instant dismissal to the notion of a woman enduring hardships beneath the authority of a disobedient husband, but the implications of Peter's instructions are often missed by the modern reader. In the 1st century Roman world, the legal freedoms of wives were much more limited than in our day. Consider the following description of the wife's standing in marriage in light of the 1st century doctrine of *patria potestas*:

> *"...a husband might inflict a death penalty on his wife if her family agreed with him that her behavior warranted such a punishment. And overindulgence in wine was apparently considered a capital offense in a wife. Although it is unlikely that many men killed their wives, with the consent of the wife's family, wife beating was not a crime; nor was it limited to the early years of Roman history. Battered wives had no legal recourse and could only hope for the intervention of their families."* [209]

When Peter penned his epistles, he wrote to a people who lived beneath a vastly different system of civil law and ethics. Adultery committed by a husband was often viewed as acceptable, whereas a wife would be deemed guilty without question.[210] The father's

---

[208]Henry, <u>Commentary on the whole Bible</u>, 1 Peter 3:1.

[209] Shelton, <u>As The Romans Did</u>, p. 278.

[210] "In Roman law up to the time of the Republic the husband has, in a case of adulterium, the one-sided right of private revenge against the guilty wife even to putting to death, whereas the

authority over all property and life within the home was such that he could, in some cases, hasten the death of a family member with very little jurisprudence. These civil standards would change within a half century, but to his immediate readers the reality of suffering under harsh conditions was quite real.[211] But Peter exhorted them to remain faithful to the Lord despite the standards of Roman law and government. Peter clearly articulated to his readers that they may even suffer in the process, but their focus must be to suffer for righteousness sake rather than for doing evil. In the case of a wife, whose husband was disobedient to the Word, Peter does not retract the call of submission, but instead he underscores the importance of her need to embrace a fearless life that reflects the godliness of Sarah:

1 Peter 3:6 ...Sarah obeyed Abraham, calling him lord, and you have become her children if you do what is right without being frightened by any fear.

Peter's instruction to the wife is in no way new, for it reflects the very call to discipleship that he received from the Lord Himself.[212] These commands may seem very distant and strange to an age of self-esteem, self-awareness, self-image, and self-preservation: this is a self*ish* age! Clearly, Satan's temptation to women has not changed since the beginning, and he continues to prey on the fears of women,

---

wife must accept the adultery of her husband." Kittel, Bromiley Friedrich, <u>Theological Dictionary</u> Vol. 4, p. 471.

[211] Will Durant affirms that Roman law did change during the reign of Emperor Hadrian (A.D. 117-138): "The second person in Roman law was the father...Rule through family and clan diminished as population became more abundant and diverse, and life more mobile, commercial, and complex; kinship, status, and custom were replaced by contract and law. Children won greater freedom from their parents, wives from their husbands, individuals from their groups. Trajan compelled a father to emancipate a son whom he had maltreated; Hadrian took from the father the right of life and death over his household and transferred it to the courts." Will Durant, <u>The Story of Civilization</u>: Part III, *Caesar and Christ* (Simon and Schuster, New York), p. 395.

[212] Matthew 10:28 "And do not fear those who kill the body, but are unable to kill the soul; but rather fear Him who is able to destroy both soul and body in hell."

whispering in their ear that they may not have all that they could possess should they remain committed to obeying God's commands. Modern counseling models tend to prey on women who are weighed down by man-centered fears,[213] offering them sham solutions to very real problems by offering the false promise that our lives can be sterilized of all suffering. But godly women of every era are to forsake worldly fear and resist the Devil while placing their hope in the Creator who made them and redeemed them by the blood of the Lamb.[214] In an age that exalts self-esteem and self-preservation, fleshly fears are often catered to in a manner that forsakes Peter's serious exhortation to godliness. This apostolic teaching must not be missed nor ignored, for *what is more important than one's self-preservation is the upholding of a godly witness in a fallen world.*

Submitting to imperfect leadership can be, humanly speaking, a fearful prospect, whether to a wicked king, a ruler, or a husband; but the woman who fears God will submit to her husband with full trust and confidence *in the Lord*. Peter does not elaborate on what forms of disobedience may be manifested in the man spoken of in 1 Peter 3:1. A list would be useless, for no matter how extensive it would be, sinful men will find ways to exceed such a list! But whether a husband represents the pinnacle of godliness, or if he is disobedient to the Word, wives are to submit to their own husbands *without being frightened by any fear.*

When 1 Peter chapter 3 is seriously considered, questions often arise regarding how far a wife should go in rendering obedience to a husband who is exhibiting severe behavior, such that he may even

---

[213] 2 Timothy 3:6-7: 6 For of this sort are those who creep into households and make captives of gullible women loaded down with sins, led away by various lusts,7 always learning and never able to come to the knowledge of the truth.

[214] 1 Peter 1:3 Blessed be the God and Father of our Lord Jesus Christ, who according to His great mercy has caused us to be born again to a living hope through the resurrection of Jesus Christ from the dead.

164

pose a danger to the wife and children. As well, in light of the fact
that she must ultimately answer to the Lord in the maintenance of
her testimony of godliness, to what extent might a woman endure
the sin of a husband before seeking outside help for conscience sake,
assuming that she can seek outside help? Such extreme cases will
occur and should be approached with great caution and care. Should
a wife's conscience be so deeply afflicted that she cannot bear up
under the weight of the influences of a man who is being disobedient
to God's clearly revealed Word then she should seek out the counsel
of the leadership of her church as a first resort.[215] In the worst of all
cases, where her life or the lives of her children are in clear danger,
she can call upon governing authorities in order to secure the safety
of the family. In such extreme cases the wife must be very careful to
invoke such secular protection as an absolute last resort, knowing
that her highest priority is not self-preservation, but it is to preserve
her life for Christ and for the sake of the Gospel. In either of these
cases, such actions should stand at the end of much forbearance; her
prayers and petitions to God, on behalf of her husband, should be
extensive; her respect for the privacy of her marriage and family
should be maintained with all integrity at every stage of such a trial;
her patient endurance and godly example, as displayed before her
husband, should long precede any final effort to seek outside help as
the Lord enables her to do. However, should she come to the end of
her ability, in good conscience, to endure her treatment in the home
then she should seek help from the leadership of the local church, or
in the worst of all cases, civil/secular authorities, remembering that
the Apostle Paul warned against the *casual* use of secular authority in
the matter of adjudicating issues within the church:

1 **Corinthians 6:1-5***:* 1 Does any one of you, when he has a case against
his neighbor, dare to go to law before the unrighteous, and not before the
saints? 2 Or do you not know that the saints will judge the world? And if

---

[215] Matthew 18:15-17, 1 Corinthians 5:1-13.

the world is judged by you, are you not competent to constitute the smallest law courts? 3 Do you not know that we shall judge angels? How much more, matters of this life? 4 If then you have law courts dealing with matters of this life, do you appoint them as judges who are of no account in the church? 5 I say this to your shame. Is it so, that there is not among you one wise man who will be able to decide between his brethren

In a world which demotes the value of the family, and which fuels such businesses as www.yourfriendlydivorce.com, it is quite evident that it is all too easy to seek out secular intervention. Many in this world are quite eager to intervene in almost any perceived crisis in the home. With circumstances permitting, the church is to be the first place of help. Especially in the case of a wife whose husband is an unbeliever, the local church is the first place to begin because it is the pillar and support of the truth and this world is not. *The believing and unbelieving husband both need the truth of God more than they need the laws of men.* Having said this, we must also recognize that secular penalties can be used of the Lord as a rebuke to sinful men; and while secular laws are a weaker witness to God's character than is the Gospel, it can still be used in God's sovereign providence. In Romans chapter 13 the Apostle Paul reminds us that governmental authority is to be seen as a *servant of God* against certain evil activities. For example, we know that the Apostle Paul invoked the protections of civil authority by disclosing his Roman citizenship during his arrest in Jerusalem.[216] By doing this he was offered protection from the angry mob that sought his death. While one may look at this action as being one where self-preservation was his paramount interest, it was not. Paul knew that these difficult times would come:

Acts 20:23-24*:* 23 ...the Holy Spirit solemnly testifies to me in every city, saying that bonds and afflictions await me. 24 But I do not consider my

---

[216] Acts 21:39.

life of any account as dear to myself, in order that I may finish my course, and the ministry which I received from the Lord Jesus, to testify solemnly of the gospel of the grace of God.

When Paul identified himself as a legal citizen to the Roman commander in Jerusalem, he actually opened up another opportunity to proclaim the Word to his kinsmen according to the flesh - *the Jews*. Rather than using the civil protections afforded to him as a means of escape, he seized the opportunity to proclaim the truth of God to the angry mob who eagerly sought his murder once again. More than self-preservation, Paul was driven to *finish the course of his ministry*. This example of godliness is instructive to all Christians of all ages, whether male or female. No matter what station of life the believer may be in, it should be his or her goal to advance the witness of the Lord Jesus Christ to all men. The godly example of Paul is the example of Christ as well: *to live is Christ and to die is gain.*[217] For wives of any circumstance, their goal should be no different. By the chaste and respectful behavior of the wife there will be the full demonstration of the humility and love of Christ to her husband and children. Let the godly wife not consider her life of any account as dear to herself that she too may finish her course and ministry as a servant of God in the home. Whether she basks in the freedoms of America, or is subjected to the oppressive standards of a Muslim nation, let her highest priority be to manifest the image of Jesus Christ, of whom it is said that *while being reviled, He did not revile in return; while suffering, He uttered no threats, but kept entrusting Himself to Him who judges righteously.*[218] Indeed, to live is Christ and to die is gain. Let the godly wife submit to her husband without fear.

Beyond such extreme circumstances, as mentioned above, it is most often the case that the average wife finds herself battling in the realm

---

[217] Philippians 1:21.

[218] 1 Peter 2:23.

of those daily struggles which involve temptations that are common to men and women. No matter how godly her husband may be, he is an imperfect man. No matter how wonderful her children are, they are the progeny of two sinners; and no matter how godly the wife is, she too battles with the flesh in her daily life. All of this is the result of living in a fallen world, but in it all, her daily responsibility is to submit herself to the Lord as the Spirit fosters Christ-like attitudes and conduct in her life. In her ministry to her family, she is to pursue godliness in her roles as wife and mother. Her first responsibility in the home is to submit to her husband's headship knowing that she should respond to him in a manner which reflects the church's submission and reverence to Christ.

In order to evaluate the true quality and nature of a wife's submission, we will evaluate her calling in light of our recent examination of the husband's calling, as described in Ephesians 5:23-33. By this analysis we find that the godly wife's labor of submission will lead her to respond well to her husband's a). *passionate love*, b). *sacrifice*, c). *leadership* and d). *care*. Let's consider these expressions of the wife's godly love, in order:

A Wife's Love for Her Husband Cont'
A. Submitting to His Passionate Love

Only a Spirit filled wife can know and understand that she is not first in her husband's life, but is second to Christ Himself. In the previous section, *The Spirit Filled Husband*, we observed that a Christ-centered husband will place his love for God above all others. It is for this reason that the Spirit-filled wife will gladly receive such a God-centered love, knowing that this is the greatest of all affections that she could possibly receive from him. Therefore, she should never want to be first in her husband's life, for that would only corrupt their relationship with one another.

168

It may seem simple enough to say that a wife ought to receive her husband's love, and yet, this can prove to be a greater challenge in real life. When a wife considers this idea of submitting herself to her husband's love and affection - accepting his expressions of love *in everything* - she must recognize that this will provide some challenges. He may not be the best with words, creativity, planning or romance, but despite his imperfections the wife is to accept his love as a blessing from God. Submission and reverence in this area will certainly remove the temptation to criticize and nitpick a husband for his imperfect expressions of love and desire. Even when a wife petitions her preferences to her husband, she should do it with the gentleness and humility that begets genuine submission. Such a principle applies to those private expressions of intimacy between the husband and wife in the bedroom as well. There, too, the wife is to receive the love of her husband:

> **1 Corinthians 7:1-5***:* 1 Now concerning the things about which you wrote, it is good for a man not to touch a woman. 2 But because of immoralities, let each man have his own wife, and let each woman have her own husband. 3 Let the husband fulfill his duty to his wife, and likewise also the wife to her husband. 4 The wife does not have authority over her own body, but the husband does; and likewise also the husband does not have authority over his own body, but the wife does. 5 Stop depriving one another, except by agreement for a time that you may devote yourselves to prayer, and come together again lest Satan tempt you because of your lack of self-control.

It is often suggested, and is most likely the case, that some within the Corinthian church were being led into the erroneous thinking that singleness, or even sexual abstinence in marriage, constituted a superior form of spirituality.[219] The impact that this teaching would

---

[219] R.C.H. Lenski, The Interpretation of St. Paul's First and Second Epistle to the Corinthians (Wartburg Press, Columbus, Ohio), pp. 272-277.

have on marriages should be obvious. There would be those who would conclude that marriage and sexual intercourse was unhealthy and unprofitable. However, Paul refuted this error and reminded husbands and wives that they are not at liberty to forsake their bonds of marriage, but that they were to fulfill their commitments in the Lord because they are one flesh. Rather than being excused from sexual intercourse, husbands and wives are commanded to fulfill their obligation towards one another in the Lord. What is true for the husband is true for the wife – neither one is at liberty to forsake their covenant before the Lord; however, such *obedience* should not be an act of mere compulsion either. Instead, the husband and the wife are to receive, joyfully, each other's love as an act of worship to Christ. Only the Spirit-filled wife can receive her husband's God-centered love and passion, and this she will do as an act of loving submission to her husband, and to the Lord. Over time the husband will learn how to express the passions of his love, to his wife, with greater care and consideration; and the best way that a wife can encourage that progress is to receive such expressions of love with joy in the Lord.

A WIFE'S LOVE FOR HER HUSBAND CONT'
B. SUBMITTING TO HIS PROTECTION

When we examined *The Spirit-Filled Husband* we observed Christ's love for the church as the perfect example for the godly husband. Like Christ, the husband is to seek the *protection* of his wife through his own self sacrifice. We also noted in that section that even the best of earthly husbands could never match the perfection of Christ's protection of His church. It would be vanity and arrogance to think otherwise! Thus it is important to acknowledge that the spiritual husband will be on a lifelong journey of growth as he learns about how he can best emulate Christ's example of sacrificial protection. This observation is significant for the wife who is called to submit to her husband and reverence him. In all of his imperfections and shortcomings, as compared to Christ, he is still God's ordained

170

means of protection for her; however, an important distinction is necessary here: the husband is a *means* of protection, and yet only the Lord can be the *sovereign source* of all protection. This distinction is important, for it should remind the wife that her husband's umbrella of spiritual protection is not her ultimate hope, but the Lord is. As we examined earlier, Sarah submitted to and obeyed Abraham despite all his frailties as a spiritual protector, therefore, as she is displayed as an example of godliness before women, so too should all wives obey their husbands *without fear*. Consider this important text *once again:*

> **1 Peter 3:3-6**: 3 And let not your adornment be merely external—braiding the hair, and wearing gold jewelry, or putting on dresses; 4 but let it be the hidden person of the heart, with the imperishable quality of a gentle and quiet spirit, which is precious in the sight of God. 5 For in this way in former times the holy women also, who hoped in God, used to adorn themselves, being submissive to their own husbands. 6 Thus Sarah obeyed Abraham, calling him lord, and you have become her children if you do what is right without being frightened by any fear.

In the eyes of the Lord genuine beauty does not consist of external adornment, with costly raiment and jewels. This is the faulty assumption of our modern culture which is infatuated with cosmetics, jewelry, and plastic surgery. The superficial beauty of our culture is clearly pictured in the wisdom of God's Word:

> **Proverbs 11:22** "As a ring of gold in a swine's snout, so is a beautiful woman who lacks discretion."

There are many ravishing women in our day whose beauty runs no deeper than that of a pig's snout, but the truly beautiful woman is the one who submits to her husband *as to the Lord.* Her submission, rendered to her imperfect husband, is the means to the greater end of submitting to the Lord of all perfection. The true *daughters of Sarah* show forth such fruit. Consider Calvin's insight into the importance of this principle as it is reflected in Ephesians 5:22:

"He [Paul] begins with wives, whom he enjoins to be subject to their husbands, in the same manner as to Christ, - as to the Lord. Not that the authority is equal, but wives cannot obey Christ without yielding obedience to their husbands."[220]

If a marriage is not God-centered, then it will falter in time. Imperfections abound in any husband and wife, and for this reason, godly forbearance is absolutely necessary in any marriage. Whether motivated by impatience or ingratitude, an immature wife may find herself seeking out the protection of her father instead of her husband; or the love and protection of another man in the church who may appear to be more godly than her husband. But Paul and Peter both correct these dangers instantly when they call upon all wives to submit to *their own husbands.*

A WIFE'S LOVE FOR HER HUSBAND CONT'
C. SUBMITTING TO HIS LEADERSHIP

Related to the thought of the husband's protection is this concept of the husband's leadership. As we examined earlier, Christ gave Himself up for the church in order that He might sanctify her by means of the Word of God. It is this model of Christ's leadership that serves as the ultimate example for any husband. Like Christ, the husband is to lead his wife to this chief end: that she would be *cleansed by the washing of water with the Word* so that she might be spotless and pure before the Lord (Ephesians 5:26). Since this is the calling of the godly husband, *it is therefore the subsequent duty of the wife to receive such spiritual leadership from her husband.* Yet unlike Christ, the man's leadership in the home will be a matter of growth

---

[220] Calvin, Commentaries, p 317.

and progress. Unlike Christ, men will struggle with the imperfections of their character as they progress as leaders. As well, some men will embrace the principles of leadership very early in their marriage, while others will grow into their ordained role with great struggle and incremental progress. In either case, the wife is called to receive his leadership with submission and reverence, knowing that her believing husband will progress as a leader over time. The greatest challenge facing women in this area is that they must accept the leadership of their husbands without attempting to subvert authority or by trying to become a co-leader in the process, because the husband is the head and the wife is the one who helps and follows. To have it any other way diminishes the Gospel testimony of the home and it confuses the parents' ministry to their children, for *no-one can serve two masters.*[221] As the husband's helper, the wife can do many things in the home, but she can never take her husband's place as the leader. This recognition is important for the wife who is learning to grow as a submissive helper to her husband. She is to receive instruction from her husband with an attitude that conveys humility and reverence, and this attitude should prevail in her every context of life:

> **1 Timothy 2:9-11:** 9 Likewise, I want women to adorn themselves with proper clothing, modestly and discreetly, not with braided hair and gold or pearls or costly garments; 10 but rather by means of good works, as befits women making a claim to godliness. 11 Let a woman quietly receive instruction with entire submissiveness.

While Paul's instructions to Timothy relate to the conduct of women in the local church, he is not teaching us that women are to be one thing in the church and another at home. The wife's garments of humility and submission are not to be seen as church clothes that she sheds when she walks through the door of her house. As well, Peter

---

[221] Matthew 6:24.

instructed wives in 1 Peter 3 to be adorned with *the hidden person of the heart, with the imperishable quality of a gentle and quiet spirit, which is precious in the sight of God.* This gentle and quiet spirit, which is eager to submit to authority, should be manifested in the church as well as in the home:

> **1 Corinthians 14:34-35:** 34 Let the women keep silent in the churches; for they are not permitted to speak, but let them subject themselves, just as the Law also says. 35 And if they desire to learn anything, let them ask their own husbands at home; for it is improper for a woman to speak in church.

The modern world normally chafes at such injunctions, but it does not realize that a Christ-like marriage is one in which the husband lovingly guides his wife into the patterns of behavior that mirror the church: *submission and reverence.* While Paul's language in 1 Corinthians 14 may seem to deal only in the realm of prohibition, it must be noted that there is a wonderful gem of positive instruction contained therein: *let them ask their own husbands at home.* In keeping with her submission to her *own husband,* the godly wife is to make frequent inquiry of her *own husband* so that she might receive his leadership. This does not negate the teaching and leadership that she receives from the local church, but it does highlight the importance of her ministry of submission to *her own husband.* This important principle must be clearly underscored: a spiritual wife should be eager to receive her husband's instructions, guidance, and leadership as her ordained head. She must understand that she is commanded in Scripture to seek out such leadership from him, and she should therefore not be discouraged from such a habit. Thus, the more she seeks out his leadership in the home, the more the husband will be encouraged to embrace-his God ordained role as the head of the home. In other words, the more a woman pursues her God-ordained calling in life, the more she will encourage her husband to pursue his ordained role! Such a ministry in the home renders a godly influence on *all members* of the family. On the other hand, the woman who rebels in contention against her husband will make life in the home difficult to tolerate:

> **Proverbs 21:9** It is better to live in a corner of a roof, than in a house shared with a contentious woman.

The clear line of distinction between a contentious woman and a woman who has a gentle and quiet spirit *is godly submission*. The woman who desires to see her husband progress as a leader will step back and let him lead, receiving his leadership with gladness as she does, and praising God for His sanctifying work in both their lives as husband and wife.

A WIFE'S LOVE FOR HER HUSBAND CONT'
D. SUBMITTING TO HIS CARE

The godly husband is called to love his wife through the practical care that he gives to her on a daily basis. He is to nourish her with this same care that he would naturally give to himself since *no one ever hated his own flesh, but nourishes it and cherishes it*. As the husband has need for food, shelter, and the comfort of a home, so must he provide the same for his wife as quickly as he would care for himself. This description of the husband's loving care for the wife was already examined in Ephesians 5:28-33:

> **Ephesians 5:28-33**: 28 So husbands ought also to love their own wives as their own bodies. He who loves his own wife loves himself; 29 for no one ever hated his own flesh, but nourishes and cherishes it, just as Christ also does the church, 30 because we are members of His body. 31 For this cause a man shall leave his father and mother, and shall cleave to his wife; and the two shall become one flesh. 32 This mystery is great; but I am speaking with reference to Christ and the church. 33 Nevertheless let

175

each individual among you also love his own wife even as himself; and let the wife see to it that she respect her husband.

As the wife reverences and submits to her husband, she will be eager to receive her husband's every expression of care for her, as well as his love, protection, and spiritual leadership. This final manifestation of the husband's imitation of Christ focuses on the practical nature of the marital relationship. Clearly, it is the husband's responsibility to provide for his wife so that she would have what she needs in order to flourish in godliness in the home. *But with this, it is the wife's responsibility to accept and receive the husband's caring provisions for her according to his ability to provide them.* This may sound quite simple as a stated principle, but it is more complicated in practical life. When a woman becomes married, she places herself beneath the protective care of her husband in every way, to include his ability to provide for her financially. The wife's submission and reverence in this area is just as crucial as in any other dimension of life. She must accept the provisions that the husband gives with thankfulness and joy, understanding that her husband is God's will for her life. In a materialistic age this can pose quite a challenge. One of the fundamental challenges to the modern household has to do with this question of our financial *necessities*. The process of defining one's wants and needs represents no small challenge for the modern family which abides in a culture of aggressive marketing strategies. What one defines as normal and necessary living can be too easily polluted by the pressures of society's commercialism. How important it is, therefore, for the wife to accept the provisions of life that are ordained for her through her husband, rather than becoming anxious for what she cannot reasonably obtain. The wife who marries a man of modest financial means should not expect to pamper herself with a lifestyle that exceeds the husband's ability to provide for the family. It is not for everyone to live in a small mansion with two new cars in the driveway! While it is the husband's responsibility to be diligent in order to provide for his family's every *need*, it is also the wife's responsibility to accept that provision and to be thankful. But when there is discontentment in the area of finances, there will be problems that can unsettle the marriage union. The temptations of this world are many and the Christian family can fall prey to a host of problems: unbearable debt, disputes over purchasing priorities, even the temptation for a mother to work outside of the home in order to establish a lifestyle that better suits their expectations. Because of these temptations, the Christian home must be on guard against the effects of materialism. Paul's example of Christ and the church is crucial in this discussion, for Christ nourishes and cherishes the church, providing for her needs as a loving husband; yet we know that throughout the generations Christian assemblies have seen times of financial prosperity as well as times of hardship. Even in the days of the Antichrist, believers will have to survive under difficult conditions since those who will have the ability to buy and sell will do so by the mark of the beast.[222] Being careful not to take Ephesians 5:29 too far (only Christ has authority over our health, well-being, and life), Paul's comparison of the wife to the church serves as a reminder that whether by prosperity or by humble means, the Christian wife can joyfully submit to her husband's provisions, giving thanks to Christ who strengthens us:

> **Philippians 4:11-13***:* 11 ...I have learned to be content in whatever circumstances I am." 12 I know how to get along with humble means, and I also know how to live in prosperity; in any and every circumstance I have learned the secret of being filled and going hungry, both of having abundance and suffering need. 13 I can do all things through Him who strengthens me.

While materialistic expectations must be avoided, we should also recognize that the man who does not at all provide for his household

---

[222] Revelation 13:16-17.

is worse than an unbeliever.[223] In the context of the local church, such a man should be confronted by shepherds who have the watchcare of the church.

Beyond such extreme situations, the wife is called to submit to her husband, receiving his provision of care as a gift that is ordained by God. Her children watch carefully as they learn from her every action and word. With an example of a godly mother before them, they will learn to be content in all things through Christ (Phil. 4:11-13). With an example of an ungodly mother before them, they will learn to complain and be discontent with whatever they have. Thus, a wife and mother must never underestimate her verbal *and non-verbal* testimony which she presents in the presence of her children. For the Spirit-filled woman, her love expressed to her husband will impact her children as they learn about the principles of godliness in marriage and family!

2. A WIFE'S LOVE FOR HER CHILDREN

Children are to be loved with the same practical, filial love that the wife is called to have for her husband: "encourage the young women *to love* their husbands, *to love their children*" [*philoteknous* > *phileō*, Titus 2:4]. Therefore the wife's ministry of love will be manifested in practical actions that are in keeping with her calling as a mother. Her labor of love to her children will be manifested in at least three crucial areas - *1. physical care, 2. spiritual nurture and 3. prayer*:

---

[223] 1 Timothy 5:8.

A Wife's Love for Her Children Cont'
A. Physical Care

The act of loving one's children with a filial love is indeed multifaceted. It includes godly counsel, discipline, instruction, prayer, and such perceptively mundane tasks as preparing a meal and changing a diaper. In a culture that defines success in terms of monetary rewards, and social acclaim, the labors of a housewife may seem to be insignificant - *but they are not*. The mother's physical care for her children is very much a part of her overall ministry to her children. From the early days of diapers, to the moment of their departure from the home, the mother's work is never trivial, but is indeed noble and challenging. The mother's every word and act of servitude is very much a part of her overall service of worship rendered to the Lord Himself:

> **Colossians 3:17** And whatever you do in word or deed, do all in the name of the Lord Jesus, giving thanks through Him to God the Father.

The challenges which face the contemporary mother often revolve around the question concerning the importance of the wife's work in the home. Fewer and fewer young mothers are learning the essentials of home-making, failing to understand the importance of this calling of God; and while modern technology is very helpful, it often fosters laziness and ignorance. Like a young student who cannot add 2 + 2 without the use of a calculator, so is the young mother who cannot prepare a meal without a frozen dinner, microwave meal, or fast-food delivery. This *"third job"* for women is suffering greatly as evidenced by the illiteracy, malnutrition, and obesity of our modern children. Young mothers are not adequately being encouraged to love their children with sound care in the home. Such a ministry of servitude not only provides for the physical well-being of children, but it also imparts the significant spiritual lesson of Christ-like servanthood:

1 Peter 4:11 Whoever speaks, let him speak, as it were, the utterances of God; whoever serves, let him do so as by the strength which God supplies; so that in all things God may be glorified through Jesus Christ, to whom belongs the glory and dominion forever and ever. Amen.

The message of servanthood is a crucial one that reflects the glory of Christ. Before the Lord was crucified on the cross, He girded Himself as a servant and washed His disciples' feet. Peter protested the moment, saying: "never shall you wash my feet." It was incomprehensible to Peter that the Lord of glory should bend down on His knees and perform such a lowly, filthy task. Culturally, it was a humble and even demeaning chore, and yet it was a necessary one:

John 13:8,12-15: 8 Jesus answered him, "If I do not wash you, you have no part with Me."...12 And so when He had washed their feet, and taken His garments, and reclined at the table again, He said to them, "Do you know what I have done to you? 13 "You call Me Teacher and Lord; and you are right, for so I am. 14 "If I then, the Lord and the Teacher, washed your feet, you also ought to wash one another's feet. 15 "For I gave you an example that you also should do as I did to you."

Humble servitude should never be a basis for shame; instead, it glorifies Christ when we follow Him in a ministry of servitude to one another. Thus, the mother's care in the home is an important one. She is the only one, by God's design, who is equipped to supply the earliest meals to her infant children. She is the one who is to care for her children making sure that they are adorned with modest and adequate clothing, being supplied with beneficial meals. She is the nurse to her ailing young and administrator who facilitates orderly conduct in the home. Her servitude in the home is unquestionably important, no matter what the task may be, or how lowly it may seem. As godly mothers render such servitude in the home, little girls and boys are gleaning the lessons of life by her daily actions. It is true of both the father and mother that their every action in the home communicates a certain set of priorities to the children. The priorities of life, to which we now expose them, will most likely become the priorities of life that they will continue with into their adult years. If a mother is discontent with the ministry of getting on her knees and washing the dirty feet of her children, then this will become woefully obvious. The manifestations of this error are too numerous to articulate here, but fathers and mothers must be on guard against the worldly thinking which says that parental care is an interruption or a third job in life. Our priorities will certainly affect our children. Here are a few questions to consider regarding the importance of a mother's care in the home:

- *Are our daughters being groomed for organized sports, professional careers, advanced education, or some other endeavor that will hinder their progress towards becoming godly single women, wives, or mothers? Such things are not evil per se, however they are the things that are often exalted above the important task of older women encouraging the younger women to love their husbands, love their children, and to be workers in the home.*

- *What are our sons learning in the home as they watch the ministry of care given by their mother?*

- *What kind of a wife will your son marry in light of the example that you have set before him? May your example in the home encourage your son to seek out a joyful, submissive, and respectful wife who will not only honor him, but also his parents as well.*

A WIFE'S LOVE FOR HER CHILDREN CONT'
B. SPIRITUAL NURTURE

While it is true that fathers are explicitly commanded to embrace the responsibility of nurturing children in the discipline and instruction of the Lord (Ephesians 6:4), this does not mean that the wife is uninvolved in such a process. This would be a dangerously false conclusion. Paul's instruction is a reminder to fathers that they are the priests and pastors of their homes. Their responsibility is to lead and direct the ministry of discipleship within the home; however, the wife is the husband's helpmeet in the home and she is therefore a crucial assistant to the father in this ministry of discipline and instruction. This is partly reflected by the fact that children are commanded to obey their parents (Ephesians 6:1) and to honor their father and mother (Ephesians 6:2). Both the husband and the wife have a ministry of the Word in the home: the husband's ministry of the Word in the home is one of leadership to all the members of the household while the wife's ministry of the Word is one of instruction to the children. Paul's instruction to Timothy concerning the ministry of the Word in 1 Timothy 2:12-15 should not be seen as a prohibition against a wife's duty of instruction to children in the home. Consider Calvin's qualification regarding 1 Timothy 2:12:

> *But I suffer not a woman to teach. Not that he takes from them the charge of instructing their family, but only excludes them from the office of teaching, which God has committed to men only.*[224]

The mother is called to instruct her children in the wisdom of the Word, and yet such a ministry of the Word to children is not an autonomous one, rather it must help and support the husband's leadership overall. Such concepts of the mother's ministry of the Word in the home is reflected elsewhere in Scripture:

- ***Proverbs 1:8*** *Hear, my son, your father's instruction, And do not forsake your mother's teaching;*

---

[224] Calvin, Commentaries, p.67. Calvin's mention of the word family in this citation connotes children in particular rather than the family in total.

- *Proverbs 6:20 My son, observe the commandment of your father, And do not forsake the teaching of your mother;*

- *Proverbs 31:1 The words of King Lemuel, the oracle which his mother taught him.*

Much more will be said on this subject in the following chapters where we will look at the examples of Lois and Eunice who trained Timothy in the Scriptures from his youth. Their example shines brightly as a guiding star for any woman who desires to raise their children for Christ, and thus she must understand that her presentation of Christ to her children is crucial in light of her special role as her husband's helper. In light of her need to instruct her children in God's Word, she must clearly understand the importance of personal godliness in the communication of God's truth. Like her husband who leads the household, the wife must watch her words and actions as she seeks to nurture her children in the Lord. Not only do children watch their fathers carefully, examining the nature of his leadership in the home, but they also watch the mother as she walks in submission and reverence to the Lord and to her husband. Therefore the wife's first key to a successful ministry of spiritual nurture to her children begins with her own walk in Christ. The following are some key components to a wife's successful ministry to her children:

- *The godly wife will endeavor to guard her times of prayer and the reading of the Scriptures. In a house bustling with children and activities, this can be a large challenge – but it is crucial that the wife secure times of private devotion in the Word. If a wife is having difficulty securing this time, let her ask her husband for help on how she can better establish a more productive schedule. The mother's ability to invest her children in the Word will depend upon her personal ability to do the same for herself.*

183

- *The godly wife is to seek every opportunity to relate the instructions of the father to her children in order to uphold his leadership in the home. Whether it is his instructions in the Scriptures through family devotions, or his directives on the daily household chores, her instruction to the children will be that which honors the Word of God and her husband as the household's head.*

- *The godly wife will understand that her life is a representation of the church's relationship to Jesus Christ, and this instruction by example is seen by her children on a daily basis. Therefore, the extent to which she joyfully submits to her husband, receives his instruction, and responds to him with godly respect will impact her children in ways that go far beyond words. Our children are learning about our Christian profession of faith at all times: may they learn the lesson of the beauty of Christian submission, humility, joy, and reverence through the example of the godly mother.*

A Wife's Love for Her Children Cont'
C. Prayer

We find in Scripture that the greatest examples of godliness among mothers are those who sought the Lord in prayer. The evidence of Scripture is quite telling as we see, for example, the prayers of women like Hannah and Mary, as recorded for all posterity. Hannah commended Samuel to the Lord and prayed fervently on his behalf (1 Samuel 2:1-10). Mary rejoiced in the blessing of Christ and exalted the Lord in prayer (Luke 1:46-55). These inscripturated prayers stand as hallmarks of true piety among women and mothers of all generations. They mark out the ultimate duty of mothers in all their endeavors. The ministry of motherhood is often fraught with anxiety and weariness, but the believer who attends the throne of grace will be guarded with the peace of Christ which surpasses all comprehension. Through prayer we seek the power and work of God for His glory; therefore it is the praying mother who seeks the glory of God to be manifested in her children through His sovereign work.

A mother's loving labor of care, instruction, and nurture for her children is an empty work if the Lord does not work in the heart of her children. It is God who provides the growth amidst the mother's tilling and planting,[225] therefore let the godly mother labor well in the fields of continual petition and prayer on behalf of her children:

> *"Without the blessing of the Lord, your best endeavours will do no good. He has the hearts of all men in His hands, and except He touch the hearts of your children by His Spirit, you will weary yourself to no purpose. Water, therefore, the seed you sow on their minds with unceasing prayer. The Lord is far more willing to hear than we to pray; far more ready to give blessings than we to ask them; but He loves to be entreated for them. And I set this matter of prayer before you, as the top-stone and seal of all that you do."*[226]

As J. C. Ryle states so well, the ministry of prayer is the top-stone and seal of the mother's ministry to her children. Her prayerful act of commending her children to the care of the Good Shepherd is her consummate expression of genuine submission to the Lord on behalf of her children.

3. A WIFE'S LABOR IN HER HOME:

The order of priority for the wife is wonderfully clarified in the second chapter of Titus: she is to render love to her husband as a first priority in the home, and then her children are to receive her significant ministry of filial love. After these priorities, the wife is to be a *worker in the home* or a house-worker. Her dwelling, while important, is not more important than her husband nor her children. Paul concludes his directions in the following manner:

---

[225] 1 Corinthians 3:6.

[226] John Charles Ryle, Train Up a Child In The Way He Should Go, The Duties of Parents, (Christian Heritage Publisher, Choteau, MT 1983).

Titus 2:5 [encourage them to be] ....sensible, pure, workers at home, kind, being subject to their own husbands, that the Word of God may not be dishonored.

The concept of a house-worker is one of great significance. The excellent wife was a woman who loved her husband, her children, and whose industry in the home was highly productive. Paul's instructions to Titus constitutes no novelty, but is instead an ancient picture of the truly pious woman:

Proverbs 31:10-13: 10 An excellent wife, who can find? For her worth is far above jewels. 11 The heart of her husband trusts in her, and he will have no lack of gain. 12 She does him good and not evil all the days of her life. 13 She looks for wool and flax, and works with her hands in delight.

Proverbs 31 is a very familiar text of Scripture that reviews the qualities of the godly and excellent wife. It is often the case that this text is reviewed on Mother's Day, or whenever the discussion of the godly woman arises in the pulpit. How can it be avoided? Perhaps more than any other text in the Bible, Proverbs 31 surveys the multifaceted characteristics of the woman of God who *loves her husband and children and is indeed a worker in the home.* Unfortunately, this text is also a rather abused one. When modern minds that have been conditioned in the ways of secularism take hold of this text it is often used as a proof-text for justifying the feminization of men and the professionalization of women.[227] But such an application of Proverbs 31 is, at best, strained and clearly contradicts the obvious instruction to mothers to be workers in the home. The industry of the Proverbs 31 woman was one that

---

[227] "This text...accomplishes a verse-by-verse demolition of the male-rulership system that issued from the fall, by showing God's ideal for women – to share fully in the responsibilities pertaining to the to the governance of community life in the family." Gilbert Bilezikien, Beyond Sex Roles What the Bible Says About a Woman's Place in Church and Family (Baker Book House, Grand Rapids Michigan), p. 77.

flourished amidst an agrarian culture which was radically different than our modern culture. She did not have a career outside of the home, but she was industrious within her home such that the surplus of her labors could be used to further the homestead. Much of Proverbs 31 carries with it the normal concepts of the ancient merchant markets of that day:

"During peace times the gate served as a gathering place for merchants (Genesis 19:1 and 2 kings 7:1). Here would be found the stalls and booths of craftsmen and hawkers as well as the produce market for the surrounding villages. Fresh produce was bartered for bread, pottery, leather goods and clothing."[228]

The merchant market of antiquity was quite different from the modern shopping mall or grocery store. Items were either purchased with money, or were traded for other goods. The agrarian family, when necessary, would come to market in order to buy, sell, and trade according to the needs of the home. Hence the expressions *"her husband is known in the gates"* and *"let her works praise her in the gates"* reflects such a family outing at the market. To suggest that this woman is some independent laborer, leaving the home for long periods of time in order to be the bread-winner for the family, requires a measure of imagination that is not supplied by the text. The godly woman of Proverbs 31 labored in love for her husband, children, and overall household:

- **Proverbs 31:15** *She gives food to her household...*

- **Proverbs 31:21** *She is not afraid of the snow for her household, for all her household are clothed with scarlet.*

---

[228] Victor H. Matthews, <u>Manners and Customs in the Bible</u> (Hendrickson Publishers, Massachusetts), p. 108.

- ***Proverbs 31:27** She looks well to the ways of her household, And does not eat the bread of idleness.*

- ***Proverbs 31:11** The heart of her husband trusts in her, And he will have no lack of gain.*

Her primary focus of servitude is not outside of her house, but it is set upon her husband, children, and her household [Titus 2:5]. She does not labor in a manner that defies her role as a woman, but labors as a worker in the homestead. Consider the insights of Matthew Henry on the industry of this woman:

> *"She applies herself to the business that is proper for her. It is not in a scholar's business, or statesman's business, or husbandman's business, that she employs herself, but in women's business: She seeks wool and flax, where she may have the best of each at the best hand, and cheapest; she has a stock of both by her, and every thing that is necessary to the carrying on both of the woolen and the linen manufacture (v. 13), and with this she does not only set the poor on work, which is a very good office, but does herself work, and work willingly, with her hands;"*[229]

The Proverbs 31 woman is such an industrious homemaker that she has a surplus with which she can offer provisions for her family, as well as for her maidservants, the needy, and the poor. But the primary industry for which she should be remembered is the industry of her personal godliness in the sight of the Lord:

Proverbs 31:28-31:
28 Her children rise up and bless her;
Her husband also, and he praises her, saying:
29 "Many daughters have done nobly,
But you excel them all."
30 Charm is deceitful and beauty is vain,

---

[229] Henry, Commentary on the Whole Bible, Pr 31:10.

188

But a woman who fears the Lord, she shall be praised.
31 Give her the product of her hands,
And let her works praise her in the gates.

At the end of the day, the evidences of her nobility in the home are clearly displayed. The spiritual profit that she brings to her husband, her children, and to the many who know her is made so evident that it cannot be hidden. She is a lover of her husband, her children, and clearly a worker in the home. She fears the Lord, and serves with joy as she looks to the future.

In all of this we are reminded that charm is deceitful and beauty is vain, but a woman who fears the Lord, she shall be praised! Here is the high calling of the wife and mother in the home: it is the imitation of Christ's love and humility, and is manifested through her respectful submission to her husband and through her care given to her children. The woman who invests herself in such godliness will not *blaspheme God's Word* but will exalt the glory of Jesus Christ before her family, within the church, and at large in the community in which she lives and serves. Her Gospel witness is a crucial one in a world that exalts careers and money over the imitation of Christ. Let no one ever doubt the importance of a mother's ministry. The godly impact of such a woman can impact generations for Christ!

THE FIRST INSTITUTION

CHAPTER 4

REFORMED PARENTING

FOR THE GLORY OF CHRIST

THE TWO PATHS OF PARENTING

In this chapter we will introduce the subject of parenting, but from the crucial vantage point of the parent's own need for maturation and sanctification. You see, there are only two real paths of parenting – *the path of the Spirit and the path of the flesh*, and the reality is that we are either travelling in one or the other. Now it is not uncommon for books dealing with the subject of parenting to deal solely with the question about *what the parent should do with their children;* however, there is a problem with this approach: *godly parenting* doesn't begin with a formula for child training – *it begins with godly parents who are being conformed to the image of Christ.* The point simply is this: if a parent wants to improve the nurture and discipline of their children, then they need to examine their own lives first. Without such a focus, parents can fall into the trap of thinking that they can simply apply some external mechanism that will change their children on a dime. Such a mechanistic approach may result in a change in their external behavior, for a season, but if one wishes to see a life *transformed*, they too must seek *transformation* in their own lives. The contextual thrust of Ephesians 5:18-6:4 clearly reveals such a notion of *spiritual transformation*. Thus, we would miss too much if we ignored Ephesians 5:22-33, as well as Ephesians 6:4, in our eagerness to examine the particulars of child training in the first three verses of chapter 6. Consider how Paul enfolds his instructions on child training within the broader emphasis of parental maturation and transformation:

Ephesians 6:1-4: 1 Children, obey your parents in the Lord, for this is right. 2 "Honor your father and mother," which is the first commandment with promise: 3 "that it may be well with you and you may live long on the earth." 4 And you, fathers, do not provoke your children to wrath, but bring them up in the training and admonition of the Lord.

We have in this section four simple commands: 1). Children *obey* your parents; 2). [Children] *honor* your father and mother; 3). Fathers *do not provoke* your children to anger, and 4). [Fathers] *bring them up* in the discipline and instruction of the Lord. Regarding children, Paul's recitation of the 5th commandment in vs. 2 reminds us that the simplicity of his instructions on child training is a kind of shorthand summary of the broader corpus of Holy Writ.[230] It is for this very reason that Ephesians 6:1-3 will serve as a launching point from which many texts will be consulted in our next chapter – *Training Children for the Glory of Christ (Chapter 5).* But before we can comprehend the particulars of such child training, we must step back and consider this broader picture of the *two possible paths that a parent can take when relating to their children.* The Apostle Paul has already revealed for us these "two paths."

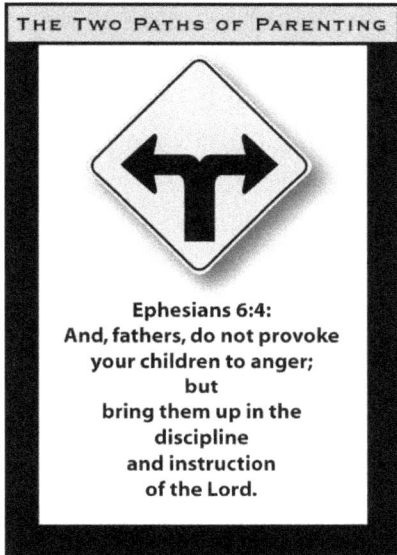

THE TWO PATHS OF PARENTING

Ephesians 6:4:
And, fathers, do not provoke
your children to anger;
but
bring them up in the
discipline
and instruction
of the Lord.

According to Ephesians 6:4, they are: the path of godly *nurture* or the path of sinful *provocation*; or we could say, the *path of the Spirit or of the flesh*:

Galatians 5:16-17: 16 But I say, walk by the Spirit, and you will not carry out the desire of the flesh. 17 For the flesh sets its desire against the Spirit, and the Spirit against the flesh; for these are in opposition to one another, so that you may not do the things that you please.

---

[230] Paul reminded the Ephesian elders why he had a clear conscience before God. It was because he proclaimed the whole counsel [*pasa tēn boulēn*] of God, Acts 20:27.

I would submit to the reader that any discussion of child training must be predicated on this more primitive question regarding the actions and attitudes of the parent. All genuine Christians understand that they are not perfect people, and that they need to grow, mature, and thereby become more and more capable of edifying and helping others. Such a pursuit of maturity will continue until death. Thus, as creatures of weakness, we will all stumble and struggle in many ways, but the Lord calls His children to continue to stand firmly in His grace.[231] With this in mind, parents must be on guard regarding their own conduct as stewards of the very children whom God has given. Their mission field is incalculably important.

As husbands and wives continue to be sanctified, they must keep in mind this aforementioned reality of the two potential paths of parenting. This is the very fork in the road that Paul presents to parents in his instructions in Ephesians 6:4. Let's now look at that text once again, but with a closer inspection of its details: "And, fathers, do not *provoke* your children to anger;[232] but *bring them up* in the discipline and instruction of the Lord." As is his habit, the Apostle gives us a didactic instruction, proverbial in nature, which exposes our potential for either *sin* or *righteousness*:

1. Sin ~ Provocation & Anger: *"...do not provoke your children to anger;"*

2. Righteousness ~ Discipline & Nurture: *"...but bring them up in the discipline and instruction of the Lord."*

This parental fork-in-the-road is a crucial one that we must comprehend well. It teaches us that if we as parents lack in the area of godly nurture, then something else will happen: a negative spirit

---

[231] 1 Peter 5:12...I have written to you briefly, exhorting and testifying that this is the true grace of God. Stand firm in it!

[232] Colossians 3:21 "Fathers, do not exasperate your children, that they may not lose heart."

will develop within our children. What this also teaches us is this: *there is no such thing as neutral parenting.* More will be said later about the myth of neutrality, as well as the implications of poor parenting, but at this point we must focus our attention on Paul's *positive path* for fathers. Fathers, says Paul, are to *bring up* their children (literally to *feed and nourish* them) in the discipline and instruction of the Lord. The English words *bring up* represent the same word that Paul used in the previous chapter concerning the husband's ministry to His wife:

> **Ephesians 5:28-29***:* 28 So husbands ought also to love their own wives as their own bodies. He who loves his own wife loves himself; 29 for no one ever hated his own flesh, but nourishes [*ektrephei*] and cherishes it, just as Christ also does the church,

When we consider Paul's repeated use of the word *ektrephete* ["nourish" - Eph. 5:29, and "bring up" in Eph. 6:4], we realize that he is pointing us to an attitude and action that considers the needs of others with a high regard. In reality, the husband's ministry in the home is a nourishing one. He cares for his wife's needs and *brings up* his children in a godly pedagogy. As we break down the nature of the Father's ministry of bringing spiritual nourishment to his children, we find that it contains two important components: *discipline* and *instruction.* Both of these terms, when brought together, form a nucleus of child training that encompasses a holy nurture of their hearts and minds. Overall, it is a spiritual nurture that is *of the Lord* (Ephesians 6:4) and *for the Lord* (Ephesians 6:1). Consider the important distinctions of these two words:

- *Discipline: The discipline [paideia] of children can include training that is positive or negative. It could be an exhortation or a reproof, a word of encouragement or a rebuke. It may be in the form of verbal teaching or the application of the rod (which we will address later).*

195

- ***Instruction:*** *Instruction [nouthesia] speaks of the parents' appeal to the heart and mind of the child. Here the emphasis is upon the inner-person of the child: their thinking, their affections as well as their internal reasoning.*

Discipline[233] [*paideia* ~ pedagogy] and instruction [*nouthesia* ~ the training of one's heart and mind] are words that, when joined together, speak of the overall shaping of a child's life, behavior, *and thinking*. It should be very clear from the combined use of these words that Paul is calling fathers to train their children in the fullest possible sense, rather than merely dealing with external behavior. His instruction also informs children regarding their spiritual responsibility: children are to receive and obey their parents, understanding that this is God's will. These instructions of Paul's give us a fundamental platform for understanding what the parents' attitude in child training should be: children are to be raised for the glory of God alone, therefore, all other priorities of parenting must fall beneath this central one. This is not an earth-shattering statement, for all that the Christian does in life is to be for the glory of God alone,[234] and yet this principle is important to state since the aberrations and defections of parenting often begin by a failure to embrace this simple principle. The fact that children are to be raised in this way should affect any serious-minded parent, for children are not personal property; they are gifts from the Lord; children are not medals to be worn by prideful parents who wish to showcase their wisdom and spirituality; children are not workhorses to be exploited according to their ability to perform for the parents; nor are they

---

[233] To discipline a child speaks of more than chastisement, for it includes the concepts of teaching, education and training as well. L. *disiplināre*: "To subject to discipline; in earlier use, to instruct, educate, train; in later use, more especially, to train to habits of order and subordination; to bring under control." The Oxford English Dictionary 2nd Edition (Oxford University Press), Electronic Edition.
[234] 1 Corinthians 10:31.

196

objects of adoration such that they should take the place of the Savior Himself. Instead, children are precious gifts from God who are to be raised in His wisdom and for His glory alone – period. Parents who bear and raise children for any other reason will most certainly fail as parents. Apart from God's gracious intervention, the natural home will only foster confusion, bitterness, resentment, envy, hostility, exasperation, and yes – anger, as Paul warned in Ephesians 6:4.[235]

Parents, through the leadership of the father, are to nurture their children in the wisdom of God, and for this to happen, they themselves must grow in wisdom. Just as an overseer is to be on guard for the church, so too must the father be for his family, for the devil knows what to attack in the economy of God's kingdom. Therefore, fathers and mothers must regularly review their motives and attitudes in their parenting, for the pollutions of their sin will often spread to their children. Satan's attack on the family comes from all sides, but he knows that the fastest path to destruction is to crumble the foundation of godly leadership in the home.

THE ONE TRUE PATH OF PARENTING

The world in which we live is filled with many wide and well traveled paths, but the Lord calls us to just one narrow path – the path of Christ alone. It is the message of Christ *alone* that truly defines the *one path of godliness for parents.* At the end of the day, after all the activities and studies are completed, the godly parent must ask this question: "Was Jesus Christ exalted in what was said and done in our home?" Such single minded parenting will continually bring the

---

[235] Such parenting is not God centered, but self-centered and will be characterized by the deeds of the flesh: Galatians 5:19-21 19 Now the deeds of the flesh are evident, which are: immorality, impurity, sensuality,20 idolatry, sorcery, enmities, strife, jealousy, outbursts of anger, disputes, dissensions, factions,21 envying, drunkenness, carousing, and things like these, of which I forewarn you just as I have forewarned you that those who practice such things shall not inherit the kingdom of God.

message of Christ to one's children, thus heralding the home as the *first of all mission fields*. But this important Gospel ministry is much more than a ministry of words: it is to be a practical ministry of genuine godliness. As stated before, it is to be a ministry which communicates the image and likeness of God through a unity that is established by Christ. Like the Apostle Paul, who represented Christ by more than just words, so too must parents take heed unto themselves in order to make sure that their actions are communicating the Gospel as well:

> **1 Thessalonians 1:5-6:** 5 ...our gospel did not come to you in word only, but also in power and in the Holy Spirit and with full conviction; just as you know what kind of men we proved to be among you for your sake. 6 You also became imitators of us and of the Lord, having received the word in much tribulation with the joy of the Holy Spirit,

Paul's important message to the church at Thessalonica was this: Christ is more than a philosophy; He is more than a collection of doctrines, truths, and principles. Christ is a real person whose indwelling presence, through the Holy Spirit, had taken Paul by storm. Christian life isn't merely a set of words to be repeated in the presence of listening audiences; it is a way of life that points to the miraculous and transformative power of God Himself. Paul's example of parental and pastoral love offers us an important corrective to those who believe that the first step towards raising children is to apply a mechanism of *training* without much concern for the conduct of the parent. It is not uncommon in our culture to hear of child training as being something that the parent does to their children, without much consideration of the parent's own example in the home. Contrarily, the first step of child training is parental maturation and godliness. Rather than focusing on one's child, spiritual parents will first take heed unto themselves with questions such as these:

198

- *Do our children see the glory of Christ in us through the power and fruit of the Spirit?*

- *Do our words match the message of our lives as we speak of Christ to them?*

- *Do our children see the glory and unity of the Godhead through our the practical union of our relationship and practice as a married couple?*

- *Do our children see in us a clear conviction of the Gospel, not just through our words, but through our conduct as well?*

- *Is the authority in our home clearly defined by Scripture alone, and is it applied with the gentleness and tender love of Christ?*

As parents, we should remember the example of the Apostle Paul. He didn't tumble into the city of Thessalonica, declaring: "Do as I say, and not as I do!" He did not riddle them with words which seemed to have no relationship to his own life, nor did he deal with them as though they were animals, or robots, commanding their mechanistic obedience with little tenderness and compassion. Such an event would have been far more destructive than anything else! Instead, Paul was just as concerned about his message to them as he was concerned about his conduct in their presence. His desire was to communicate Christ by word *and deed* so that they might hear and see Christ through him. This was Paul's important mission to the churches *and it is the same calling that parents have in the mission field of their own homes*!

The importance of this ministry and stewardship is well described by Mr. Thomas Manton in his *Epistle to the Reader* contained in the Confession of Faith of the church of Scotland:

"CHRISTIAN READER, I CANNOT suppose thee to be such a stranger in England as to be ignorant of the general complaint concerning the decay of the power of godliness, and more especially of the great corruption of youth. Wherever thou goest, thou wilt hear men crying out of bad children and bad servants; whereas, indeed, the source of the mischief must be sought a little higher: it is bad parents and bad masters that make bad children and bad servants; and we cannot blame so much their untowardness, as our own negligence in their education. The devil hath a great spite at the kingdom of Christ, and he knoweth no such compendious way to crush it in the egg, as by the perversion of youth, and supplanting family duties. He striketh at all those duties which are public in the assemblies of the saints; but these are too well guarded by the solemn injunctions and dying charge of Jesus Christ, as that he should ever hope totally to subvert and undermine them; but at family duties he striketh with the more success, because the institution is not so solemn, and the practice not so seriously and conscientiously regarded as it should be, and the omission is not so liable to notice and public censure.

Now the devil knoweth that this is a blow at the root, and a ready way to prevent the succession of churches: if he can subvert families, other societies and communities will not long flourish and subsist with any power and vigour; for there is the stock from whence they are supplied both for the present and for the future. For the present: A family is the seminary of church and state; and if children be not well principled there, all miscarrieth: a fault in the first concoction is not mended in the second; if youth be bred ill in the family, they prove ill in church and commonwealth. By family discipline, officers are trained up for the Church, (1 Timothy 3:4). Upon all these considerations how careful should ministers and parents be to train up young ones whilst they are yet pliable, and, like wax, capable of any form and impression in the knowledge and fear of God."[236]

---

[236] The Confession of Faith, the Larger and Shorter Catechisms (William S. Young, 173 Race Street, Philadelphia, 1851), pgs. 5-6.

There is a right and a wrong path in parenting, but there is never neutrality. The right path is one that *nurtures* children in the *discipline* and *instruction* of the Lord – *for the glory of God alone*. What the Apostle Paul has given us in Ephesians 6:4 is a simple roadmap for Christian *discipleship*. Such a concept of discipleship goes beyond just correction or chastisement. Biblical discipleship, as modeled after Christ and His disciples, is a multifaceted *relationship* that encompasses many forms of teaching, training, and communication; but amidst it all is the wonderful centerpiece of Christ Himself. Parenting is so much more than a didactic mechanism: *it is the imitation of Christ Himself in the presence of one's children.*

THE HEART OF PARENTING

As I mentioned at the beginning of this chapter, the one true path of godly child training is one that begins in the heart of the parents. For parents to be effective soldiers in the battle for the family they must first look to the conflicts that stir within their own souls. Satan knows that the heart of effective parenting is the love of God. How crucial it is, therefore, for parents to comprehend that the love of Christ must reign supremely in the hearts of fathers, mothers, and children in order for the Christian home to thrive in godliness. But when parents falter in such love, it is then that sinful attitudes breed and grow in the home.

But we cannot hope to understand the heart of parenting without first looking to the heart of God in His dealings with us as His children. In order for our conduct to be transformed for the better, we must seek out the example of one who is worthy of imitation. Above any other, the Lord Himself is such an example. His love, forbearance, patience, compassion, and faithfulness is infinitely perfect and exemplary, for our Lord is called by name, *Father*,[237] and as our Father He *disciplines* us as His children with a purpose:

> **Proverbs 3:11-12:** 11 My son, do not reject the discipline of the Lord, Or loathe His reproof, 12 For whom the Lord loves He reproves, Even as a father, the son in whom he delights.

God the Father's example of love is unmatched by any. His is a perfect love that manifests itself in many ways. Here are just a few:

- *He is a loving and kind Father: Ephesians 1:5 In love He [the Father v. 3] predestined us to adoption as sons through Jesus Christ to Himself, according to the kind intention of His will.*

- *He is infinitely good and compassionate: Matthew 7:11 If you then, being evil, know how to give good gifts to your children, how much more shall your Father who is in heaven give what is good to those who ask Him! Matthew 6:8 ...your Father knows what you need, before you ask Him.*

- *He is a protective Father: Matthew 18:6,10-11 6 but whoever causes one of these little ones who believe in Me to stumble, it is better for him that a heavy millstone be hung around his neck, and that he be drowned in the depth of the sea. 10 "See that you do not despise one of these little ones, for I say to you, that their angels in heaven continually behold the face of My Father who is in heaven. 11 [For the Son of Man has come to save that which was lost.]*

---

[237] Several references can be cited, but for brevity – Ephesians 1:2-3, Rom. 15:6, 1 Cor. 1:3, 1 Peter 1:2. Even Christ is described as Father as our head, protector and provider: Isaiah 9:6 6 For a child will be born to us, a son will be given to us; And the government will rest on His shoulders; And His name will be called Wonderful Counselor, Mighty God, Eternal Father, Prince of Peace.

- ***He is even merciful to those who are not His:*** *Matthew 5:44-45 44 But I say to you, love your enemies, and pray for those who persecute you 45 in order that you may be sons of your Father who is in heaven; for He causes His sun to rise on the evil and the good, and sends rain on the righteous and the unrighteous.*

- ***He is a Holy Father:*** *Hebrews 12:5-10 5 and you have forgotten the exhortation which is addressed to you as sons, "My son, do not regard lightly the discipline of the Lord, Nor faint when you are reproved by Him; 6 For those whom the Lord loves He disciplines, And He scourges every son whom He receives." 7 It is for discipline that you endure; God deals with you as with sons; for what son is there whom his father does not discipline? 8 But if you are without discipline, of which all have become partakers, then you are illegitimate children and not sons. 9 Furthermore, we had earthly fathers to discipline us, and we respected them; shall we not much rather be subject to the Father of spirits, and live? 10 For they disciplined us for a short time as seemed best to them, but He disciplines us for our good, that we may share His holiness.*

THE HEART OF PARENTING

Deuteronomy 6:6-7:

"And these words which I command you today...

...shall be in your heart...

...and you shall teach them diligently to your children, and shall talk of them when you sit in your house, when you walk by the way, when you lie down, and when you rise up."

Without the love of God, our world would be a perpetual place of darkness, misery, and condemnation. In many ways, a home that is devoid of the love of God is not any different. But parents who walk in love do so because of Him who *first loved us.*[238] Let it be known that God's love is the eternal well from which the Christian family should drink

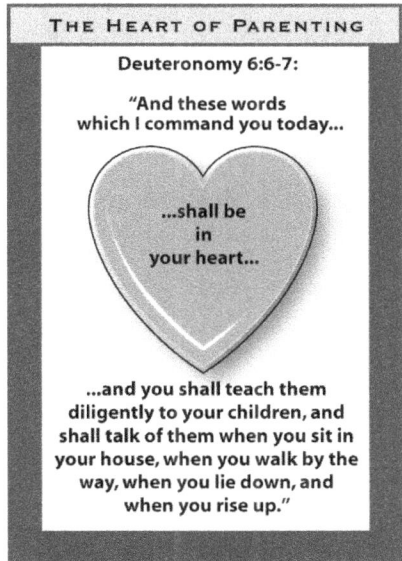

---

[238] 1 John 4:19.

regularly, for the fountain of this affection is that which sustains the Christian home amidst this drought-ridden world. Where the Lord's love does abide, there you will find parents who genuinely seek to raise their children for Christ. It is this very priority of God-centered love that is the centerpiece of the godly family:

> **Deuteronomy 6:4-5** – 4 Hear, O Israel! The Lord is our God, the Lord is one! 5 And you shall love the Lord your God with all your heart and with all your soul and with all your might.

Our Lord and Savior referred to this text in Matt. 22:36-40 as being the first commandment upon which all of the law and the prophets depends. This *greatest commandment* therefore has centrality for all Christians in every stage of life, to include husbands, wives, and children. In a sense, this principal command of love is the very starting point of all duties and activities in the home, for the Lord desires that we serve Him, and one another, from a heart of godly love. But if parenting were simply a matter of applying a set of rules for children, then many more homes would be havens of spirituality.[239] And if child training were simply a matter of laying down laws and requiring the mechanical obedience of children, then life would be, perhaps, much more simple. However, the Lord is not satisfied with heartless obedience, instead, He desires a servitude that is genuine:

> **Psalm 51:16-17:** 16 For Thou dost not delight in sacrifice, otherwise I would give it; Thou art not pleased with burnt offering. 17 The sacrifices of God are a broken spirit; A broken and a contrite heart, O God, Thou wilt not despise.

---

[239] Ted Tripp, Shepherding A Child's Heart (Shepherd Press by Calvary Press Publishing, Amityville, NY), pp. 19-24.

Parents who only seek the mechanical obedience of their children, without a regular examination of their child's attitude and intention, are running the risk of nurturing the bad seed of Pharisaism. But this is not the characteristic of the Christian home which has at its center the Love of Christ. It is in a home such as this that the *greatest commandment of all* regularly serves as a corrective to heartless duty and devotion. As we look further in Deuteronomy 6 we see that an additional command is given in verse 7 to parents instructing them to teach their children the priority of devotional love for God. However, sandwiched between the first great commandment and the commandment to parents is the heart of parental leadership:

> **Deuteronomy 6:6-7:** 6 And these words, which I am commanding you today, shall be on your heart; 7 and you shall teach them diligently to your sons and shall talk of them when you sit in your house and when you walk by the way and when you lie down and when you rise up.

The lesson here is quite clear: parents must be examples of godly love if they are to serve well as His representatives. When Moses says "these words" (v. 6) he refers to the preceding context to include the commandment of love in verses 4-5. Therefore, Moses' commandment to parents could be paraphrased in this way: "*These commandments (including the commandment of love for God) must first be on your heart before you seek to teach your children.*" Moses' order of instruction is important: in order for parents to teach their children about the priority of loving God, they (the parents) must first have this sacred duty upon their own hearts. What this instruction then prohibits is the hypocrisy which says: "Do as I say and not as I do!" Parents are to call their children to obedience *in the Lord* (Eph. 6:1), but they must do so as the living, breathing examples of such loving devotion to Christ. God the Father *lovingly* disciplines His children for their good; however, the home that is lacking godly love will become a dark haven of harsh discipline or lawless

205

negligence. Both realities are the product of an unloving environment, producing children who are filled with resentment, despair, and anger (Ephesians 6:4). There simply are no viable substitutes for godly love, and therefore, children must not be driven with harshness, nor cajoled with trickery. Consider the wise thoughts of J. C. Ryle on this matter:

> "Love should be the silver thread that runs through all your conduct. Kindness, gentleness, long-suffering, forbearance, patience, sympathy, a willingness to enter into childish troubles, a readiness to take part in childish joys, - these are the cords by which a child may be led most easily, - these are the clues you must follow if you would find the way to his heart."[240]

Ryle's emphasis on love is quite needful. May our homes be havens of godly love where Christ is first! Let every believing father and mother seek to manifest the love of Christ to their children. May parents lead by way of example as fervent lovers of God such that their lives yield as much instruction as do their lips! Consider the following review questions concerning the heart of parenting:

- *God the Father is our Perfect Model: God disciplines us as an act of love and for our good. Any other basis or goal is a deviation from the standard of God. How could you improve in this area? How often do you pray before teaching or chastising your children? When you do chastise, how often do you explain your motives to them?*

- *God Calls His Children to Genuine Obedience: In your parenting, do you find yourself correcting behavior rather than correcting sinful attitudes? Have you developed a pattern where you are content with a child's external obedience, knowing that their heart is corrupted with rebellion?*

---

[240] Ryle, <u>Train Up a Child</u>, p. 23.

- *God is Perfect and We are Not: When you discipline your children in a manner that is unloving or full of anger, do you confess that sin to God and to your children? If you fail to do so, what are you teaching your children by failing to admit your failings?*

THE HEART OF PARENTING APPLIED

Having looked at the parents' perfect model of love, we now come to this important question: *How can parents know if they are manifesting godly love within the family*? An immediate answer from Scripture comes to us in Paul's treatise on love to the Corinthians:

1 Corinthians 13:4-7: 4 Love is patient, love is kind, and is not jealous; love does not brag and is not arrogant, 5 does not act unbecomingly; it does not seek its own, is not provoked, does not take into account a wrong suffered, 6 does not rejoice in unrighteousness, but rejoices with the truth; 7 bears all things, believes all things, hopes all things, endures all things.

Paul's instructions to the Corinthian church may not seem entirely applicable to our discussion, however, we know that the family is, in some respect, a microcosm of church life[241] and therefore it must be included in our study. Overall, godly love is godly love, whether it is manifested in the local church or in a family. Paul's treatise on love in 1 Corinthians 13 was given to a church that was busy with religious function and activity, but they had one central problem: much of what they did as a church was done *without the love of Christ.* Paul's antidote was clearly needed, for the carnal Corinthians were becoming a bustling, noisy, and unspiritual assembly. In like manner, a home that is lackluster in the genuine love of Christ will become too much like that rebellious lot at Corinth. Like the weakened leadership at Corinth, parents who become indifferent to their

---

[241] 1 Timothy 3:5 (but if a man does not know how to manage his own household, how will he take care of the church of God?).

children often end up exposing their young ones to experiences that endanger them spiritually. This serves as a warning to all parents concerning the priority of godly love in the home. It should be noted that a parent's attitude is oftentimes a reflection of their Christ-like love, or the lack thereof. Where there is patience, kindness, humility, gentleness, compassion, selflessness, longsuffering, forgiveness, holiness, faith, and hope – there is the love of Christ. Loving one's child, therefore, goes well beyond the giving of a hug or a kiss. It goes beyond feeding them food, giving them clothing, and a good education. All these tasks can be performed by an unbeliever! However, the Christian parent seeks to *nurture their children in the discipline and instruction of the Lord* with a *heart of genuine love.* Such an environment of love will then produce the very qualities that Paul described in 1 Corinthians 13:4-7. This brings us to the important application of the parents' loving ministry in the home. 1 Corinthians 13:4-7, and texts like Galatians 5:22-23, can in many ways be used as a measuring rod to evaluate one's attitude in the home, for they provide us with the answer to that important question: *"How can I be sure that I am exhibiting love within my family?"* In the following pages we will examine several Biblical standards that will help us genuinely apply Christ-like love in our homes. We will consult portions of 1 Corinthians 13:4-7, harvesting several godly attitudes that are always necessary in any parent's life. There are many details that could be unfolded by studying Paul's description of love, however, for the purpose of this work we will examine the heart of parental love by looking at four attitudes of Christian love. By these we will learn about the importance of parents being: *Humble, selfless, hopeful and zealous for truth.* By examining these attitudes, we can learn how to minister the love of Christ to our children with greater care and wisdom.

HUMILITY: Paul instructed the Corinthians as follows: *"...love does not brag and is not arrogant, does not act unbecomingly."* This is another way of saying: "love begets humility." The importance of humility in the lives of Christian parents is inestimable. God has granted to the husband and wife a remarkable authority and stewardship over their children. Being a parent is an incredible responsibility! It is oftentimes intimidating to consider the seriousness of the task of parenting and yet it is a necessary reflection, *for the privilege of parenting should produce greater humility in the heart of any Christian parent*. When armed with such humility, the Christian parent will be endowed with greater sobriety and conviction. Contrarily, human pride seeks to prevail in every dimension of life. When pride creeps into the heart of a parent he/she is less likely to confess sin or admit a mistake. Where there is pride, you will find

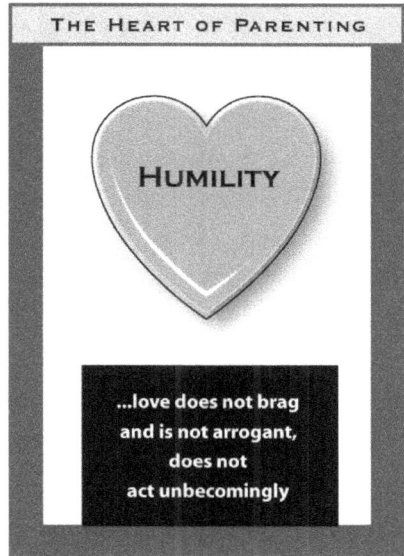

THE HEART OF PARENTING

HUMILITY

...love does not brag and is not arrogant, does not act unbecomingly

parents who (in their thinking) do no wrong and therefore need no input or wisdom from others.[242] The resultant transgressions that follow from this sinful attitude are beyond cataloguing. What is helpful for parents to remember is that humility is the beginning of wisdom:

Proverbs 4:7 The beginning of wisdom is: Acquire wisdom; And with all your acquiring, get understanding.

---

[242] In our modern culture there have been a growing number of home-schooling families in our country. This has been a good trend overall, and yet there are many who are within this home-schooling culture who have become convinced that they do not need the accountability of a local church. Such isolation is un-Biblical and is often the product of pride and an unwillingness to tolerate even the smallest differences among genuine brethren.

Only a humble parent will confess his regular need for the washing and cleansing of God's Word in every aspect of life, including parenting. The person who can confess "I must acquire wisdom" is the one in whom genuine humility resides. Simply put, such a parent as this is ready to become a better parent! This is godly leadership in action, and this stands against the false form of leadership where one tries to drive others to a standard that he does not uphold nor believe. Christ Himself, against such pharisaic notions, led his sheep by way of a holy example. Such an example of godly leadership ought to impact the actions and motives of parents who desire to train up their children for Christ. As overseers must do for the church, so too must parents take *heed unto themselves* before they can adequately shepherd their little flock of sheep.[243] It is often the temptation for parents to think that the first step to a better family is to fix their children. However, if there is a problem with one's children in the home, then there is most likely a problem with the parents in the first place. In fact, it is the father who bears the chief responsibility for the progress or decline of any home. Hence it is a first key step for any struggling family to admit, in humility, their need for the wisdom of the Lord for their life and struggles. As the family grows in wisdom and maturity, so too will their humility. How crucial it is for parents to take heed unto themselves before they apply their duties of discipline and instruction. The privilege of parenting is a wonderful, sanctifying experience, and those who are trained by it will yield the peaceful fruit of righteousness.[244] As weak and sinful parents we will sin, but even in this the humility of a confessional and prayerful life will impact our children for the sake of the Gospel:

> **Luke 18:10-14** 10 Two men went up into the temple to pray, one a Pharisee, and the other a tax-gatherer. 11 The Pharisee stood and was praying thus to himself, "God, I thank Thee that I am not like other

---

[243] Acts 20:28.

[244] Hebrews 12:11.

people: swindlers, unjust, adulterers, or even like this tax-gatherer." 12 "I fast twice a week; I pay tithes of all that I get." 13 But the tax-gatherer, standing some distance away, was even unwilling to lift up his eyes to heaven, but was beating his breast, saying, "God, be merciful to me, the sinner!" 14 I tell you, this man went down to his house justified rather than the other; for everyone who exalts himself shall be humbled, but he who humbles himself shall be exalted.

Progress in our children should not lead the parent to self-exaltation, instead, a spirit filled parent will exalt the One who alone can supply every perfect gift from above. He is the Father of lights, with whom there is no variation or shifting shadow, and it is in Him that we boast. Here are some questions for consideration:

- *What do your children see in your life respecting the matter of humility? Do you confess sin when you are guilty of transgression?*

- *Do your children see in your life the confession that says "the beginning of wisdom is: Acquire wisdom?" By this, what priorities are your children learning as they see your devotion to the Word and your faithful participation in a local church?*

- *Do your children see humility in their mother through a godly submission to the father's leadership?*

- *Fathers, do your children see a humble, sacrificial love exemplified through your love for your wife?*

SELFLESSNESS: Paul tells us that love "does not seek its own," or in other words - *love is not selfish*. As the descendants of Adam and Eve, we struggle with pride and selfishness on a daily basis. Therefore, this attribute of love (*selflessness*) is crucial for a healthy attitude within the Christian parent. Godly parents do not raise children for their own sake, but for the ultimate sake of God and His glory. They understand that, on the one hand they will always be a

211

father or mother to their children, yet on the other hand, their parental stewardship is temporary and will change dramatically when their children leave the home in order to establish new familial institutions of their own. There is a tender balance to be upheld in this. In one way, a godly parent cherishes their time with their children as being a precious and brief stage of life. In another sense, they also look forward to that day when their children can subsist in a godly lifestyle without their assistance. There will come that day when we as parents will leave this life. When that will happen, we do not know, but we should understand that our parental stewardship is temporary and it fades away quickly with the increasing passage of time; therefore, we must seek to do God's will as *long as it is day*.[245] Like the Savior, this is the heartbeat of one who is selfless. A selfless parent understands that children are a special and temporary stewardship, therefore, the goal of the godly parent will not be that their children would grow up, marry, and then live right next door to mom and dad such that "dinner is at 6pm, and don't be late." Such parental possessiveness as this is a historic problem that reaches back to the earliest descendants of our first parents. Parental neglect, another form of selfishness, is just as pervasive. The key to avoiding both extremes is, again, to consult God's Word. When we understand whose possession they ultimately are, we can better understand the nature of our stewardship:

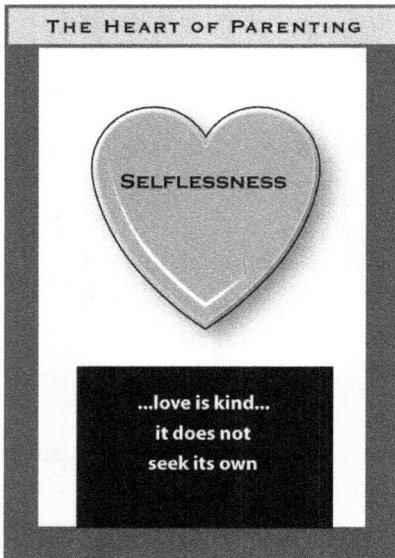

THE HEART OF PARENTING

SELFLESSNESS

...love is kind...
it does not
seek its own

---

[245] John 9:4.

Psalm 127:3 Behold, children are a gift of the Lord; The fruit of the womb is a reward.

In principle, there are two key truths that Solomon gives us in this Psalm: *1. God is the final source of children, for he is the one who opens and closes the womb;*[246] *and 2. These precious gifts and rewards from God are a special stewardship, entrusted to parents.* In simple terms: They are ours, but ultimately they are His! Knowing that children are His gifts to us compels us to remember their inexpressible value – they are gifts from heaven above and should be treated as such. Such knowledge ought to nurture a deeper respect and love for children. What a stark contrast this is to the modern wisdom of this world that has reduced these gifts of God to a mere mass of flesh that can be cut out with a surgeon's knife with little or no thought at all! It is often the attitude of this culture (as it has been in many cultures throughout the ages), that children are a necessary burden of society to be tolerated only for the propagation of the human race. Such an attitude is evidenced when careers or recreational activities are deemed as more important than the genuine privilege of raising a child. The truth that children are a gift *of the Lord* reminds the Christian parent that they must raise their children *for the Lord* who gave them in the first place. Such an understanding keeps the parent from a host of sinful attitudes ranging from possessiveness to neglect. Their goal will not be to raise children for their own purposes, but for God's purposes such that they will become sharp arrows who will spring forth and fly from the quiver of the home someday.[247] Additionally, *since they are gifts to the parents* (even rewards/possessions), they are therefore the parents'

---

[246] Gen. 29:31, 30:22; Job 3:10; 1 Samuel 1:5-6.

[247] Psalm 127:4-5 4 Like arrows in the hand of a warrior, So are the children of one's youth. 5 How blessed is the man whose quiver is full of them; They shall not be ashamed, When they speak with their enemies in the gate.

responsibility. This truth is a corrective to those who would tend to neglect their children or try to surrender the responsibility of parenting to another. As long as the parents are alive and capable of raising their offspring, there should be no attempt to substitute their role. One of the greatest disasters of our modern culture stems from a growing unwillingness of parents to raise the children whom God entrusted to them. It is not the school teacher, youth minister, daycare, siblings, or friends who can replace the father and mother: *The privilege of being a father or mother is a direct gift from God.* Children are not interruptions nor are they burdens. They are not invaders whom we seek to get out of the house as soon as possible, nor are they objects of adoration who take the place of the Lord. Parental selfishness can be manifested from both extremes of neglect and possessiveness, but God calls us to neither. Rather, He calls us to the loving act of raising these precious gifts for His glory. Fathers...bring up your children in the discipline and instruction of the Lord!

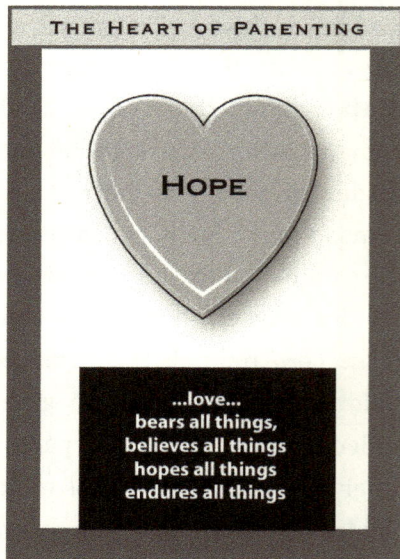

THE HEART OF PARENTING

HOPE

...love...
bears all things,
believes all things
hopes all things
endures all things

HOPE: Any honest parent would have to admit that they have, at times, become frustrated in the process of training their children, and therefore, it is important to recognize that the privilege of parenthood is not an immutable experience of success and victory. There are difficulties and hardships that come along the way and it is no wonder: you as parents are sinful, and your children were born after your sinful likeness. With a household full of sinners, something is bound to go wrong! But thanks be to God that this is not the end of the story concerning Christian parenting.[248] Wherever Christ's love is, thoughts and feelings of frustration, bitterness, and anger will regularly dissolve into longsuffering, patience, and hope, because love *"...bears all things, believes all things, hopes all things, endures all things"* (1 Corinthians 13:7). The loving and Christ-centered home is not a place of perpetual despair and frustration, rather it is a place that is largely characterized by faithful longsuffering, patience, *and hope*. This last quality of hopefulness is very crucial. The Scriptures refer to God-centered hope as being that which is an anchor to our souls.[249] As well, in the Christian home it is foundational for the parents' perseverance in their child training. Consider the following wisdom from the book of Proverbs:

Proverbs 19:18 Discipline your son seeing there is hope, and set not thy heart on his destruction. (ASV)

This precious gem of wisdom offers us an abundance of truth concerning the parent's loving attitude of hope in the home. Let's first look at the conclusion of this verse: "And set not thy heart on his destruction" (death – NASB). This statement most likely has to do with the attitude of the parent's heart rather than the punitive laws of the O.T. for rebellious children.[250] This should be clear by the contrasting attitudes of hope at the beginning of the verse and the *desire* for destruction/death at its end. Only a heart of hatred and abandonment could lead a parent to desire the death of their child.[251] Such an extreme shows us the ugly end that awaits those who harbor hatred for their offspring. Too often do we hear about child abuse

---

[248] 1 Thessalonians 5:8 But since we are of the day, let us be sober, having put on the breastplate of faith and love, and as a helmet, the hope of salvation.

[249] Hebrews 6:17-20.

[250] Exodus 21:15 "And he who strikes his father or his mother shall surely be put to death." Leviticus 20:9 "If there is anyone who curses his father or his mother, he shall surely be put to death; he has cursed his father or his mother, his blood guiltiness is upon him."

[251] 1 John 3:15.

and murder in the news, and we are thereby reminded of the sinfulness of the human heart. The polarity of proverbial teaching is helpful for us, for we are again reminded that there are two general paths that husbands and wives can take in their journey of parenting: the path of hope/life versus the path of indifference, hatred, and death. How crucial it is for parents to minister to their children with godly hope! Failure to do so will lead to despair,

THE TWO PATHS OF PARENTING

Proverbs 19:18

Chasten thy son seeing there is hope...

And set not thy heart on his destruction.

discouragement, and anger. Looking again at Proverbs 19:18, we see an important detail in the Hebrew text that is best revealed by the ASV and NIV translations: Proverbs 19:18 "Discipline your son seeing there is hope" and "Discipline your son, for in that there is hope" respectively. Both translations correctly convey the sense of the textual construct [*ḳiy-yeś*], literally: *"for this is hope."* Rather than thinking that parents can determine, for themselves, how long they might hold on to hope for their children, the text actually indicates that the process of loving discipline is itself a basis for hope. The point of application here is crucial: parents are never called upon to give up hope, rather, what is being profoundly stated in this wise expression is that parents must keep their focus upon their duties as parents, *for this is their hope:* not the discipline itself *per se*, but the discipline and instruction *of the Lord.* They are to discipline [LXX – *paideue*] or disciple their children *in the Lord* with an enduring perseverance. Parents who give up on their children, or who forsake their duties as parents, are erroneously taking it upon themselves to declare their children as *hopeless.* Such actions are at best hateful and full of death. This principle of hope and faithfulness is evident

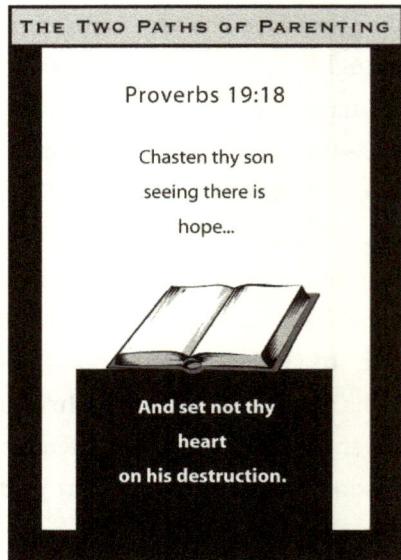

216

elsewhere in Scripture. As we studied earlier, God the Father is faithful and loving in the discipleship of His children such that He disciplines us *for our good* (Hebrews 12:10), therefore those who are disciplined by Him have hope.[252] In the extreme examples of church discipline we find that the Apostle Paul, who ministered gently to the churches as a *nursing mother,* was faithful to deliver over to Satan those whose lives were full of the rebellion of sin *with the hope* that they would someday be restored.[253] In like manner, the father of the prodigal son gave his rebellious child over to the afflictions of the world, not out of vengeance, *but in hope that what had been lost would someday be found.*[254] Reproof that is administered out of anger is an act of punitive vengeance, which is the sole prerogative of God; but the Lord prohibits us all from this imitation.[255] The Christian parent is called to walk in His holy love,[256] thus discipline that is given in loving hope is that which reflects the heavenly Father who faithfully disciplines his children for their good. Because the Christian parents' hope is in the Lord, they must never stop ministering in hope to their children. It is often the case that parents who are inconsistent in their discipline will resort to the extremes of overindulgence or harshness. Such a relationship is provoking, both for the parents and for the children. This is the path of indifference, despair, frustration, and anger – in the most extreme case, it is the path of death. But the path of life in the Christian home is found

---

[252] Hebrews 12:7-8 7 "It is for discipline that you endure; God deals with you as with sons; for what son is there whom his father does not discipline?" 8 "But if you are without discipline, of which all have become partakers, then you are illegitimate children and not sons." Here it is very clear that the absence of discipline is an indication of an absence of true hope. Those who are disciplined by the Lord have a great hope and confidence that they are being loved by the God and Father of our Lord Jesus Christ.

[253] 1 Thess. 2:7, 1 Corinthians 5:5 I have decided to deliver such a one to Satan for the destruction of his flesh, that his spirit may be saved in the day of the Lord Jesus.

[254] Luke 15:11-32. The father's attitude towards the son is clearly revealed in verse 20. The father had compassion his son, and embraced him with great love when he returned.

[255] Deut. 32:35.

[256] Ephesians 5:1-21.

along the way of God-centered hope. It is here that one will find the act of loving discipleship. Consider the following questions in order to examine your own ministry of *hopeful discipleship:*

- *How often do you consider your own attitude towards your child? Do you minister with a God-centered hope, or are you filled with despair when you go to correct a child?*

- *Are you ever angry? If your eagerness to discipline is born out of anger, rather than love, then you're not ready to discipline in the pattern of God's discipline.*

- *Are you being careful to maintain a faithful prayer life to include regular prayer and petition for your children, praying for their redemption, or if they are saved, for their continued sanctification in Christ?*

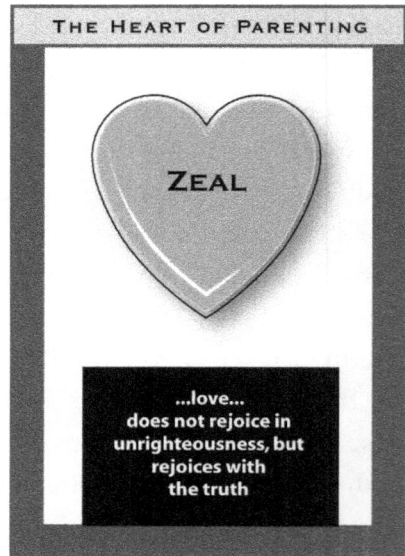

THE HEART OF PARENTING

ZEAL

...love... does not rejoice in unrighteousness, but rejoices with the truth

ZEAL: The contemporary church has popularized the thought which says that *love* and *doctrine* are utterly incompatible. "Doctrine divides" as the saying goes, therefore truth should never be emphasized too much! However, the Biblical definition of love is one that not only accepts God's truth as crucial, *but embraces it with great zeal: 1 Corinthians 13:6 "[love]...does not rejoice in unrighteousness, but rejoices with the truth."* This simple statement teaches us that the child of God is one whose heart is not thrilled by sin, instead he disdains it because it is loathsome to his Lord. Instead, what thrills his soul is truth, because the Lord Himself is truth. The Apostle's statement in verse 6 reflects a form of antithesis that is frequently presented in the O.T. wisdom literature: *"not unrighteousness...but truth."* Such antithetical language is very important, because it is not enough to say that we should rejoice in truth, but we must also refuse and reject behavior that denies the truth! From this principle of love, we must remember that if practical parenting can be summarized in one way, it would be this: parents are called upon, by God, to love their children by guiding them *into truth* while directing them *away from unrighteousness*. Such is a ministry that does not exclusively emphasize one or the other, rather both processes of instruction and correction are necessary, and when they are brought together into a home where there is godly love, then you have an environment of godly nurture. This, in many ways, brings us back to Paul's instructions in Ephesians 6:4: "And, fathers, do not provoke your children to anger; but bring them up [*nurture them*] in the *discipline* and *instruction* of the Lord." The spiritual father is to *Discipline* [*paideia*, positive training and reproof] and he is to give *instruction* [*nouthesia*, the training another's heart, mind, and reasoning] to his children. The father who thus nurtures his children is constantly involved in this loving process of encouraging his children to *rejoice in truth* as he exhorts them to *reject unrighteousness,* all of which evidences godly zeal. This is the very heart of proverbial wisdom in the Old Testament: there is truth, and there is error; there is righteousness and there is unrighteousness; there is a right way that leads to life and there is the path that leads to death; there is right vs. wrong; good vs. bad; wisdom vs. foolishness etc. It is quite clear that godly discipleship embraces both a positive and negative element of training, thus, parents who love their children will train them with the full bounty of understanding that comes from Biblical discipline and instruction. Our Lord's discipleship of His apostles more than amply illustrates the point in all four gospel accounts (Matt 16:13-23), in that He nurtured them in the truth, praying that they would be sanctified by it:

John 17:17 Sanctify them in the truth; Thy word is truth.

Of the many manifestations of love that we see exhibited by the Savior, it is most evident that He *rejoiced in truth* while *rejecting unrighteousness.* He is the way, the truth, and the life (John 11:4) and so He called upon all who heard Him to come to Him and receive Him freely. This He did with diligence and faithfulness as a laborer who knew that night was coming:

> **John 9:4** We must work the works of Him who sent Me, as long as it is day; night is coming, when no man can work.

In principle, this text applies to all aspects of Christian life, including parenting, and therefore it should be remembered that the time is coming when a parent's labors will be through. Because of this, parental privileges should be embraced with joy, eagerness, and diligence. Our joyful pursuit of truth is one that should be characterized by an earnest zeal, after all, God's precious Word is the Christian's great joy (Psalm 119:111), treasure (Psalm 119:11), and prize (Proverbs 4:8-9). Therefore, it is the spiritual parent who will *earnestly desire* that their children embrace the prize of God's Word.[257] Parents who rejoice in truth will do this, as they eagerly enfold their children in the cleansing water of the Word of God with faithfulness and diligence. This is not a forced feeding, but a *nurturing in the Lord* that takes into account the age and progress of the child. However, when love wanes, such joy for truth diminishes, and when this pattern increases, faithfulness and diligence in parenting suffers. These conditions are normally manifested through inconsistent parenting, poor family worship habits, harsh or negligible discipline, and ultimately, a tarnished representation of

---

[257] Proverbs 4:8-9 8 "Prize her, and she will exalt you; She will honor you if you embrace her. 9 "She will place on your head a garland of grace; She will present you with a crown of beauty."

Christ in the home. However, where love abides, there you will find parents who disciple their children with diligence. How crucial it is for parents to look to themselves first before they seek to reform their children. Lethargy in parenting is inexcusable, but diligence is a sign of Christian love. Consider the following principle expounded in the book of Proverbs:

> **Proverbs 13:24** He who spares his rod hates his son, but he who loves him disciplines him diligently.

There are many rich truths found in this important verse. The very simple contrast that it supplies yields an important point: *discipline is loving, but negligence is hateful.* The mention of the rod in Proverbs 13:24 will be addressed in chapter 5 *Training Children for the Glory of Christ (The Profit of Reproof and The Profit of Correction)*, but for now our focus is upon the latter portion of this verse which teaches that genuine love is manifested through parents who not only discipline their children, but do so *with diligence.* The picture presented in v. 24 is one of a parent who is *zealous for truth* to such an extent that all of the tools of discipleship are employed for the child's benefit, including the rod of reproof. Reproof is only a part of the discipleship (discipline) process, but it is an important one. The withholding of the rod is hateful, but the application of discipline [*musar* – teaching, instruction or reproof] is loving. However, the application of discipline should not be thought of in terms of chastening alone, but must include the broader spectrum of training: *the process of immersing one's child into God's truth by every pedagogical means.* Yet there is much more being revealed in this verse than just the mechanism of training. Proverbs 13:24 in fact shows us the heart of a godly parent: "...he who loves him disciplines him *diligently* [*śiḥarō*]." This Hebrew word - [*šaḥar*, pronounced *shachar*] - is normally translated in the Old Testament as *early* or *dawn*, such that Satan is called the star of the morning and the "...son of the *dawn*" [italics mine]. The NASB translators chose the word - *diligently* - in order to convey the idea of one who does not delay or ignore an opportunity for discipline. The NKJV uses the word – *promptly* - and the KJV employs the word – *betimes* - both of which capture the temporal concept of our word in question. Thus, the core concept of this term - *diligently* [*śiḥarō*] - conveys this thought of applying discipline *early*. The point is quite clear: a loving parent does not delay the matter of immersing their children in the standards of God's truth. The withholding of discipline is a serious matter, therefore the discipleship process is not to be stalled, thwarted, nor delayed by anyone or anything. The dark reality of withheld discipline is ultimately illustrated for us by the author of Hebrews:

> **Hebrews 12:8** But if you are without discipline, of which all have become partakers, then you are illegitimate children and not sons.

In the imitation of God's fatherly care for His children, Christian parents must promptly seek to nurture their children *in the discipline and instruction* of the Lord, avoiding the habits of neglect or abandonment. Such an attitude will foster several responses. First, the *prompt* parent will understand that the discipleship relationship begins as soon as a child is born, not when they are two or three years of age. Second, the *prompt* parent will bathe their children in truth without harmful delay, no matter what their age. This means that parents will not put their children on the back burner of life, ignoring particular sins or ongoing patterns of rebellious behavior. In both cases, prompt and diligent parenting is an evidence of godly zeal and eagerness for God and His truth. From beginning to end, such a parent rejoices in truth not only for their own benefit, but also for the benefit of their offspring. This is clearly illustrated in the life of Timothy, whose upbringing is described by the Apostle Paul in this way:

2 Timothy 3:14-15 14 You, however, continue in the things you have learned and become convinced of, knowing from whom you have learned them; 15 and that from childhood you have known the sacred writings which are able to give you the wisdom that leads to salvation through faith which is in Christ Jesus.

Timothy's mother and grandmother were believers in Christ,[258] and it is for this reason that he was nurtured in God's Word *from childhood* such that he learned the Scriptures and became convinced of its truth. The wisdom that he was taught in Holy Writ led him to saving faith and it was in those earliest lessons of life that the Apostle Paul called Timothy to persevere. The details of Paul's description of Timothy's upbringing should not go unnoticed. Paul described just how early Timothy's tutelage in the Word began when he says that *"from childhood* you have known the sacred writings." Of the four words that Paul could have used for *child*,[259] he used the one word which speaks most often of a newborn baby or infant [*brephos*]. This detail clearly shows us that Timothy was deeply embedded within a diligent discipleship ministry from the very beginning:

2 Timothy 1:5 For I am mindful of the sincere faith within you, which first dwelt in your grandmother Lois, and your mother Eunice, and I am sure that it is in you as well.

Timothy lived in an environment of *sincere faith* where the Scriptures were read and taught ever since he was a newborn baby. Timothy's mother did not wait until he was a teenager to enfold him

---

[258] Acts 16:1, 2 Timothy 1:5.

[259] Five words for child are compared here: G. 1. *teknos* – Generally speaks of a child in the sense of offspring without an emphasis on age; 2. *paidion* – A broad word speaking of a little or young child to a more advanced child; 3. *huios* – A word used for son to speak of male offspring of any age; 4. *nēpios* – Speaks of younger children and even infants; 5. *brephos* – used almost exclusively as a newborn babe or infant.

with the wisdom of God, instead, it was there from the very beginning. From his birth he continued to learn wisdom such that he became convinced of the truth that constantly surrounded him. Sincere faith and genuine love cannot help but produce such an environment of wisdom. It is an environment that does not rejoice in unrighteousness, but rejoices in the truth – here is the environment of genuine Christian love! In all of this, we are reminded that the ultimate goal for any parent is to present back to God the very children that He gave in the first place, such that they would passionately love the Lord God with all their heart, soul, mind, and strength.

Without a right heart and attitude towards God, the act of parenting will become a shallow experience for children and parents. Those who desire to reform their parenting must first take careful inventory of their own devotional relationship with the Lord as well as their marital union. Through the husband's spiritual leadership in the home, there should be an ongoing transformation of heart taking place within the mother and father:

> **Proverbs 4:23** Watch over your heart with all diligence, for from it flow the springs of life.

It is from this heart-transformation that the home itself is transformed. Without such a God-centered perspective, one that seeks the genuine worship of God, parenting could take the form of religious sterility, like the religious leaders in Jesus' day:

> **John 5:39-40** 39 You search the Scriptures, because you think that in them you have eternal life; and it is these that bear witness of Me; 40 and you are unwilling to come to Me, that you may have life.

CHAPTER 4 – REFORMED PARENTING FOR THE GLORY OF CHRIST

The religious leaders whom Jesus addressed were well versed in the Scriptures, however, they approached the Word as a mere mechanism. They knew about God *without actually knowing Him or His Son.* By contrast, a spiritual home will seek to be immersed in the Scriptures that it might be immersed in the Lord Himself. Parents must therefore desire for their children what the Lord desires from us all: loving obedience from the heart (Deuteronomy 6:4-7). As the hearts and minds of parents are transformed, by the Spirit and truth of God, they become better examples for their children to follow – this is leadership by example as manifested by the Apostle Paul:

1 Corinthians 11:1 Be imitators of me, just as I also am of Christ.

Paul's call to the Corinthian church was not to imitate him *ultimately*, but to imitate him in the *imitation [G. mimētai] of Christ.* Paul's goal in life was to *mimic* the Lord Jesus Christ as he called others to join him in the same. This priority in Paul's life must be the priority of every parent for their children! Our goal is not to reproduce little replicas of ourselves, but to raise our children to be imitators and lovers of the Lord God Himself. This is what is meant by Paul's instructions to fathers that they bring up their children in the discipline and instruction *of the Lord.* It is not just a pedagogy that is from Him, but it is one that leads to Him as well.

Parents must instruct their children to listen to them and obey them, but in the end the goal must be that the child's obedience would ultimately be directed to the Lord Himself. The great challenge for parents in this task is to be involved in this process without getting in the way! From their earliest days children love, respect, trust, admire, and mimic their parents. What the parent must strive for is that this love, respect, trust, admiration, and mimicry would soon be devoted to Jesus Christ. This is the *practical* core of a Gospel- centered, Christ centered, and love-filled home. It is in this context that

225

parents can discipline and instruct their children with integrity. We as parents are not simply passing on information to our children, but we are looking to represent the Lord Jesus Christ Himself to them, and as we do so, God is at work on us as parents to sanctify and cleanse our hearts and minds for His glory.

Godly parenting is not a formula, *it is a way of life.*

For from Him and through Him and to Him are all things.
To Him be the glory forever. Amen. Romans 11:36

CHAPTER 5

TRAINING CHILDREN

FOR THE GLORY OF CHRIST

A CHILD'S OBEDIENCE, HONOR, AND DISCIPLESHIP

In the following sections we will focus more specifically on the practical aspects of child training. To do this we will continue along the path of Ephesians 6:1-4. Paul's very brief yet profound command to children gets right to the point in verses 1 and 2: Very simply, children are to 1. *obey* and 2. *honor* their parents. Well that was easy! What's so hard about parenting? Well, the principles are not complicated to understand *per se*, but the practice of these

> **OBEDIENCE**
>
> Ephesians 6:1
>
> Children, obey your parents in the Lord
>
> **For this is right**

principles is where the difficulty lies. As we examine these two commands in order, we find that they formulate the centerpiece of a child's responsibility in the home. Paul's first instruction to children concerns obedience (Ephesians 6:1): *Children, obey your parents in the Lord, for this is right.* Despite its simplicity, the profundity of this command could pass by the reader too easily. The word *obey* comes from a construct of two Greek words which speak of *hearing* and *submitting* to authority [*hupakouete*].[260] In Scripture, this word is even used of a servant who attends the entry of a house, opening it when a knock at the door is *heard*.[261] The important relationship between *hearing* and *obeying* must be clearly understood. In order to obey, children must first exercise the discipline of listening to their parents. This detail of Paul's command is reflected in the proverbial

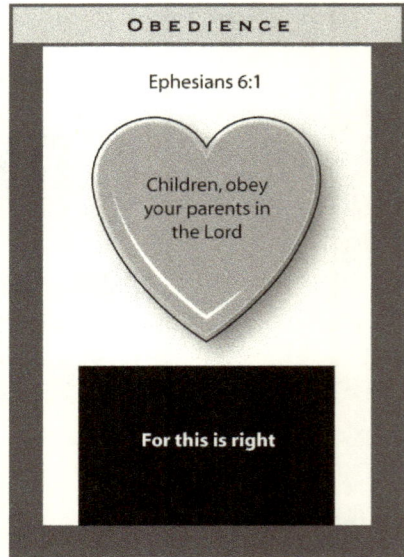

---

[260] *hupakouein* is commonly used for the Hebrew word *šm'* (to hear) in the LXX. In order for one to obey, they must first hear the instructions given to them. G. Abbott-Smith, <u>A Manual Greek Lexicon of the New Testament</u>, (T & T Clark LTD, 59 George Street, Edinburgh), p. 456.
[261] Acts 12:13.

injunctions concerning the need for children to listen to their parents. Consider the repeated instructions concerning this principle:

> **Proverbs 4:1-22:** 1 Hear, O sons, the instruction of a father, and give attention that you may gain understanding, 2 For I give you sound teaching; Do not abandon my instruction. 4...."Let your heart hold fast my words; Keep my commandments and live; 5 Acquire wisdom! Acquire understanding! Do not forget, nor turn away from the words of my mouth... 10 Hear, my son, and accept my sayings, and the years of your life will be many... 13 Take hold of instruction; do not let go. guard her, for she is your life... 20 My son, give attention to my words; incline your ear to my sayings. 21 Do not let them depart from your sight; keep them in the midst of your heart. 22 For they are life to those who find them, and health to all their whole body.

The command offered to children to hear, receive, and take hold of the instructions of parents is oft repeated in the Old Testament Scriptures. It may seem to be too simple to be needful, however, it is an important principle to grasp: *the first step towards obedience is this act of hearing and embracing instruction.* Consider the following four steps towards a child's obedience:

1. CHILDREN MUST UNDERSTAND THEIR NEED TO HEAR

The necessity of hearing is regularly taught throughout the books of wisdom in the Old Testament, as well as throughout other portions of Scripture. Listening to wisdom and counsel is the very opposite to the way of a fool, therefore this lesson of hearing is fundamental for children:

Proverbs 1:5,8 – 5 A wise man will hear and increase in learning, And a man of understanding will acquire wise counsel... 8 Hear, my son, your father's instruction, And do not forsake your mother's teaching;

Children learn to listen when they better understand that *they need counsel* and that *it is right* that parents instruct them. The sooner that this lesson is impressed upon the hearts of little ones the better. For parents to wait to teach such a fundamental lesson is a fatal error. As children develop intellectually, they will become more tempted to do what is right in their own eyes. A *loving* parent will seek to impress upon the child, at the earliest stages, the truth that children need the loving leadership of their parents for their own good. However, this will not happen within a vacuum of activity. In order for children to learn the skill of listening, parents must always take an active role in communication and instruction with their children. A child that is indifferent, impatient, and has a short attention span is a child that has subsisted in an environment of little communication and leadership. Indifference, impatience, and inattention are all the bad fruits of parental neglect of some sort; however, the opposite of parental neglect is an active relationship that is saturated in instruction and communication. Communication is the first step towards teaching your children to *listen*.

2. CHILDREN MUST HEAR WITH CLARITY

Is your child disobedient or just plain confused? This is an important question at all times for all parents! When parents give instructions to their children, those instructions must be clear. The words used, their meanings, and the expectations associated with each must all be clearly clarified for the child at a level that they can comprehend. Without this, children become exasperated as they try to obey and please their parents. This can even occur when a father and mother both give separate, contradictory instructions. Both sets of instructions may be crystal clear, but if they are in opposition to one another then children can become confused and frustrated. Such errors, if frequent, point back to a problem in the father's leadership and possibly the wife's unwillingness to submit to her husband. Such problems are then amplified in a home of contradiction. It is important to understand that parents can diminish the confidence of their children by failing to give unified instructions. While the source of this problem can vary remarkably, the effect is often the same: confusion, provocation, and exasperation. As believers, we take great confidence in the fact that the Lord's Word does not return to Him void. As well, He does not lie, nor relent, nor change His mind.[262] His protection and care for us is assuring, for the Lord is faithful. While parents will never be perfect, their goal must be to nurture an environment of trust and confidence which comes through a faithful and godly life. Children can *hear* us best when we have a comprehensible message to give them! In addition, it is often necessary to have children ask questions about our instructions. It is a good habit to ask the child: "do you understand?" Whether it is a three year old helping to clear off the table, or a teenage boy learning to use a power saw for the first time, clarity and comprehension is always necessary in the reception of instruction.

3. CHILDREN MUST BE RESPONSIVE WHEN HEARING

How a child responds to instruction is another crucial aspect of obedience. Not only should the parent be concerned about what actions their child will take, but even their countenance and especially their attitude must be carefully considered when calling for obedience. The Bible frequently speaks of the countenance of a person as that which gives an indication of their attitude, whether

---

[262] Is. 55:10-11, 1 Samuel 15:29, Mal. 3:6.

good or bad. Hence the word *face* in the Hebrew (*pāniym*) is always given in the plural most likely to denote the multifaceted facial features that indicate the attitude of an individual. A crossed brow, a frown, a smile, sorrowful eyes, or a host of other features constitute a person's overall countenance.[263] It is for this reason that a person's sinful pride is difficult to mask: Proverbs 21:29 "A wicked man shows a bold face." By this, it is often the case that a child's countenance can inform a parent concerning how ready the child is to hear them. This principle of observing another's countenance is important, not only for the child but also for the parent, because the countenance of the parent is crucial in communicating authority and love. The Scriptures remind us that the Lord *turns his face* away from the wicked,[264] but shines His glorious countenance upon His children.[265] Thus, it would be difficult to imagine parents never looking their children in the eye when they speak. It should be just as unimaginable for children to nurture the same habit with their parents.

When children receive instruction, they are not only receiving information but they are also receiving guidance from their parents concerning the attitude in which those instructions are received. Parenting is more than an information exchange, it is a relationship between parents and their children. If a child's heart is not ready to receive instruction, the parent must be careful to seek out the root issue of rebellion and disobedience. Like adults, children can often render a mechanical obedience that is joyless and even resentful. While it is true that children must obey their parents no matter what

---

[263] "This particular word always occurs in the plural, perhaps indicative of the fact that the face is a combination of a number of features. As we shall see below, the face identifies the person and reflects the attitude and sentiments of the person. As such, *pāniym* can be a substitute for the self or the feelings of the self." Laird, Harris, Archer, and Waltke. Theological Wordbook, p. 727.

[264] Psalm 132:10.

[265] Psalm 4:6.

their attitude, the parent must be most concerned about the heart-attitude of their children over and above anything else. As the Lord is not satisfied with sacrifices that are heartlessly rendered, so neither should the parent be satisfied with the child who obeys on the outside but who is full of rebellion on the inside.[266] When parents detect that a child is not responding well to instruction, they must work to correct the attitude first before instruction can be given and embraced.

The condition of the heart is crucial, therefore communication must be meaningful for the parent and child. In the hustle and bustle of daily life it is often tempting for parents to instruct their children without considering the nature of the child's response, but the Christian parent cannot be merely satisfied with the raw mechanics of communication and obedience. They should seek to engage in a relationship with their children, carefully observing the child's demeanor as they hear and respond to our instructions. The child's responsiveness to parental instruction is crucial, for it constitutes the difference between genuine obedience and covert disobedience. It is therefore a helpful pattern of behavior for parents to relate openly to their children with godly words and a loving countenance,[267] while observing the countenances of their children in order to understand the nature of the child's response to parental leadership.

Such advice should not be taken to an illogical extreme however. Instructions given for taking out the trash, or picking up one's shoes may be given and received without as much as a glance at times. Clearly, parents need to apply sound wisdom according to the need of the moment, being careful to make sure that children take seriously this matter of receiving instruction.

---

[266] Psalm 51:16-17.

[267] Acts 6:15.

4. CHILDREN MUST BE RESPONSIBLE
FOR WHAT THEY HEAR

When the parent gives an instruction to their child it is then necessary for that parent to hold the child accountable to respond in obedience. The importance of the parental instruction should not be devalued through lethargy or disregard. If a child does not obey parental instruction, it is a sin in light of the simple instructions of Scripture (Ephesians 6:1, Colossians 3:20). It is at this point that the parent is to apply *diligence* in their discipline. Ignoring the child who ignores you will teach them that your word and authority are essentially meaningless. This was not Paul's approach to the local church: "But as God is faithful, our word to you is not yes and no" (2 Corinthians 1:18). Like that apostle, our message to our children must be *yes* or *no*, but not both by our refusal to uphold our instructions in the home. When a parent speaks to a child, that child must experientially know of the resolve of the parent without doubt. Unless the parent has been unclear, there should be no good reason for a parent to have to repeat an instruction: children are commanded to *hear* and *obey*! When a child does not swiftly obey (within a reasonable time), that child is ultimately disobeying. The parent must carefully distinguish between a child who is genuinely confused versus a child who is sinfully using a delay tactic in order to stall or forgo compliance. This then becomes the moment of opportunity for a parent to teach their child that *yes means yes and no means no*. With patient and loving discipline, the parent is to correct the child such that they will learn to respond with diligence to their parents' command. It is too often a temptation for parents to try to compete with a disobedient child in such a setting. If a parent engages in a form of competition, arguing, debating, repeating commands, or perhaps even threatening, then they have already lost their parental opportunity. God commands children to hear and obey. If they do not do so, then they are committing sin and are to be lovingly chastened for that disobedience – there should be no debating, no negotiation, no argumentation, no threatening or repeating instructions, but loving discipline so that they might be taught to *hear* and *obey*. It is in this area that the majority of parents struggle the most, in terms of applying diligence, and yet it is so crucial in light of the foundational importance of a child's need to learn how to heed the instructions of his or her parents.

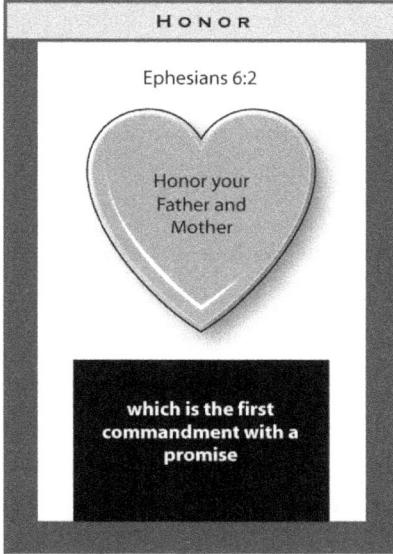

Having examined the Apostle's first command to children (*obey*), we must now consider his second instruction as it relates to *honor*:

> **HONOR**
>
> Ephesians 6:2
>
> Honor your Father and Mother
>
> which is the first commandment with a promise

Ephesians 6:2-3 – 2 Honor your father and mother (which is the first commandment with a promise), 3 that it may be well with you, and that you may live long on the earth.

This second imperative reveals the importance of a child's valuation of the father and mother. Paul's injunction in Ephesians 6:2-3 reveals that parents are to be held in high regard as being the very representatives of the Lord Himself. When we consider the broader significance and meaning of *honor*, we understand that it is one of the chief components of love and respect, after all, brethren are to show honor to one another (Romans 12:10); the husband is to honor his wife (1 Peter 3:7); wives are to honor and respect their husbands (Ephesians 5:33) and we are to honor all men including those who are in governing authority (1 Peter 2:17). The act of honoring others is a significant part of the Christian life and it is to be one of the earliest lessons impressed upon children *from* their parents and *for* their parents. Paul taught this principle by drawing from the Old Testament Scriptures:

> **Exodus 20:12** Honor your father and your mother, that your days may be prolonged in the land which the Lord your God gives you.

> **Deuteronomy 5:16** 'Honor your father and your mother, as the Lord your God has commanded you, that your days may be prolonged, and that it may go well with you on the land which the Lord your God gives you.

At the heart of this "first commandment with a promise" is the concept of life and wellness. Like many Old Testament conditional statements, this is not necessarily *guaranteeing* longevity for obedient children, but it does describe the blessings of life that are often availed to children who respect and honor their parents. The crucial concept here is this: children are safest in this life when they readily subject themselves to the protective care and covering of their parents. This stands in opposition to the child who dishonors his parents by rejecting discipline and instruction. A rebellious child who dishonors and rejects parental tutelage is choosing to live outside of the umbrella of God's ordained protection. Such a child is essentially living on his own without the protective graces afforded to him through the parents. What we learn from this instruction to children is this important truth: parents are a gift from God to their children! This is essentially the mirrored truth of the teaching found in Psalm 127 where we saw that children are *a gift of the Lord*. Additionally, we must note that such honor does not come naturally, hence children are to be regularly taught to honor their parents in an active way. Such relationships of honor have a point and purpose and it is this: The chief end is that God would be honored in all things (Malachi 1:6).

Malachi 1:6 A son honors his father, and a servant his master. Then if I am a father, where is My honor? And if I am a master, where is My respect? says the Lord of hosts...

Parents are to regard the value of their children, and children are to regard the value of their parents *in the Lord.* These relationships of honor must then point us to the greatest matter of honor over all others: *the honor and glory of God.*

A Child's Obedience, Honor, And Discipleship Cont'

In Chapter 4 (The Two Paths of Parenting) we examined the details of Ephesians 6:4. It was there that we learned how Fathers are not to *provoke* or *exasperate* their children, rather they are to *nurture* them in the Lord. The reason why we began with verse 4 was so that we could examine the parent's responsibility in the home *first.* Now that we have taken a look at 6:1-3, we can better synthesize the full text as a unit. Overall, Ephesians 6:1-4 is teaching us that children will either be led into a path of 1. provocation and exasperation, or 2. obedience and honor. When we looked at these two paths of parenting, our focus was set upon the positive notion of godly nurture. However, we need to extend our examination of this section to include the full spectrum of exhortation *and warning,* for the simple reason that God's warnings are no less important than his positive exhortations:

Colossians 3:21 Fathers, do not exasperate your children, that they may not lose heart.

Paul's choice of words in Ephesians 6:4 and Colossians 3:21 are quite telling. Respectively speaking, provocation (Eph. 6:4, *parorgizō: to be angered*) and exasperation (Col. 3:21, *erethizō: to become resentful*) are to be seen as very real hazards in parenting when godly discipleship is absent. It is interesting to note that the Apostle Paul does not say how such responses might come. However, the antithesis of Ephesians 6:4 is essentially self explanatory:

> **Ephesians 6:4** And, fathers, do not provoke your children to anger; but bring them up in the discipline and instruction of the Lord.

The two commands go together as *poison* and *antidote*: *don't provoke* but *nurture*. When parents lovingly nurture their children in the Lord, they minimize any justification for a child's provocation and resentment. The absence of such nurture and discipline will often lead to children whose disposition is characterized by anger, resentment, provocation, disrespect, and exasperation. In such an environment, the source of provocation can come from a lengthy list of deficiencies in the home. By analogy, this was the very environment in which the Lord Jesus Christ found the multitudes when He ministered on the earth. The spiritual leaders of the day did not lovingly nurture the people in truth, rather they established a man-centered religion that was mechanistic and fell quite short of the *discipline and instruction of the Lord:*

> **Matthew 9:36** And seeing the multitudes, He felt compassion for them, because they were distressed and downcast like sheep without a shepherd.

The absence of genuine shepherding left the people in this downcast state through their man-centeredness and neglect of true spirituality. Such ungodliness has this effect, not only on adults, but on children as well, therefore the task and privilege of shepherding the Christian home must be upheld with a serious mind and godly determination. With this principle laid down clearly, we must now consider how such a ministry of truth is to be upheld. Consider once again the

Apostle Paul's reminders to Timothy about the importance of being trained in the Word of God:

> **2 Timothy 3:1-2, 13-17:** 1 But realize this, that in the last days difficult times will come 2 For men will be lovers of self, lovers of money, boastful, arrogant, revilers, disobedient to parents, ungrateful, unholy...13 But evil men and impostors will proceed from bad to worse, deceiving and being deceived.14 You, however, continue in the things you have learned and become convinced of, knowing from whom you have learned them; 15 and that from childhood you have known the sacred writings which are able to give you the wisdom that leads to salvation through faith which is in Christ Jesus. 16 All Scripture is inspired by God and profitable for teaching, for reproof, for correction, for training in righteousness; 17 that the man of God may be adequate, equipped for every good work.

In Paul's warning to Timothy, regarding the future state of mankind in the last days, he gave his son in the faith an important reminder of his beginnings in Christ. Paul exhorted Timothy to continue in the things that he had learned and become convinced of: the Scriptures that led him to salvation and that had nourished him in wisdom throughout the years. Verse sixteen is especially helpful, for it shows us how God's Word instructed and sanctified Timothy's heart ever since his youth.

> **2 Timothy 3:16** All Scripture is inspired by God and profitable for teaching, for reproof, for correction, for training in righteousness;

As noted earlier, Timothy *profited* spiritually in a home that upheld the glory of Christ through the Scriptures. Timothy was regularly *taught* the Scriptures (v. 15 & 16) in a positive, proactive environment, ever since he was a little child. It was through this active process of *teaching* that Timothy learned about the path of life and the path of death; the way of wisdom and the way of foolishness;

such that when Timothy sinned, he was *reproved, corrected and trained in righteousness* by means of God's Word.

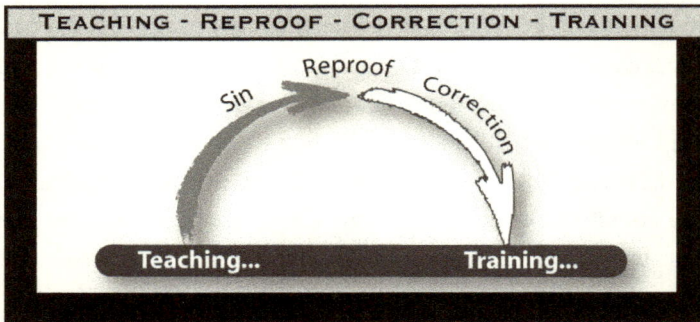

In summary, the components of *teaching, reproof, correction and training in righteousness* are all crucial elements of discipleship, in their respective order. *Teaching* represents the active process of presenting the Scriptures, both in their exhortative and corrective elements. *Reproof* is a negative form of instruction, offering a rebuke to the sinner by teaching him that he must repent and turn away from the path of sin. *Correction* is necessary since it shows the one who has sinned which way he should go: a child can be told not to go out into a street (reproof), but he then needs to know where a *correct* alternative place to play is. The final step, *training in righteousness*, is the place where one *rehearses* the lessons gleaned through *teaching, reproof and correction*. This cycle of training is what the Lord used in the life of Timothy in order to make him adequate, prepared for every good work.

THE PROFIT OF SCRIPTURE

Before we examine these four components of a child's discipleship, it is imperative that we first consider what Paul has to say about Scripture. Scriptural *teaching, reproof, correction* and *training in righteousness* are all *valuable* components of discipleship *because of*

240

the profitability of Scripture itself. It is therefore crucial to note that no matter what takes place in a child's discipleship there must never be a corruption of their understanding of the *value of God's Word.* For most conservative families, this may seem to be a point that is too obvious to make. The affirmation of the inerrancy of Scripture is commonplace among most who would embrace the label *evangelical,* and yet this principle can be vastly undermined in very subtle and even unnoticeable ways. In a Christian culture that has countless ministries which focus on children, it is surprising to consider that, in many cases, the principle of Scripture's profitability is actually diminished, if even unintentionally. Both in the church and para-church contexts there is often the temptation to offer various enticements, prizes, and awards to children in order to give them an incentive to learn God's Word. Such a philosophy of ministry has its adult version as well, especially as we see the modern church sinking further into an environment of entertainment, rather than Scriptural discipleship. The error is the same for adults as it is for children: such models of ministry fail to see that Scripture's real profit leads us to that which is pleasing to God, rather than that which pleases our own flesh. Young people who are nurtured in an environment of temporal enticements, entertainment, prizes, and awards from their youth programs tend to grow up and populate churches that do the same for adults. But the Christian has been called to a different standard, as was Timothy and thus the godly family of every generation is to be governed by Scripture and not by popular wisdom. As parents seek to nurture their children in

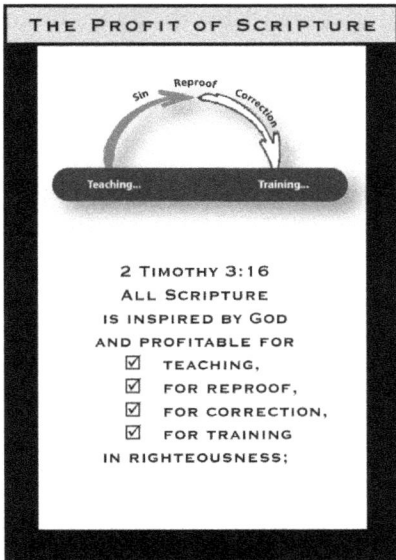

THE PROFIT OF SCRIPTURE

Reproof
Sin
Correction
Teaching...
Training...

2 TIMOTHY 3:16
ALL SCRIPTURE
IS INSPIRED BY GOD
AND PROFITABLE FOR
☑ TEACHING,
☑ FOR REPROOF,
☑ FOR CORRECTION,
☑ FOR TRAINING
IN RIGHTEOUSNESS;

the Lord they must recognize the clear and repeated message of Scripture: we are to prize God's wisdom above all else:

> **Proverbs 4:8-9**: 8 Prize her [godly wisdom], and she will exalt you; She will honor you if you embrace her. 9 She will place on your head a garland of grace; She will present you with a crown of beauty.

The governing imperative in verse 8 (*prize her!*) comes from the Hebrew root *sălāl* meaning to exalt or esteem. As a negative example, it was Pharaoh who *esteemed* [*sălāl*] himself above God and His people in his pride and arrogance (Exodus 9:17). Sadly, we live in a culture that regularly preaches self-esteem as though it were a mathematical constant in the equation of life; however, God's Word gives us very different counsel on the subject of esteem: rather than esteeming ourselves and our own wisdom (Proverbs 3) we are to esteem and prize God and His Word (Proverbs 4). The end result is this: wisdom will present us *with a crown of beauty.* In other words, *wisdom is itself the prize* to those who embrace it. The motivation for embracing God's profitable Word could not be clearer. Rather than being motivated by entertainment, games, prizes, or awards, the instruction of Solomon to his sons is that wisdom itself is our *crown and prize.*

There is another important truth regarding the pleasure of pursuing wisdom. Not only is wisdom a prize granted to those who embrace it, but there is another source of motivation involved in a child's learning the wisdom of God's Word and it is based on the foundation of two very important relationships: their relationship with their parents and their relationship with God:

> **Proverbs 10:1** A wise son makes a father glad, But a foolish son is a grief to his mother.

Colossians 3:20 Children, be obedient to your parents in all things, for this is well-pleasing to the Lord.

The child who heeds godly wisdom is a child who brings great joy and satisfaction to his parents, and ultimately to God Himself. When children seek to do things that are pleasing to their parents they are doing that which is right (Ephesians 6:1) and that which is pleasing to the Lord (Colossians 3:20). Such truths point to a motivation that is based upon godly relationships rather than monetary rewards. Wisdom is a prize, but so is the satisfaction of pleasing one's parents and ultimately the Lord Himself. The satisfaction that children gain by making a father glad (Proverbs 10:1) is an earthly reflection of the joy that is found in the believer's relationship with God:

> **Ephesians 5:8-10***:* 8 ...you were formerly darkness, but now you are light in the Lord; walk as children of light 9 (for the fruit of the light consists in all goodness and righteousness and truth), 10 trying to learn what is pleasing to the Lord.

Christians are children of light who are to learn what is pleasing to the Lord. How true it is that the believer's central joy in life is to live for the satisfaction and pleasure of God, and what is good for the Christian parent is also good and acceptable for the child in the home. Scripture is profitable and therefore obedience to it brings wisdom, satisfaction to the parents, and pleasure to the Lord. Here is the profit, gain, and prize of Scripture. Such an emphasis on the spiritual blessings of Scripture does not nullify the truth that wisdom is often accompanied with temporal blessings, while foolishness is often met with affliction (Proverbs 21:5; 10:4; 13:4). There are temporal blessings that come to those who embrace wisdom, but such gifts are not the chief end or purpose of embracing the wisdom of God. Godliness is a means of great gain if we understand the

nature of our ultimate prize in Christ. Paul's earlier instructions to
Timothy addressed this important matter:

> **1 Timothy 6:6-11:** 6 But godliness actually is a means of great gain, when
> accompanied by contentment. 7 For we have brought nothing into the
> world, so we cannot take anything out of it either. 8 And if we have food
> and covering, with these we shall be content. 9 But those who want to get
> rich fall into temptation and a snare and many foolish and harmful
> desires which plunge men into ruin and destruction. 10 For the love of
> money is a root of all sorts of evil, and some by longing for it have
> wandered away from the faith, and pierced themselves with many a pang.
> 11 But flee from these things, you man of God; and pursue righteousness,
> godliness, faith, love, perseverance and gentleness.

These instructions given by Paul to Timothy were a corrective to
those false teachers at Ephesus who taught that the purpose of
pursuing godliness was for seeking temporal advantage and blessings.
Paul gently moved such a false notion to the Biblical standard by
reminding Timothy (and us) that godliness is a means of great gain,
not so much in terms of temporal wealth (v. 9), but in terms of the
pursuit of righteousness, godliness, faith, love, perseverance, and
gentleness (v. 11). Parents – Godliness is a means of great gain, and
the Scriptures are indeed profitable. Therefore, as we endow our
children with the temporal blessings of food and covering and
various other gifts that show our love and affection, let us be very
careful that our children learn the value of Scripture without bribery
and manipulation. Once again, as children obey their parents in the
Lord they will find delight in the substance of wisdom and from the
God ordained satisfaction of pleasing their parents in the Lord.
Rather than clouding the satisfaction of wisdom and obedience with
temporal prizes and awards, parents should be very careful to
nurture an environment that is grounded in godly relationships –
especially with the Lord Himself. This is not to say that temporal
rewards are never to be used in any context, however, *parents should*

be clearly warned about the danger of a rewards-based spirituality. How profitable Scripture is to those who find its genuine value! It is more *desirable* than gold, than much fine gold and it is sweeter than the honey of the honeycomb (Psalm 19:10). With this preview of the profitability of Scripture, we will now press on to the treasury of 2 Timothy 3:16 which shows us how to use and apply God's profitable Word through God's ordained means of *1. teaching, 2. reproof, 3. correction and 4. training in righteousness.*

1. THE PROFIT OF TEACHING

Life is never a neutral experience. Human beings, whether young or old, are constantly learning, changing, and being transformed in one way or another. Such a transformation will take only one of two paths: *the path of wisdom or the path of foolishness.* This is why the sons and daughters of Adam and Eve require a regular diet of God's Word, for by it we

THE PROFIT OF TEACHING

↑ ONE WAY (TEACHING)

2 TIMOTHY 3:16
ALL SCRIPTURE
IS INSPIRED BY GOD
AND PROFITABLE
☑ FOR TEACHING,
☐ FOR REPROOF,
☐ FOR CORRECTION,
☐ FOR TRAINING
IN RIGHTEOUSNESS;

are transformed by the renewing of our minds:

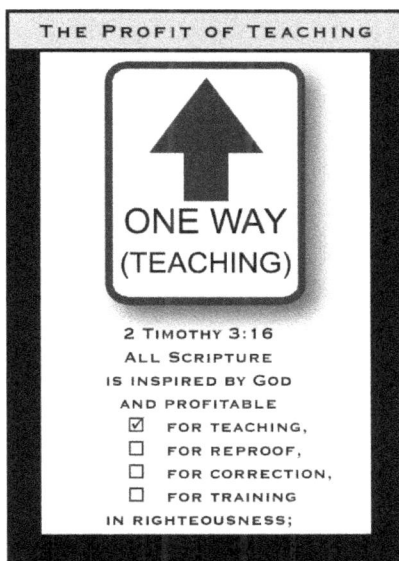

> **Romans 12:2** ...do not be conformed to this world, but be transformed by the renewing of your mind, that you may prove what the will of God is, that which is good and acceptable and perfect.

As already stated, the path of one's life can take only one of two directions: *the path of wisdom or the path of foolishness.* Our minds are in a constant state of flux such that without the regular input of God's profitable Word, we decay in the morass of our own

245

corruption. And what is true for the adult is no less applicable to children. By this principle it is crucial to stress that the entry point of discipleship for children is this discipline of teaching and instruction in the home. It is, however, a misconception to think that the absence of such regular teaching leaves a child in a merely neutral environment – it does not. Instead, the absence of Biblical instruction is a negative and destructive one. A parent could even remove the television, radio, along with every harmful magazine and book possible, but a child who is left to himself is still in danger because of his own sinful *heart and mind*. Without outside help, he will go into the way of foolishness and destruction! Consider the wisdom of C. H. Spurgeon on this matter:

> *"I heard of a man who said that he did not like to prejudice his boy, so he would not say anything to him about religion. The devil, however, was quite willing to prejudice the lad. If ever you feel it incumbent upon you not to prejudice a piece of ground by sowing good seed in it, you may rest assured that the weeds will not imitate your impartiality. Where the plow does not go and the seed is not sown, the weeds are sure to multiply. And if children are left untrained, all sorts of evil will spring up in their hearts and lives."*[268]

This is a crucial duty of parents – to sow the seed of God's Word in the hearts of their children, regularly. It is a necessary work that must be constant, knowing that Satan, the cares of this world, and the deceitfulness of the human heart are constantly working against the labors of parents.[269] God's Word is profitable for *teaching* - which means that it is a comprehensible revelation that clearly instructs sinners about the nature of God and man, the person of Christ and His salvific work, the nature of worship, along with the final consummation of God's overall plan of redemption and judgment.

---

[268] C. H. Spurgeon, <u>Bringing Sinners to the Savior</u>, Sermon delivered on August 22nd 1880.
[269] Matt. 13:1-9.

246

All that is needed pertaining to life and godliness is provided through God's revelation and it is this good seed that parents are to plant without relenting. Therefore, in light of our ongoing need for Scripture, it is important to point out that the Christian home must be a place where God's Word is taught *actively* and *reactively*. *Active* teaching seeks to survey the whole counsel of God because it is understood that *all Scripture* is inspired by God and is profitable. Therefore such *active* instruction does not wait for a crisis or disaster of any sort, but approaches the Word of God with the design of harvesting and presenting the full counsel of the Scriptures to those who need to hear it. This was the Apostle Paul's principal approach to shepherding as articulated in his farewell address to the Ephesian elders in Acts 20:

> **Acts 20:20, 26:** 20 ...I did not shrink from declaring to you anything that was profitable, and teaching you publicly and from house to house... 26 Therefore I testify to you this day, that I am innocent of the blood of all men. 27 For I did not shrink from declaring to you the whole purpose of God.

The Apostle Paul had clarity of conscience before God because he was not a hobby horse preacher, but was a messenger of God who delivered the full measure of Biblical revelation to the church at Ephesus. This he did despite the opposition and hostility that he received during his ministry there (Acts 19:21-42). Active teaching is a philosophy of ministry which comprehends that life's circumstances cannot always affect the teacher's decision as to what truths from God's Word should be taught. For example Christ was often confronted with false admiration (Luke 4:15), hostility from Jewish leaders (John 8:48), and even foolish queries from His followers (John 6:25), but in these circumstances He did not *shrink back* from declaring the profitable Word to His audience. Despite the external distractions of this world, such a ministry as this seeks to proceed through the full spectrum of God's revelation.

On the other hand, there is also a Scriptural precedent for a form of *reactive teaching*. It is this form of instruction which recognizes that there are times when special needs must be met with special instruction. It is here that a teacher will respond to a specific need in a particular moment. We need not go far in the epistles to find examples of such a reactive ministry – Paul's correction of the legalism at Galatia; Peter's exhortations of perseverance to a suffering and dispersed church; John's warnings against idolatry to the churches in Asia Minor, not to mention the corrective instructions in the seven epistles in the book of Revelation. Christ, who is the greatest example of active instruction also taught his followers in view of their circumstantial needs: The woman at the water well (John 4:7-8), those at Lazarus's gravesite (John 11:35), as well as the multitudes whom Jesus fed (John 6:1-58) to name only a few.[270] All of these examples point out an approach to teaching which seeks to deal with the circumstances and needs of the audience. The important distinction between *active* and *reactive* ministry is this: *Active teaching* represents the normal pattern of instruction of the whole counsel of God whereas *reactive teaching* addresses special needs and problems according to the need of the moment.

> **Ephesians 4:29:** 29 Let no unwholesome word proceed from your mouth, but only such a word as is good for edification according to the need of the moment, so that it will give grace to those who hear.

---

[270] It must be noted that such language employed such as *reactive* and *active* teaching, as applied to Christ's ministry, should not be thought of in merely human terms. Christ foreknew what and when He would teach (John 6:6). But from the human standpoint, there are certain occasions when Christ taught without respect to the circumstances that surrounded Him (active); and there were times when He taught specific lessons which were tailored to an event, a debate, or a question (reactive). These terms are more *anthropomorphic* as they might be applied to Christ, however, with respect to any other teacher of the Word – they are all the more applicable.

In imitation of Christ and the Apostles, a conscientious parent will endeavor to present the Word of God in the fullness of its wisdom, while not neglecting the special needs which will crop up in the lives of their children. Like a pastor of a church, it is important for the father to plan out regular times of Biblical study with his family so that the Word of God can have a regular import into the home. However, with this regular schedule at hand there must be an attitude of flexibility too. Sometimes a father may change his plans in his family devotions in light of a particular circumstance or need. This may be done as an interruption to a regular devotional series through the Gospel of Matthew or the book of Proverbs. If his family has a particular need to pause and consider the sin of gossip, or anger, or covetousness (for example) then he should freely exercise his leadership prerogative to take such a pause and then return to his series when appropriate. The father is to apply the wisdom of a shepherd in order to understand the genuine need of his family, without being too distracted by every circumstance and change – it is the careful walk of a leader who leads the sheep in straight and beneficial paths. The maintenance of such a ministry ought to be carried out in much the same way that our Lord did with His disciples. Many times we find the Savior preaching sermons to the crowds where his disciples listened and learned. At other times our Lord responded to their questions or even their poor doctrine. Oftentimes, occasions like a meal became opportunities to teach on the sovereignty and power of God. At other times, Christ rebuked his disciples for their sin and then proceeded to instruct them in a corrective manner. Usually He addressed the twelve while at other times he taught individuals or just a few at a time. If ever there was an example of one who *taught diligently when he sat down and when He walked by the way, when He laid down to rest and rose up again* (Deuteronomy 6:7) it certainly was the Lord Jesus Christ, without comparison. His ministry of teaching and discipleship was relentless and faithful. While no parent can match the perfection of Christ's example of discipleship, we must understand that He stands as our perfect standard and example of faithful shepherding. His was a ministry of the Word that was supplied for the good of His sheep and for the glory of the Father. Consider the following helpful principles regarding the parents' ministry of the Word in the home:

- *Teaching by Example: The parents' most significant ministry of the Word is upheld by their example of godliness. We have already addressed the need for parents to represent Christ to their children through the example of their lives in The Heart of Parenting, however it is a necessary reminder to parents that the ministry of God's Word must begin within our own hearts: These things (God's Word) shall be on our hearts (Deuteronomy 6:6) before we seek to minister the Word to our children. Parents are the direct representatives of Jesus Christ in the home, and their representation is one that is established by actions in addition to words. Children mimic parental behavior very early in life. Their natural tendency towards imitation can be a great blessing when they reside in a home where the imitation of Christ is to be found. How crucial it is to remember that the pedagogy of our children begins with a godly example set by the parents just as Christ sought the Father's will for the sake of His disciples (John 17:19).*

- *Teaching in the Wayside: As already stated, Christ stands as the greatest example of one who taught the Word of God diligently. His ministry to the disciples was therefore one that reflected the diligence that parents should have with their children as seen in Deuteronomy 6:6-7. Christ's ministry of the Word was not only found in formal times of preaching, but it encompassed every circumstance of life such that we even find in the Gospels that some of the richest times of instruction came in the midst of the regular experiences of daily living. Christ's shepherding ministry was one that pursued every event in life as an opportunity to speak about the glory, wisdom, authority, and power of God. Christ's theocentricity was compelling. Unlike the man-centered scribes and Pharisees, who faithfully upheld the weekly meetings in the* synagogue, Christ's pursuit of truth went well beyond the regimen of a weekly Bible study. Our Savior's eagerness for truth reflects the zeal of the psalmist in Psalm 119:117: "Uphold me that I may be safe, that I may have regard for Thy statutes continually." Such a zeal for God's Word cannot be concealed, but will overflow in one's actions and words. The times of teaching our children therefore cannot be constrained by a calendar or a clock, but we should seek every God ordained moment and circumstance in order to present God's truth. This is the discipleship pattern of our Savior.

- *Teaching in Family Worship:* The Lord Jesus Christ's ministry to His disciples was one that was continually grounded in the truth. As the Good Shepherd (John 10) he led His disciples into the paths of truth and righteousness (Psalm 23:3); and as their Rabbi, He carefully instructed with clarity and authority. As we have already noted, Christ's ministry of the Word was both active and reactive. He carefully employed times of both formal and informal instruction in a manner that clearly reminds us of His perfection as Shepherd and Teacher. The father who seeks to love his family in the manner which reflects Christ's love for His sheep will seek to establish a regular pattern of instruction that remains consistent, according to the father's ability. Such a ministry, patterned after the Savior, will be characterized by regular times of formal instruction (Matthew 11:1), prayer (Luke 22:45), and praise (Matthew 26:30). Like Christ, who taught truth with seriousness and determination, fathers are to nurture their children faithfully in these disciplines. This time of instruction, prayer, and praise (or family worship) is a crucial time for all Christ-centered homes. Not only is it a key time for the father to unfold the Scriptures to his family explicitly, but it is also a time in which godliness is modeled through the faithfulness of the father. A father communicates his reverence for God and His Word most by his faithful and diligent investment in it, both in personal devotion as well as in family devotions. It is in these times of family worship that God is exalted through the teaching of His Word accompanied by reverent prayer and praise. The family worship time is a key opportunity to rejoice in truth through the worship of God Himself.

251

Consider the wise reflections of James W. Alexander on the subject of the father's leadership in family worship:

> *"The hour of domestic prayer and praise is also the hour of scriptural instruction. The father has opened God's Word, in the presence of his little flock. He thus admits himself to be its teacher and under-shepherd. The example of a father is acknowledged to be all-important. The stream must not be expected to rise higher than the fountain. The Christian householder will feel himself constrained to say: 'I am leading my family in solemn addresses to God; what manner of man should I be! How wise, holy, and exemplary!' This undoubtedly has been, in cases innumerable, the direct operation of Family-Worship on the father. As we know that worldly men, and inconsistent professors, are deterred from performing this duty by the consciousness of a discrepancy between their life and any acts of devotion, so humble Christians are led by the same comparison to be more circumspect, and to order their ways in such a manner as may edify their dependants. There cannot be too many motives to a holy life, nor too many safeguards to parental example. Establish the worship of God in any house, and you erect around it a new barrier against the irruption of the world, the flesh, and the devil."[271]*

The godly impact of family worship is found not only in the explicit message given through Biblical instruction, but it is also found in the implicit message of the father's faithfulness. As the father leads his family in worship, he should consider the following principles: 1. Prayer must be a high priority. By prayer the worshipper enters into the presence of God by the merit of Christ and calls upon the Lord for the Spirit's guidance, leadership, illumination, and aid in worship. By prayer we confess sin and acknowledge our need for Christ's daily grace to stand firm and serve Him as His children. Christ taught His disciples concerning the of importance and need for prayer as being

---

[271] Alexander, James W., Thoughts on Family Worship (Soli Deo Gloria Publications, Morgan PA) pp. 49-50.

the means by which we hallow God's name, admit our dependence upon His sovereign care, confess our transgressions, and petition for His shepherding guidance (Matthew 6:5-15). The time of family worship is but a mere mechanism if it consists of Scriptural study without the discipline of prayer. The father should lead his family in a time of prayer requesting the Spirit's work in their midst so that they might genuinely worship in spirit and in truth (John 4:24). 2. Praise must saturate the time of family worship. It is important to understand that when we use the word worship we are speaking of the specific act of *ascribing to God his worth;* that is, declaring to God His *worthiness* to be praised.[272] Praise and thanksgiving are both crucial aspects of worship. The Old Testament book of Psalms is filled with profound expressions of praise and thanksgiving. Even in the darkest expressions of despair and anxiety, the psalmist often resolves to praise God and give thanks. The importance of this aspect of worship should not go without adequate consideration, for the act of praise and thanksgiving nurtures humility and joy in the heart, and is therefore critical medicine for the soul (Psalm 33, Psalm 43:4). The time of family worship may even be focused on a difficult subject, or may even emphasize a family's tragedy, and yet it can always be said that declaring the blessedness of God is good and pleasing in His sight (Job 1:20-22). 3. Biblical instruction must be central since the time of prayer and praise is upheld by the truth of God's Word. There is an interdependency between prayer, praise, and Scripture that must be recognized. Without prayer and praise, we are like the Pharisees who viewed worship as mere duty. On the other hand, without God's truth, we are left with a form of prayer and praise that is devoid of genuine substance. Therefore, the father should often seek to make the time of Scriptural study that which is central to the

---

[272] The word *worship* comes from the old English word *weorthscipe* (*weorth* ~ worth and *scipe* ~ ship). The primitive idea of this English word is that of "the condition (in a person) of deserving, or being held in, esteem or repute; honour, distinction, renown." The Oxford English Dictionary 2nd Edition (Oxford University Press), Electronic Edition.

family worship time. The truth of God's Word should not just be studied, but it must also be meditated upon through prayer and praise. The following are some helpful ideas for fathers as they seek to establish a pattern of teaching in their homes:

- *The family worship time should be clearly led by the father, but it must also involve all members of the family at the same time, therefore, it should be presented in a manner that will ultimately seek to engage all of the children at their various levels. The father should carefully prepare his lessons in such a manner that addresses the various stages and capabilities of his children: their age and spiritual condition should be carefully considered in this way. The father's priority in the time of family worship should be to teach the Word of God in such a way that his family can have time to listen and respond with questions, as often as possible.*

- *The family worship meeting should be held at a time that will make maximum use of the family's schedule. There will be nights where the father's work schedule may prevent him from leading a family worship time: of course, in lieu of the father's presence, the mother can guide the children in a time of worship and prayer in his stead. But it should be noted that there is a great need for parents not to treat a family worship time with superstition (i.e., it must be done every evening or else!); but neither should the family justify the habitual neglect of family worship for the sake of a schedule and routine that should ultimately be trimmed back in order to restore better priorities. It is helpful for the father to outline a schedule for his family, at least for his own sake, and then to approach that schedule with the understanding that he may need to adjust it according to the needs of his family. His drive in this should not be a schedule or calendar, rather it should be born out of an earnest desire to shepherd his family in Christ.*

- *The father's lessons can consist of studies in various books of the Bible, or in other books that focus the reader's attention to the*

254

Scriptures themselves. His overall goal must be to present a Christ-centered and Christ-glorifying message to his family.

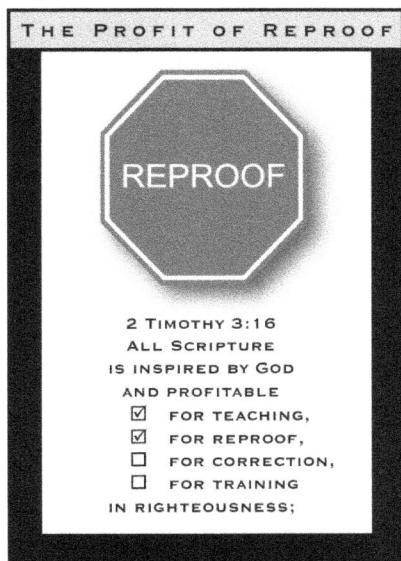

2. THE PROFIT OF REPROOF

THE PROFIT OF REPROOF

REPROOF

2 TIMOTHY 3:16
ALL SCRIPTURE
IS INSPIRED BY GOD
AND PROFITABLE
☑ FOR TEACHING,
☑ FOR REPROOF,
☐ FOR CORRECTION,
☐ FOR TRAINING
IN RIGHTEOUSNESS;

Having discussed the profitability of God's Word for teaching, we now consider its profit of reproof. As noted earlier, reproof is a punitive response to sin. Its focus is a negative one, whereas correction offers a positive resolve to reproof. As sinners, we all need godly reproof. Without it we would be left to wander away from the path of truth. Godly reproof is like the shepherd's staff that prods sheep away from the path of danger; therefore it is a very necessary tool for parents who love their children in the Lord. The environment of reproof can either be a healthy one, or if imbalanced, a very poor one. When we consider what the Scriptures have to say regarding reproof, we see that there are essentially two forms of godly reproof described: 1. *The rod of reproof* and 2. *Consequential reproof.*

THE PROFIT OF REPROOF CONT'
THE ROD

The subject of the rod, or the use of corporal punishment, has become a tabooed discussion in our nation. Whereas the use of the rod in disciplining children was commonplace in America in the past few centuries, today it is almost universally shunned as barbarous and cruel. Since the earlier part of the 20th Century the predominant

255

influences of psychology in America have greatly accelerated many faulty views of child training and discipline. Rather than employing the use of the rod in discipline, parents of this generation are often scolded into the belief that children must be psychologically coerced towards obedience, rather than being instructed, commanded, and led into it. In addition to this motif, parents are frequently given the mantra regarding a child's need for "self-esteem," that is, if there is any hope that they will love others, then they must first learn to love themselves. However, the principles of Scripture run entirely contrary to this world's system of wisdom. In order for children to love others well, they must first be directed to the love of God as their highest priority in life. The Scriptures call us to *esteem* the Lord first, our neighbors second, and then we fall into third place. Additionally, the Scriptures call parents to exercise a loving yet commanding leadership in the home, rather than that of psychological coercion. A crucial component to their loving leadership is mediated by the rod of reproof. In this book the rod of reproof is presented, not as a human philosophy, but as a biblical principle that must be maintained in the Christ-centered and loving home. It is often hard for parents to comprehend well, but the rod of reproof is an instrument of care and compassion rather than of hatred. In fact, parents who withhold the use of the rod on their children are actually *hating them*, as the Scripture declares:

Proverbs 13:24 He who spares his rod hates his son, but he who loves him disciplines him diligently.

In our last mention of this verse, we focused on the concept of *diligent discipline (or early discipline)*. But here, this verse is presented in order to remind parents that the withholding of chastisement is actually a *hateful thing to do*. Sadly, many child's-rights activists today, who oppose corporal discipline of children and laud themselves as the great protectors of children, will oftentimes be the greatest supporters of abortion and familial socialism. The logic of our society is strained at best, but the reality is quite clear: what lies at the heart of those who kill the unborn child, as well as those who withhold the rod of discipline, *is hatred*. The difference between these two actions is simply a question of magnitude. It is a difficult but painfully true reality that cannot be minimized. Such hatred of children is Satanic and stands against the loving nature of God:

> **Proverbs 3:12** For whom the Lord loves He reproves, even as a father, the son in whom he delights.

Unfortunately, the subject of chastisement is often accompanied by discussions of child abuse. Our contemporary culture normally equates the two as though they were the same. Obviously, there are those cases where parents will resort to something other than loving chastisement. Clearly, child abuse is a serious problem where it is actually the goal of the parent to injure the child, or to take out their rage on the child to the extent that the child's safety is truly in question. Such extremes are stark and must be resisted. But the parent must remember this: what the Bible calls unloving and abusive is the parent who refrains from the use of the rod! *Loving* reproof is one of the ways that parents provide protection for their children. It is like that shepherd's staff that redirects his sheep from the dangerous and errant paths of the wilderness. For David (who was a shepherd himself), the Lord's rod and staff were sources of great comfort to him:

> **Psalm 23:1, 4:** 1 The Lord is my shepherd, I shall not want... 4 Even though I walk through the valley of the shadow of death, I fear no evil; for Thou art with me; Thy rod and Thy staff, they comfort me.

This metaphor of Scripture, concerning the loving care that God gives as a shepherd, is one that serves as a perfect model for parents.

Like God the Father, parents are to apply the rod of reproof with great love, and for the greater good of the child. Several principles of Scripture come into play at this point. When parents opt to apply the rod of discipline, they should take the time to consider the following:

- *Prayer: God's discipline is given out of the perfection of His own nature. He always and only disciplines us out of a holy love. However parents must take heed unto themselves and examine their motives in delivering the rod. If they are filled with anger or frustration, it means that it is a good time to pause and pray. This is not to say that prayer must always precede the application of the rod, but it does point out the need to consider one's motive and attitude before applying chastisement.*

- *Preparation: Within sound spiritual judgment, the parent must then consider the need for reproof. When the rod is deemed necessary, then parents must apply it. When there are other providential means of reproof available (this will be explained in the next section) then those options should be considered too. While the rod is the principal tool of parents to reprove their young, it is not the only tool, but if the rod is appropriate, then it is in this moment of preparation that the parent should communicate to the child what is about to happen and why. Along with these times of explanation there will often be opportunities for the parent to pray with the child before or after the application of the rod (or both). Our Heavenly Father disciplines us for our good, and so it must be for parents and their children. In order for reproof to be effective, children must be told why they merited the rod. The rod is best applied when it is joined with wise words of reproof:*

Proverbs 29:15 The rod and reproof give wisdom...

Proverbs 29:15 clearly explains the importance of joining the physical rod with the verbal presentation of reproof, and all in the same moment of discipline. This is the very point of the rod. Without a Biblical understanding as to why one is being reproved, the act of chastisement will seem arbitrary. The pain of the rod must therefore be associated with the reality of sin; and sin must be identified by the standard of God's Word – The rod and reproof give wisdom.

- **Perseverance:** *It is often challenging for a parent to apply the rod faithfully to a child who has sinned. As parents, we don't ever like to see our children in any form of pain. This calls to mind the common expression: "this is going to hurt me more than it will hurt you." But as unpleasant as it may seem at times, the parent must persevere and be consistent in their chastisement and reproof. While the parent is not looking to injure or bruise the child, neither is he merely looking to pat the child on the backside: If your children can assemble a puzzle or play fiddle sticks while you are chastening them, then it's time to apply greater force! What oftentimes happens is that children will feign severe chastening in order to coerce the parent into a lighter reproof of the rod. Parents – persevere!*

> **Proverbs 23:13-14** 13 Do not hold back discipline from the child, Although you beat him with the rod, he will not die. 14 You shall beat him with the rod, and deliver his soul from Sheol.

In addition, phony crying, excessive noise, or any protests to the rod should not be tolerated; it is necessary that children not be permitted to resist the rod, rather they are called upon to accept their reproof as that which is good for them:

> **Proverbs 3:11** My son, do not reject the discipline of the Lord, or loathe His reproof...

> **Proverbs 15:31-32**: 31 He whose ear listens to the life-giving reproof will dwell among the wise. 32 He who neglects discipline despises himself, but he who listens to reproof acquires understanding.

- ***Parental Love:*** *Finally, it should be said that throughout the process of the application of the rod of reproof, it must be the goal of the parent to communicate parental love to the child. This is not just the human parental love of the father and mother, but the perfect parental love of God the Father. It is God who has ordained the standards of parenting and therefore children should be reminded that the purpose of the rod and reproof are founded in God's good and perfect will:*

    Hebrews 12:9-10: *9 Furthermore, we had earthly fathers to discipline us, and we respected them; shall we not much rather be subject to the Father of spirits, and live? 10 For they disciplined us for a short time as seemed best to them, but He disciplines us for our good, that we may share His holiness.*

    This lesson ought to permeate every phase of the event of reproof with as much consistency as possible. It is often helpful for the parent to conclude such discipline with the tender reminders of God's purposes in such discipline.

Prayer, preparation, perseverance, and parental love should characterize the reproof of a child who has sinned. However, by contrast, the act of spanking a child is fairly easy, but the act of loving discipline takes great effort and *time*. One of the greatest challenges among parents is this commodity of *time*. It takes *time* to identify sin correctly, rather than ignore it. It takes *time* to apply the rod of discipline in a meaningful way such that children understand its profit and benefit. It takes *time* to look our children in the eyes and express our affection and concern for them when we reprove them. But rest assured, meaningful discipline is never a *waste of time* for our children!

The rod is the most basic tool of the parent in administering reproof to their children. It offers the most fundamental and universal form of language that transcends all borders, tongues, and ethnicities: it is the language of pain through chastisement. Children at their earliest stages can understand such language before they can comprehend or speak their first word. But as children grow and develop, their comprehension of language will increase and with it the Biblical wisdom of reproof. In time, children will grow in their ability to discern biblical standards of right and wrong to the point where verbal reproof alone will become increasingly effective. Eventually, there will be a shift in the effectiveness of the rod in their lives:

> **Proverbs 17:10** A rebuke goes deeper into one who has understanding than a hundred blows into a fool.

Children are most foolish in their youngest years, but as they grow their understanding and wisdom will increase, therefore while the rod of reproof is extremely useful and effective, it is not intended to be used with children with no end in sight. There comes a time when other forms of *rebuking* are more effective than the blows of a rod, *even a hundred blows*! This leads us to another means of reproof other than the rod: consequential reproof.

THE PROFIT OF REPROOF CONT'
CONSEQUENTIAL REPROOF

In the broadest sense of meaning, the expression *consequential reproof* is being used here to refer to God's provision of chastisement by means of specific *consequences* for sin. This aspect of reproof is very important in light of the fact that it is a universal form of rebuke that will follow us throughout the rest of our lives. Because of this, children should be trained in such a way that they can learn to appreciate this form of reproof. The Scriptures give us several examples of what consequences may come as a result of sin, for

261

example: if you don't pay your bills then you will receive the consequences for such negligence (Proverbs 6:1-2); if you fail to take care of your household then it will decay and become broken down (Proverbs 24:30-31); and the perverse use of one's mouth will bring ruin (Proverbs 6 & 18). Foolish behavior will be met with the *consequential reproof* of the Lord. This reproof is providentially given by God Himself, especially to those who are His children for their greater good. However, we must remember that great caution must be applied when attempting to ascertain if God's hand of reproof is being applied for specific sins. When we attempt to interpret life's experiences we must guard against the error of merely assuming that all hardships are the direct result of particular sin. For example, when the disciples encountered the man who was born blind from birth in John 9, they queried about what sin the blind man or his parents had committed such that this ailment came to be. The Lord's answer clearly redirected their thinking, for it was neither that he sinned nor his parents, *but that the works of God might by displayed in him* (John 9:1-3). When difficult circumstances come our way, it is in keeping with wisdom and humility to seek the Lord in an attempt to understand the purpose of His providences (2 Corinthians 12:7-10). However, it is also important to exercise great wisdom and caution when attempting to interpret such circumstances. Sometimes our comprehension of trials will be very clear, at other times we may have to admit our inability to comprehend God's immediate purposes. However, if you break the law and go to jail for it, wonder not! Whether we suffer for doing good, or evil (1 Peter 2:15-20), God's profitable Word reminds us that He is working all things together for good (Romans 8:28).

These broader principles of life also apply to the family, including children. As parents, we are in the process of learning how to ascertain life's circumstances appropriately; that is, Biblically. As we grow in wisdom in this area, we must aid our children such that they too will think biblically about their circumstances. It is certain that they will experience the natural consequences for sin, and when they do they will need the wisdom of the Word to understand the Lord's loving reproof in it all. Parents should avoid the superstitious approach of the disciples, but if a child burns his hand on a hot iron after being commanded - "No! Do not touch!" - then there should be little mystery concerning the relationship between their failure to obey and the injury they received! Consequential reproof can take many forms, arising in many contexts. There will be times when consequential reproof will come by means of events that take place outside of the parent's direct influence (i.e., the child who touched the hot iron when ignoring the parent's warning). At other times, consequential reproof can be supplied by specific events that are initiated and governed by parents. In this latter category it is the parent who directly supplies the *consequences for sin.* Consider the following examples.

- ***Temporary isolation for gossip:*** *Proverbs 20:19 He who goes about as a slanderer reveals secrets, therefore do not associate with a gossip.*

- ***Temporary isolation for selfishness:*** *Proverbs 21:13 He who shuts his ear to the cry of the poor will also cry himself and not be answered.*

- ***Temporary isolation for mockery:*** *Proverbs 22:10 Drive out the scoffer, and contention will go out, even strife and dishonor will cease.*

- ***Removal of various privileges for selfishness or laziness:*** *Proverbs 13:4 The soul of the sluggard craves and gets nothing, but the soul of the diligent is made fat.*

- ***The temporary loss of responsibilities in the home because of sin:*** *Proverbs 28:10 He who leads the upright astray in an evil way will himself fall into his own pit...*

- ***A loss of a meal for laziness:*** *Proverbs 20:4 The sluggard does not plow after the autumn, so he begs during the harvest and has nothing. (2 Thessalonians 3:10 "...if anyone will not work, neither let him eat.")*

- ***Temporary removal of property for disobedience:*** *Proverbs 13:18 Poverty and shame will come to him who neglects discipline, but he who regards reproof will be honored.*

The loss of privileges for the sins of gossip, selfishness, mockery, laziness, or general disobedience can be very effective in offering punitive reproof to children. Like the use of the rod, the use of *consequential reproof* should be designed in order to offer a safe but effective rebuke to the child. A loss of a single meal will not lead to malnutrition; nor will an hour of isolation lead to insanity. The extent to which these methods of reproof are employed should be measured with careful consideration in order to achieve a balance of compassion and a needful rebuke. Parents will learn, over time, what forms of reproof are most effective with their children. For some children, an hour of isolation can be a small vacation for them, while for others the loss of certain responsibilities in the home could be a great victory. But it could also be that for these same children the removal of certain possessions of theirs, or the loss of a meal, could capture their attention and cause them to consider their sin more clearly. The point is simply this: what is effective for one child may not be as effective for others, therefore, parents must watch, listen, and learn as they apply such reproof.

It is oftentimes argued that such reproof caters to a *fleshly* motivation for obedience. Such a concern is well advised since it is true that fleshliness should always be a concern in all matters of obedience to God's Word. However, the concern over fleshly motivation actually applies not only to devices of *consequential reproof*, but it also applies to *the rod of reproof*. This is so because both means of reproof deal in the language of grief and pain. The pain of the rod, the pain of hunger, the pain of isolation etc., all bear the common root of this universal language of grief and pain. Therefore, there will always be a danger that children would obey only so that they might avoid the pain of any of these forms of reproof. While it is true that the avoidance of pain will have some part in one's motivation in obedience, it cannot be the goal of the parent for this to be the principal source of motivation. Our highest motivation must be the love of God and His good pleasure, and secondarily, the love of our neighbor. The fear of consequences for sin should take on a tertiary role of importance, at best. This concern of motivation never ends however; not only in parenting, but even in the lives of mature Christians. What parents should do in order to direct their children to a right motivation is to use the pain of reproof (whether by the rod, or by circumstantial reproof – *or both*) as a tool to show them the ugliness of sin and thus direct them to the goodness of the Savior, Jesus Christ, who came in order to *save His people from their sin.*[273]

The goal of our *teaching, reproof, correction, and training in righteousness* is to direct our children to Christ. As they mature, their exposure to the Word of God will grow. As well, our methods of reproof will change in time, as generally represented in the following chart:

---

[273] Matthew 1:21 "And she will bear a Son; and you shall call His name Jesus, for it is He who will save His people from their sins."

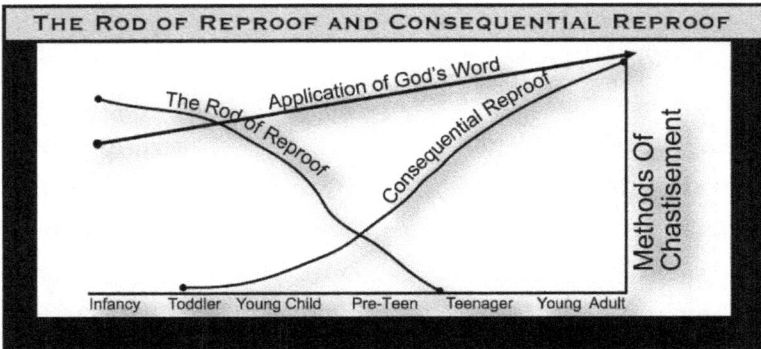

THE ROD OF REPROOF AND CONSEQUENTIAL REPROOF

As a child's understanding of the Scriptures increases, their responsiveness to verbal and consequential reproof will increase; as this occurs, the usefulness of the rod will diminish over time. The means of reproof will shift and vary, but the constancy of God's Word cannot.

No reproof offered can ever stand without the standard of Holy Writ. Without Scripture men will tend to resort to standards that subsist within the domain of human speculation and opinion. This is the pattern of foolishness that is seen among the Pharisees who constantly reproved the Lord for His contradictions against human tradition. However, Christ-centered churches and families must constantly guard against the temptation of seeking the profit of reproof from anything else other than God's Word. The Lord reproves and disciplines His children for their good so that they will not be ensnared with sin, but rather be guided into the path of righteousness. This model of love, established by the Lord Himself, stands as an example for fathers who would endeavor to reprove their young for their spiritual protection.

266

THE PROFIT OF REPROOF CONT'
IMPLICATION FOR PARENTS

In order for parents to teach their children the profit of reproof, they must again consider their own example as those who respond well to God's chastening, whether it is administered by the local church, by the general trials of life, or by the specific consequences of sin. Our children watch us very carefully as they continue to learn about life and godliness. Our message to our children is: *"...do not reject the discipline of the Lord, nor loathe his reproof."* But as we are eager to call them to this obedience, so too must we demonstrate this godliness in their presence.

In our discussion of the *Heart of Parenting* we spoke of the importance of hope in the Christian home. Those who are being sanctified by the grace of God will be characterized by genuine hope, even when trials do come. The saint who understands that the Lord's reproof is profitable is a saint who walks in hope and genuine joy:

> **Romans 5:1-4** Therefore having been justified by faith, we have peace with God through our Lord Jesus Christ, 2 through whom also we have obtained our introduction by faith into this grace in which we stand; and we exult in hope of the glory of God. 3 And not only this, but we also exult in our tribulations, knowing that tribulation brings about perseverance; 4 and perseverance, proven character; and proven character, hope;

Like an inter-connected chain, genuine hope is that link which is indelibly tied to the overall process of sanctification, which includes the tribulations and trials of life:

THE FOUR LINKS TO GENUINE GODLINESS

Romans 5:2-4

Tribulation ...brings about... ...brings about... perseverance ...brings about... proven character ...brings about... hope

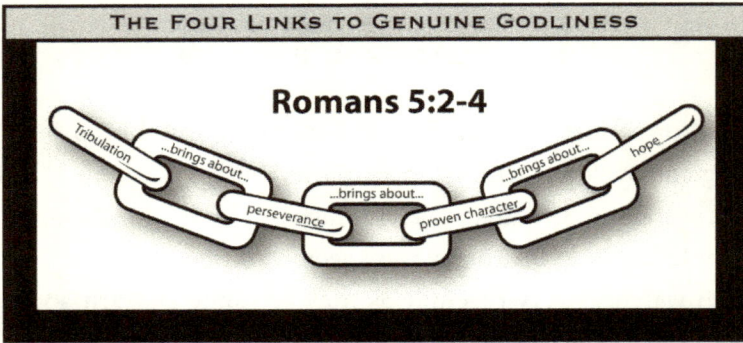

It is often the case that believers will try to achieve hope and joy in life without going through this God ordained process. When we resist trials and tribulations we resist God's method of establishing proven character and thus godly hope; breaking such a chain is not only harmful to ourselves, but it is harmful to our children as they watch our every action and attitude in life. But parents who *exult in tribulation* demonstrate to their children this crucial principal: those who love the Lord do not loath His reproof! How crucial it is that we lead our children by word and *by example.*

3. THE PROFIT OF CORRECTION

THE PROFIT OF CORRECTION

Correction

2 TIMOTHY 3:16
ALL SCRIPTURE
IS INSPIRED BY GOD
AND PROFITABLE
☑ FOR TEACHING,
☑ FOR REPROOF,
☑ FOR CORRECTION,
☐ FOR TRAINING
IN RIGHTEOUSNESS;

In our continuing discussion of the profitability of Scripture we have seen how God's Word is constantly pruning the believer with respect to sin, and thereby fostering greater growth in godliness and wisdom. And concerning the subject of reproof, it is clear that we need Scripture's chastening to keep us from entering the path of sin. These needful benefits of Scripture are just as necessary for

268

children as parents train them up in the Lord. Having considered the importance of godly reproof in the life of a child, we now continue with an examination of the Word's profit in correction. As stated earlier, it is not enough to tell a child that they are wrong in light of their sin; rather, they need to know how their way can be *corrected*. The commandments and ordinances of God's Word certainly tell us much about the reality of sin, and we are thereby convicted by its standard. However, the prohibitive nature of God's commandments and ordinances are designed to point us to something more than our sin, for the law of God was given to us to be our tutor to lead us to Christ:

> **Galatians 3:23-25:** 23 But before faith came, we were kept in custody under the law, being shut up to the faith which was later to be revealed. 24 Therefore the Law has become our tutor to lead us to Christ, that we may be justified by faith. 25 But now that faith has come, we are no longer under a tutor.

The punitive nature of God's Word is designed to show us the spiritual death and corruption of our sinful nature, and if this were our only use of God's Word, then we would be left with a *ministry of death*.[274] Like the religious leaders of Christ's day, theirs was a ministry of death such that they looked to the law *alone* as their chief hope,[275] thus ignoring Christ who is the law's end and fulfillment:

> **Romans 10:4** For Christ is the end of the law for righteousness to everyone who believes.

The distinction between reproof and correction is very important, and it is this distinction which further informs us about the profitability of Scripture: the reproof that God's Word supplies is

---

[274] 2 Corinthians 3:7.

[275] John 5:39-42.

indeed profitable, *but only so far as it continues with the profit of correction.* The greatest purpose in the Word's work, of pointing out our sin, is that we would thereby be directed to Christ. This is the very essence of the word *correction* [*epanorthōsis*], which means to restore or reform. Consider for a moment the reflections of that Reformer, Martin Luther, on the aforementioned text of Galatians 3:23-25:

> *"...the law is a word that shows life and drives men to it. Therefore, it is not only given as a minister of death, but its principal use and end is to reveal death, that it might be seen and known how horrible sin is. The office therefore of the law is to kill, but only so that God may revive and quicken again."*[276]

It is entirely crucial that parents apply the punitive standards of God's Word, not as an end, but as a means to the greater end of directing their children to the sufficiency and sacrifice of the Savior who alone gives life.[277] This is true, not only for children who are not yet redeemed, but is also true for regenerate children. Christ is our only hope whether young or old; whether as an unsaved sinner in need of salvation, or as a child of God seeking to grow in Christ. As parents apply reproof and correction in the home it will be their desire to learn more about the hearts of their children; whether they are redeemed or not. The redeemed in Christ are commanded to *walk in a manner that is worthy of the calling with which they have been called.*[278] But those who are not redeemed are called upon by the Scriptures to *repent* and *believe* in the Lord Jesus Christ:[279] Until they are forgiven, redeemed, and indwelt with the Holy Spirit, their

---

[276] Martin Luther, <u>Commentary on Galatians.</u>(Simpsonville SC: Christian Classics Foundation), Galatians 3:24.

[277] John 5:21 "For just as the Father raises the dead and gives them life, even so the Son also gives life to whom He wishes."

[278] Ephesians 4:1.

[279] Acts 20:21.

pedagogy in the Scriptures will focus on their need for salvation. As the unsaved, their ability to uphold the standards of God's Word with a genuine heart simply won't be there. This is a crucial point of consideration that should lead a parent to greater caution concerning their expectations: a child that is unsaved does not have the same motivation as the child in whom the Spirit dwells. Unsaved children are to obey their parents, as are redeemed children, however the heart orientation will be different between them both. These distinctions are much harder to discern when children are younger, but it becomes much more apparent when they mature in age. Cain and Abel may have seemed like very similar young men growing up, however the realities of their hearts were revealed when they were old enough to offer up their own sacrifices to the Lord. Cain and Abel, like all children, were called to obey their parents in the Lord, and this they undoubtedly did as children. However, their hearts were filled with different goals and objectives in rendering such obedience. At some point in time Abel came to saving faith in the Lord, such that the sacrifice he offered evidenced such trust:

Hebrews 11:4 By faith Abel offered to God a better sacrifice than Cain, through which he obtained the testimony that he was righteous, God testifying about his gifts, and through faith, though he is dead, he still speaks.

However, Cain never placed his trust in the Lord, but remained in the family as an unbeliever. The evidence of his rejection of the Lord became most obvious when he shed his brother's blood. But until then, the reality of his rebellion may have remained undetected to his parents.[280] Cain's legacy is the legacy of spiritually dead and religious men who offer up meaningless sacrifices to God. This is the legacy of man-centered religion. It is the legacy of all men who, from

---

[280] Jude 4, 12.

childhood, learn how to be religious without having genuine faith in the living God:

> **Jude 11-12:** 12 Woe to them! For they have gone the way of Cain, and for pay they have rushed headlong into the error of Balaam, and perished in the rebellion of Korah. 12 These men [Cain, Balaam and Korah] are those who are hidden reefs in your love feasts when they feast with you without fear, caring for themselves; clouds without water, carried along by winds; autumn trees without fruit, doubly dead, uprooted...

The Scriptures make no small distinction between the lives of Abel and Cain. Abel's heart was filled with faith in the Lord, but Cain's heart was not. And the corruption of Cain's heart was clarified when he was reproved by the Lord Himself. From this clear reality it is important to note that the moment of reproof and correction is an important one, for it becomes a key opportunity for the parent to comprehend, more fully, the heart of their children in light of their response to the Word. When a child's sin is found out, it is not enough to correct mere behavior. Busy parents can often be tempted to be satisfied with the mere compliance of a child; however the godly parent's goal must always be that children obey their parents *in the Lord.* A child's sin is an opportunity for godly confrontation and counsel, and how they respond to such Biblical counsel will inform the parent concerning the heart attitudes of the child. Genuine sorrow for sin is an encouraging sign that points to the Spirit's work of conviction; however, worldly sorrow is short lived and leads to regret:

> **2 Corinthians 7:10** For the sorrow that is according to the will of God produces a repentance without regret, leading to salvation; but the sorrow of the world produces death.

A child who has been caught in a particular sin will either show a genuine sorrow for the sin itself, or they will evidence a worldly sorrow: usually the sorrow of being caught or embarrassed. Such worldly sorrow can even be manifested through anger and resentment, rather than sorrow for sin:

> **Genesis 4:4-6:** 4 And Abel, on his part also brought of the firstlings of his flock and of their fat portions. And the Lord had regard for Abel and for his offering; 5 but for Cain and for his offering He had no regard. So Cain became very angry and his countenance fell. 6 Then the Lord said to Cain, Why are you angry? And why has your countenance fallen?

The true nature of Cain's sorrow was written all over his face – *literally.* It was not to be confused with the righteous sorrow that believers will have when they realize that they have sinned against God, and have grieved Him, thereby struggling over the painful reality of their disdainful offense. Rather, Cain's sorrow was a selfish one that led to hatred and death: the death of his brother. The example of Cain and Abel is crucial, for it gives parents a clear warning and reminder that the highest calling of the Christian home is this precious ministry of the Gospel.

May it never be that we as parents should be satisfied with a home that is filled with children who obey us on the outside, but who disobey the Lord from within their heart! May it never be that we as parents should be satisfied with a home that is filled with children whose lives are rich with activities, programs, and personal possessions, but who are poor in the things of the Christ! The opportunity of reproof and correction is more than just an opportunity to correct external behavior; rather it is a God ordained opportunity to direct our children to Christ, for He alone is the solution for our sin and for the *correction* of our errant lives. With these principles in mind the parent is better equipped to train his children in righteousness.

4. THE PROFIT OF TRAINING

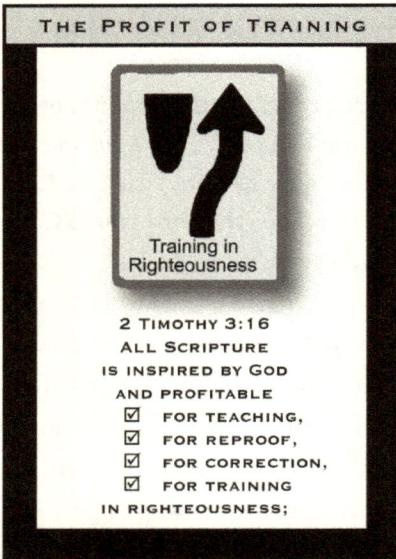

THE PROFIT OF TRAINING

Training in
Righteousness

2 TIMOTHY 3:16
ALL SCRIPTURE
IS INSPIRED BY GOD
AND PROFITABLE
☑ FOR TEACHING,
☑ FOR REPROOF,
☑ FOR CORRECTION,
☑ FOR TRAINING
IN RIGHTEOUSNESS;

The Scriptures are profitable for teaching, for reproof, for correction, *for training in righteousness that the man of God may be adequate, equipped for every good work.* It is in this final stage of *training in righteousness* that the profit of God's Word is brought to bear in the lives of the children of God. This concept of training [*pros paideían*] corresponds to the *English* word *pedagogy* which speaks of the act of tutoring or guiding another. It is the same form of the word in Ephesians 6:4, Hebrews 12:5, 7, 8 & 11 which speaks of a father's *discipline.* A variant of this word is used in Galatians 3:24 to speak of the Law as a *tutor* that leads us to Christ. In all of these examples it should be clear that the concept of training in 2 Timothy 3:16 is one of *guidance and leadership.* This is what the Word of God does in our lives: it guides us and leads us in the paths of righteousness. Along with this, the Scriptures call us to the profitable act of rehearsing, or practicing righteousness. Such a rehearsal of righteousness is the true path of wisdom, for we understand that the learning of truth is not enough; it must be practiced and rehearsed. The Old Testament books of the Psalms and Proverbs address the fact that there are at least three different ways in which we learn and apply the Word of God in our lives, and this is through: *1. Private study in the Word; 2. Public exhortation in the Word and 3. Daily experience with the Word.* It is through this cycle of learning that the believer better comprehends the profit of teaching, reproof, correction, and training in righteousness.

Therefore, it is this same process that is to be applied to children who are being nurtured in the discipline and instruction of the Lord. Consider the wisdom of Proverbs concerning this important cycle of learning:

1. PRIVATE STUDY

Psalm 119:144: Thy testimonies are righteous forever; Give me understanding that I may live: Every student of the Bible is trained in the Word by means of private study and devotion. The medicinal prodding of the Word faithfully brings reproof, correction, and calls to righteousness by means of personal devotion and worship. Thus, as soon as children are taught to read, they should have opportunity to possess and search out their own copies of the Scriptures; and with this, parents can do many things to encourage their children in a personal study of the Word:

- *Give children a designated time to have devotions in the Word and in prayer. Talk to them about what they are reading, how well they understand it, and how they are seeking to apply it in their lives.*

- *Talk to your children about your own time in God's Word, explaining to them what the Lord is teaching you. The best teachers among men are sound students themselves.*

- *Encourage your children to search out and investigate the Word in light of what they are hearing in their times of family worship or in church. Younger children who have difficulty focusing on Sunday's sermons will be greatly aided by parents who bring the discussion of the preached Word to their home. It is an especially good idea for parents to have a sermon-review night as part of their family worship regimen, in order to reinforce and strengthen their private comprehension of such public instruction.*

- *Fathers should assign private reading assignments to their children (according to their ability) in order to strengthen what is being taught in your family worship times.*

- *Children of all ages can always profit by listening to the Word on tape – such resources are too many in number to list here, but local Christian book stores will normally have the Bible on tape or CD.*

2. Public Exhortation

Proverbs 1:5 A wise man will hear and increase in learning, and a man of understanding will acquire wise counsel: Until young children are equipped to read the Word on their own, they rely most heavily on verbal exhortations from the Word. This is, of course, the central ministry of the father and mother. It is crucial for young children to learn of the importance of wise counsel through public exhortation, admonishment, and encouragement in the Word. With this in view, one of the greatest ministries that parents can have to their children is to exemplify a consistent and regular pattern of worship in a local church. It is there that children witness the value of the public exhortation of the Word through their parents' faithful reception of it under a pulpit ministry. If it is our desire that our children be trained in righteousness, then we as parents ought to set an example for our children in this way. Children must not only be directed to be wise themselves, they need to see wisdom personified in their parents who, in humility, faithfully receive the teaching, reproof, correction, and training that they need through the public exhortation of the Word.

3. Daily Experience

Psalm 1:1 How blessed is the man who does not walk in the counsel of the wicked, Nor stand in the path of sinners, Nor sit in

the seat of scoffers!: There is no substitute for the experience of obeying God's Word. Our conviction of the profitability of God's Word is strengthened most when we walk in obedience to it. It is not that our experience with the Scriptures makes the Word more sure, rather our depth of conviction of the Word's importance grows when we see the wisdom of God in action:

> **Proverbs 4:10-12***:* 10 Hear, my son, and accept my sayings, and the years of your life will be many. 11 I have directed you in the way of wisdom; I have led you in upright paths. 12 When you walk, your steps will not be impeded; and if you run, you will not stumble.

The language employed here of *walking* and *running* speaks of this process of *living out the truth of God* in daily life. As parents train their children in the Word, they will need to guide them in this process of experientially applying truth. There will be many experiences in life that will afford parents unique opportunities to teach the Scriptures to their children. Principally, the Christian home should be the first haven for positive opportunities of teaching through the godly example of parents. As well, the local church provides multiple examples of godliness through believers whose lives represent the Savior. There will also be opportunities for teaching that will arise due to sin, either in the home, the church, or in the world at large, by the sin of children, or of parents, or of outsiders in general. When such experiences occur, it is the responsibility of the Christian parent to embrace such circumstances as opportunities to unfold the Word so that children can understand how to relate to their experiences – this is part of the process of being *trained in righteousness:*

- *A death in the family can become an opportunity to consider the brevity of life and our need for Christ who is the source of all life.*[281]

---

[281] John 1:4, 5:26.

- *As we considered earlier, acts of sin in the home become opportunities to review our need for Christ's forgiveness and cleansing.*

- *Acts of evil in world affairs provide opportunities for parents to teach their children about our world's fallen condition, as well as God's providence in everything.*[282]

- *There will be times when children will witness the suffering of the righteous, and even the unrighteous. In moments like these, children must understand the purpose of trials and tribulations; such an opportunity will help them to understand that God sometimes allows His children to suffer for righteousness sake as He did with His only Son.*[283]

- *As we exist in a fallen world, it is inevitable that evil events will be seen and even experienced by all members of the family, in one way or another. When these providential moments come, it is important for parents to teach their children not just the paths of righteousness, but also to instruct them concerning the paths of wickedness. Such lessons become strong warnings to our children to avoid the wickedness of the world:* **Proverbs 4:10-17** *10 Hear, my son, and accept my sayings, And the years of your life will be many. 11 I have directed you in the way of wisdom; I have led you in upright paths. 12 When you walk, your steps will not be impeded; And if you run, you will not stumble. 13 Take hold of instruction; do not let go. Guard her, for she is your life. 14 Do not enter the path of the wicked, And do not proceed in the way of evil men. 15 Avoid it, do not pass by it; Turn away from it and pass on. 16 For they cannot sleep unless they do evil; And they are robbed of sleep unless they*

---

[282] Proverbs 21:1.

[283] 1 Peter 2:13-25.

make someone stumble. 17 For they eat the bread of wickedness,
And drink the wine of violence.

The parents who are devoted to training their children in righteousness will engage in an ongoing discipleship relationship with them, understanding that children need help in considering the direct application of the Scriptures to daily life. As they grow in Christ, they will grow in discernment, being equipped for every good work. Their lifelong lesson will then continue beyond the home such that they will seek to live lives that are spiritually profitable and are pleasing to the Lord.

When we consider the important task of child training it is helpful to remember that the book of Proverbs is crucial for parents because it is a book of wisdom that reminds us of the weakness of the flesh, and how we should deal with those weaknesses. We will sin, and our children will sin, but as this battle goes on we must guard against the ugly temptation of thinking that our children are the enemy! Our calling as parents is not to fight with our children, but to love them, lead them, discipline them, and guide them within the context of compassionate discipleship. We must live with our children in an understanding way, knowing that they are weaker vessels in light of their youth. Consider the following principles that will help parents to remember the very nature and purpose of Scriptural training:

- *Children must understand their greatest need in life – [Proverbs 19:3 The foolishness of man subverts his way, And his heart rages against the Lord]: Left to themselves, our children would grow up in the paths of destruction and rebellion against the Lord. It has already been stated, within the body of this material, but it is worth repeating: children are like any other member of the human race – they need the Lord. Until they are born again[284] their lives are at risk*

---

[284] John 3:3-8.

of going the way of destruction. This important truth is a reminder to parents that there is no cruise control or autopilot in parenting. God is sovereign and He will successfully save His elect, however such truth should never send the parent into the easy-chair of presumption or laziness. The home is the parents' first and greatest mission field above all else, therefore it is crucial that parents understand that their expectations of their children should be measured by the knowledge that children need to be born again. Until they are, their struggle in the home will be greater in light of their unregenerate nature. Children must obey their parents, but it will be the parents' prayer that this obedience will someday be a genuine obedience that is ultimately rendered to the Lord Himself.

- ***Children are naturally destructive** – [Proverbs 14:1 The wise woman builds her house, But the foolish tears it down with her own hands]: Whether young or old, children will spend their days at home learning how to value the world around them as good stewards. What is true of children is also true of adults, and yet the learning curve is much greater for us all earlier in life. It is therefore necessary for parents to understand this as they raise their children. Whether it be a little child who carelessly breaks an expensive piece of china, or a teenager who damages a car through negligence, the hazards of such foolish destruction will populate the experience of child training – it is inevitable. This does not make it excusable; however, it should temper a parent's thinking regarding how well they are teaching their children the principles of stewardship and respect of others' property. Rather than waiting for disasters to come, parents can actively teach their children the importance of being good stewards of their personal possessions. This would include the wisdom of not giving our children more than they can handle or appreciate in light of their age. What they must learn is that the person of wisdom builds his house rather than tears it down.*

- ***Children are naturally deceptive** – [Proverbs 14:8 The wisdom of the prudent is to understand his way, But the folly of fools is deceit]:*

280

As foolishness is bound up in the heart of a child, so too is this tendency towards deceit. Every parent has had that first experience with their children where they catch them red handed in some sin, but then the child denies their guilt no matter how obvious it may to a roomful of witnesses! This is the same foolishness that we saw exhibited by our first parents in Genesis 3, after Adam fell in sin. Their deceitful blame-game went on as though it had been rehearsed somewhere else before. Children who may never see such deception exhibited by others, will do so naturally on their own, because the folly of fools is deceit. Such deception by children can be very frustrating to parents. It seems inconceivable that such adorable children can produce such treachery, but they do by nature, just like we all do apart from the grace of God. But the wisdom of the prudent is to understand his way and the way of a child is naturally inclined towards foolish deception. Like the Lord, we should go to the core of their sin and offer loving but firm reproof rather than taking their deception too personally. Their sin is against God more than it is against us.

• ***Children do not understand the gravity of sin - [Proverbs 14:9*** *Fools mock at sin, but among the upright there is good will]: All men, by nature, do not understand the seriousness of sin. But what is true for all adults is even more true for children in light of their spiritual and moral naïveté. If anyone understands this principle in Proverbs 14:9, it would especially be those who produce the TV shows and movies that populate the entertainment industry. Many of these programs rely on the fact that fools mock at sin. With the plethora of video games and movies that target our children, the Christian parent should stand guard over their homes with greater vigilance. It is the natural tendency for children to make light of their sin, or the sin of another, but among the upright there is good will. Rather than mocking at sin, children should be seriously warned about the gravity of sin: that it is an offense against God:*

Ephesians 5:3-5: 3 But do not let immorality or any impurity or greed even be named among you, as is proper among saints; 4 and there must be no filthiness and silly talk, or coarse jesting, which are not fitting, but rather giving of thanks. 5 For this you know with certainty, that no immoral or impure person or covetous man, who is an idolater, has an inheritance in the kingdom of Christ and God.

- *Children can be quick-tempered – [Ecclesiastes 7:9 Do not be eager in your heart to be angry, For anger resides in the bosom of fools. Proverbs 14:29 ...he who is quick-tempered exalts folly]: Rage and anger are some of the most natural responses of the sinful human heart ever produced. When we do not get our way, it is very tempting to feel enraged and cheated in life. This is the natural impulse of the flesh and it is that which runs contrary to the Spirit. No one ever had to send a child to school in order for them to learn how to become angry, jealous, or hostile when things do not go their way. This is the way of Cain; it is the natural way of all of the descendents of Adam and Eve. As in all these principles, it is never acceptable, but it is understood as a natural tendency of children and must be dealt with by means of Scripture:*

    James 1:19-20: 19 This you know, my beloved brethren. But let everyone be quick to hear, slow to speak and slow to anger; 20 for the anger of man does not achieve the righteousness of God.

- *A child's foolishness multiplies with little effort – [Proverbs 14:18 The naïve inherit folly, But the prudent are crowned with knowledge. Proverbs 14:24 The crown of the wise is their riches, But the folly of fools is foolishness]: Without being demeaning to their children, parents should remind them of their weakness as children so that they will be less inclined to trust in themselves, even more than their parents. Children will often attempt to get their own way, but such a desire should not be readily granted:*

Proverbs 29:15 The rod and reproof give wisdom, But a child who gets his own way brings shame to his mother.

- **Children should be taught to accept their parents' wisdom and authority:** *It is needful for children to understand their own weakness as children so that they will seek out godly wisdom and help, rather than associating with poor influences. A child's influence upon himself or others can quickly gravitate towards error:*

    Proverbs 13:20 He who walks with wise men will be wise, but the companion of fools will suffer harm.

- **A Child's Tongue is Prone to Error** – *[Proverbs 15:2 The tongue of the wise makes knowledge acceptable, But the mouth of fools spouts folly]: There will be times when children will say things that will shock us quite dramatically. In a fit of rage, or in a moment of mindless talking, children can exhibit foolishness than can seem unrecognizable. But a patient parent will understand that this is part of the process of child training. Children should not be allowed to reveal their own mind, or lash out at others with their tongue, rather children should be taught to measure their words carefully:*

    Proverbs 25:11 Like apples of gold in settings of silver is a word spoken in right circumstances.

- **Children do not naturally embrace wisdom** – *[Proverbs 15:14 The mind of the intelligent seeks knowledge, But the mouth of fools feeds on folly]: It is of course true that only the Holy Spirit can instill a genuine appetite for God's Word in the heart of an individual, however children should be discipled in such a way that they are taught to embrace God's truth as their only hope for true wisdom in this world. Like our Shepherd who leads us beside quiet waters, for spiritual refreshment, so too must parents teach their children the value of Scripture.*

- *Children must be taught to use their time well – [Proverbs 24:9 The devising of folly is sin, And the scoffer is an abomination to men]:* Like the mind, time is a dangerous thing to waste. Men who have the time to devise folly thereby demonstrate that they have failed to make full use of their time as stewards of God. In like manner, children should be taught to use their time as wise stewards, knowing that it does not take much to squander precious moments. It is a great danger in our American culture to devote our time to entertainment and folly. It is even a greater danger for parents to use their TV as an artificial baby-sitter, rather than exercising the discipline of engaging our children in activities that will spur them on to godliness. Time is a gift of the Lord – let the family of God use it well for His glory.

- *Children must hear and obey their parents – [Proverbs 1:8-9 8 Hear, my son, your father's instruction, And do not forsake your mother's teaching; 9 Indeed, they are a graceful wreath to your head, And ornaments about your neck.]:* As discussed earlier, this is a crucial aspect of a parent's training of their children that must be nurtured from the earliest stages of life. It is again mentioned here in light of the consideration of a child's propensity towards foolishness. Naturally, children will want to resist this process of listening and obeying:

  Proverbs 18:2 A fool does not delight in understanding, but only in revealing his own mind.

  Part and parcel of a child's composition is this natural tendency to want to be heard rather than to listen to sound counsel. When this form of rebellion arises within children, parents should neither be surprised nor resort to sinful anger. It is a predictable course of conduct that will be a fundamental one throughout the child's life, especially when they become a teenager. During their latter years, children will often develop greater confidence in their skills and knowledge of life. This growth spurt in their lives will often be met

284

with the temptation to believe that they know more than they really do[285] – education and knowledge can often lead men to think more highly of themselves than they ought to think. But the parents who model humility to their children will demonstrate, through their own lives, the value of godly counsel and wisdom.

In Chapter 2 (*The First Child*) we examined the realities of the fallen nature of our children. In that section we considered the reality of a child's original sin and the resultant corruption of foolishness which prevails within their heart. We also examined the nature of foolishness, recognizing that while children are not naturally innocent, they are foolishly naïve and are therefore very susceptible to the corruptions of the world. Such truth must never be used in order to belittle children, nor embarrass them, rather it serves as a reminder to parents as to how their children will tend to behave according to the course of their nature. Parents who are convinced that their children are little angels will surely be disappointed!

"We must not expect all things at once. We must remember what children are, and teach them as they are able to bear. Their minds are like a lump of metal – not to be forged and made useful at once, but only by a succession of little blows." [286]

To think any other way about our children is to set ourselves up for great disappointment, frustration, and even anger. A parent who believes that his children are little angels will sinfully expect too much from them. Our hope is not in our children, or in *their ability*

---

[285] Romans 12:3 For I say, through the grace given to me, to everyone who is among you, not to think of himself more highly than he ought to think, but to think soberly, as God has dealt to each one a measure of faith.

[286] Ryle, Train Up a Child, p. 28.

to come to a knowledge of the truth – rather it is in Christ alone who has the power to call, save, and guide His lambs in the paths of righteousness for His name's sake.

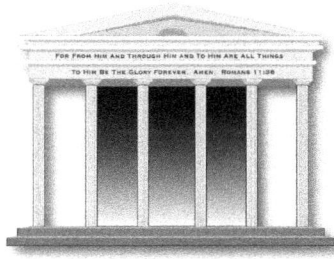

THE FIRST INSTITUTION

CHAPTER 6

CONCLUSION TO

THE FIRST INSTITUTION

CONCLUSION

TO HIM BE THE GLORY FOREVER

Revelation 19:7
"Let us rejoice and be glad
and give the glory to Him,
for the marriage of the Lamb has come
and His bride has made herself ready."

Romans 11:33
For from Him and through Him
and to Him are all things.
To Him be the glory forever.
Amen.

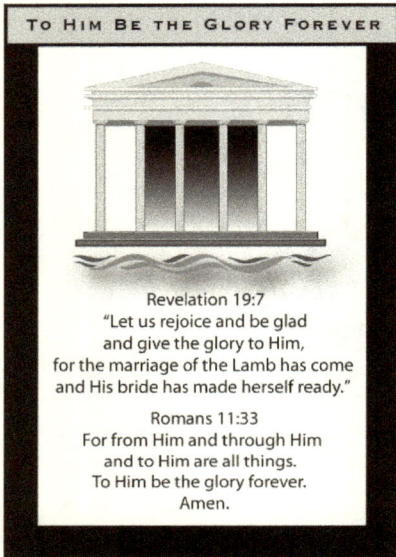

As we now come to the end of *The First Institution*, I am mindful of the fact that this is not really the end, but the beginning of a great privilege: the privilege of *practicing* God's truth. We have examined several theological truths concerning marriage, family life, and child training, but now we must now conclude that our work has really only begun. I begin our conclusion in this manner, in view of Paul's own *finale* to the believers at Philippi:

Philippians 4:9 The things you have learned and received and heard and seen in me, practice these things; and the God of peace shall be with you.

After laying out four chapters of theology, instruction, and exhortation, the Apostle Paul gave the Philippians an important command: *practice* these things![287] This is often the pattern of Biblical writers, to give important theological truth and then to call the audience to obedience in light of that truth. In like manner, we now come to a similar juncture in *The First Institution*. It is one thing to be equipped with Biblical truth regarding the family – it is another to

---

[287] [*prassete*] To practice; to experience or engage in the events of life (godly living). "to carry out some activity (with possible focus upon the procedures involved)—'to do, to carry out, to perform, deed.'" Louw, Johannes P., and Eugene Albert Nida. Greek-English Lexicon of the New Testament : Based on Semantic Domains. electronic ed. of the 2nd edition., Vol. 1, Page 511. New York: United Bible societies, 1996, c1989.

engage in the rehearsal of that truth. As parents we must resolve to practice God's Word in our daily lives, and as we do, we must keep before us the right goals for our children. Like the runner who sets his sights on the prize at the end of a race[288] so too must parents look to the God-ordained end of Biblical parenting. Proverbs chapter 3 gives us such a goal. It comes in the midst of Solomon's instructions to his son regarding the importance of wisdom. Here, Solomon explains to his son what will come to those who heed the wisdom of the Lord:

Proverbs 3:23-26: 23 Then you will walk in your way securely, And your foot will not stumble. 24 When you lie down, you will not be afraid; When you lie down, your sleep will be sweet. 25 Do not be afraid of sudden fear, Nor of the onslaught of the wicked when it comes...

...26 For the Lord will be your confidence, and will keep your foot from being caught.

In these verses we have the ultimate result of God's gracious work through wise and loving parenting: *children who trust in the Lord.*[289] Our chief goal is not that our children would develop a trust and confidence in us (as an end), but that God Himself would be their ultimate trust and *confidence.* It is this God-centered trust (v. 26) that is the basis of a bold walk in the Lord (23-25). This is what the Apostle Paul spoke of when he called children to obey their parents *in the Lord.*[290] It therefore behooves us as Christian parents to

---

[288] Phil 3:14, Heb 12:1-2.

[289] [H. 'āz] Used only six times in the book of Proverbs, this adverbial particle denotes a temporal climax: "at that time..." or "then". It essentially gives us the ultimate goal of training children in wisdom

[290] Calvin: "Besides the law of nature, which is acknowledged by all nations, the obedience of children is enforced by the authority of God. Hence it follows, that parents are to be obeyed, so far only as is consistent with piety to God, which comes first in order." Calvin, *Commentaries Vol. XXI*, p. 326.

practice the truth that we have learned for the good of our children and for the glory of God!

The greatest legacy that parents are to seek in their children is the spiritual one, such that by the sovereign grace of God their offspring would be more than their descendents in the flesh, but spiritual offspring who love the Lord their God with all their heart, soul, mind, and strength. The challenges to this priority are many in our contemporary culture which is a culture filled with philosophies of career-worship, materialism, self-esteem, and the exaltation of countless other forms of man-centered living. In order for the family of God to sail successfully through the storms of this life, they must trail behind the Captain of our salvation: the Lord Jesus Christ. The family of God must reject the bankrupt philosophies of men and embrace the profitable Word of God alone. There is such a great need for reformation in our nation and world: we must return to the priorities of those Reformers of old who embraced *Christ alone*, by *grace alone*, through *faith alone*, being grounded in the *Scriptures alone*; all *for the glory of God alone*. At the end of our lives nothing else will matter at all - not our wealth, education, power, prestige, or influence in this world. In that final day of judgment, men will be measured by whether they trusted Jesus Christ as their Lord and Savior, or not. And for the children of God who do trust the Savior, no deed in this life will have any value, save those which were accomplished by the power of God and for the glory of Christ. Such a simple truth as this is both powerful and life changing for those who know the Savior. With this in mind, parents ought to be consumed with the priority of living for the glory of God such that they spend their days commending their children to the Lord, through their prayers and through their training, knowing that their frail lives are as a fleeting breath. As well, let husbands and fathers find their true satisfaction in the spiritual growth and maturation of their families as they labor as priests and shepherds in their homes. This was the Apostle John's great joy with respect to the church:

> **3 John 4** I have no greater joy than this, to hear of my children walking in the truth.

The Lord created the institution of marriage and family for His own glory, and it is this earthly institution of marriage that serves as a type of that eternal marriage between the Lamb of God and His redeemed people. Let men therefore glorify Jesus Christ through a God-centered, loving, and self sacrificing leadership in their homes, in the church, and in their communities. Let women glorify Jesus Christ through a godly humility and servitude which exalts the Lamb of God whose own humility, servitude, and self-sacrifice will be the reigning theme of worship in heaven.

May the Lord raise up a new generation of such godly men and women who will fearlessly embrace the truths of God's Word, for no matter what true godliness may cost us in this life, it will never compare to the matchless worth of the Bridegroom of the church – the Lord Jesus Christ.

THE FIRST INSTITUTION

APPENDIX

THE FIRST PROMISE

IN FAMILY WORSHIP

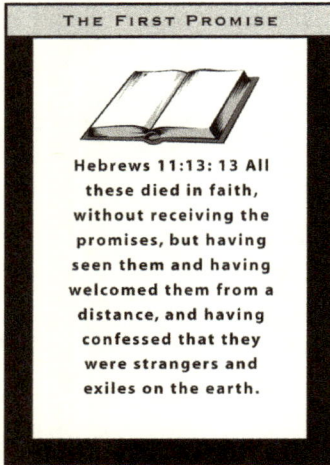

God's standards for the first institution did not change after the fall. Having the promise of God's coming seed, along with the type of the blood sacrifice for their covering, the first family passed on their heritage of truth and hope to the generations that followed them. And those who sought God in faith during this time of history, who evidenced their trust through obedience, did so with the limited revelation that was entrusted to Adam and his wife:

> THE FIRST PROMISE
>
> Hebrews 11:13: 13 All these died in faith, without receiving the promises, but having seen them and having welcomed them from a distance, and having confessed that they were strangers and exiles on the earth.

Hebrews 11:13-16: 13 All these [Abel, Enoch, Noah, Abraham & Sarah] died in faith, without receiving the promises, but having seen them and having welcomed them from a distance, and having confessed that they were strangers and exiles on the earth. 14 For those who say such things make it clear that they are seeking a country of their own. 15 And indeed if they had been thinking of that country from which they went out, they would have had opportunity to return. 16 But as it is, they desire a better country, that is a heavenly one. Therefore God is not ashamed to be called their God; for He has prepared a city for them. [Bold, italics mine]

These stellar examples of faith all welcomed the promises of God *from a distance*, being temporally removed from the first advent of Christ, and yet they worshipped God in the light of the revelation of His promise. We see in many of these Old Testament examples the preservation of the principle of family worship. Now, I must remind the reader that when selecting examples of family worship from the

294

Old Testament we must do so cautiously, knowing that the Old Testament carries some good examples along with many more bad examples. In order to focus on the discussion of family worship at this point, we will direct our attention to three men who are clearly lauded for their godliness and priority of family worship: Noah, Job,[291] and Abraham.

THE FIRST PROMISE

NOAH

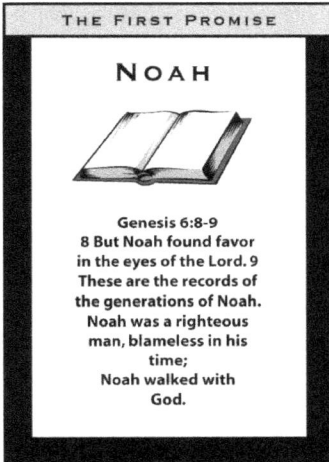

Genesis 6:8-9

8 But Noah found favor in the eyes of the Lord. 9 These are the records of the generations of Noah. Noah was a righteous man, blameless in his time; Noah walked with God.

NOAH

By God's grace, Noah was a worshipper of God. He is spoken of throughout Scripture as an example of piety and worship.[292] Spiritually speaking, he was a lone island in a vast sea of utter corruption, for the people of his generation were "eating, they were drinking, they were marrying, they were being given in marriage."[293] Now the reader should note that eating, drinking, and marrying isn't sinful *per se*, but what is conveyed here is that the world was populated with men whose first priority of life was their own pleasure rather than the good pleasure of God. They lived for themselves and were filled with violence of heart and action. Amidst it all, Noah worshipped the Lord *alone.*

- *2 Peter 2:5,9:* 5 *[God]...did not spare the ancient world, but preserved Noah, a preacher of righteousness, with seven others, when He brought a flood upon the world of the ungodly; 9 ...the Lord knows how to rescue the godly from temptation, and to keep the unrighteous under punishment for the day of judgment,*

---

[291] Job, 1:1-5; Ezek. 14:14-20.

[292] Ezekiel 14:14 even though these three men, Noah, Daniel, and Job were in its midst, by their own righteousness they could only deliver themselves," declares the Lord God. (Ezek 14:20).

[293] Luke 17:26.

- *Genesis 6:8-9:* 8 ...*Noah found favor in the eyes of the Lord. 9 ...Noah was a righteous man, blameless in his time; Noah walked with God.*

The next time you feel spiritually isolated in this corrupt world, consider Noah who was *entirely* alone in the world as a *worshipper of God.* Noah wasn't popular. He wasn't perceived as having any common sense. He wasn't a defender of environmental protection, nor was he normal by the world's standards. However, Noah's family would be protected because of the piety wrought in Noah. By God's grace Noah labored in faith, and in obedience to the will of the Lord. In *reverence* he prepared the ark, which was a type of the coming Christ who would deliver His people from the wrath of God.

> *Hebrews 11:7 By faith Noah, being warned by God about things not yet seen, in reverence prepared an ark for the salvation of his household, by which he condemned the world, and became an heir of the righteousness which is according to faith.*

It is very clear that Noah had the priority of heart, mind, and strength to prepare a haven of protection (the ark) *for the salvation of his household.* Noah's guardianship, rendered on behalf of his family, was not just physical (i.e. the preservation of their biological lives), but spiritual: for the promise of God's coming seed had yet to be fulfilled in Christ who would be born of a woman. In other words, the preservation of the human race was needful for the fulfillment of God's promises, and therefore the hope of the Lord's promise was mediated through Noah's completion of the ark. In view of this it is quite clear that Noah, in his generation, provided *salvation* for his family which is a type of the salvation that Christ would accomplish for His own.[294]

---

[294] 1 Peter 3:20-21 20 ...when the patience of God kept waiting in the days of Noah, during the construction of the ark, in which a few, that is, eight persons, were brought safely through the water.21 And corresponding to that, baptism now saves you—not the removal of dirt from the flesh, but an appeal to God for a good conscience—through the resurrection of Jesus Christ,

Noah is set forth as a clear example of godly, spiritual leadership. We see with this early patriarch a clear priority of worship, as evidenced through his obedience to God's Word and through his acts of worship which were Gospel-centered:

> **Genesis 8:20-21 – 9:1:** *20 Then Noah built an altar to the Lord, and took of every clean animal and of every clean bird and offered burnt offerings on the altar.21 And the Lord smelled the soothing aroma; 1 And God blessed Noah and his sons and said to them, "Be fruitful and multiply, and fill the earth…"*

The pages of Scripture are stained with a trail of blood that leads to the cross of Christ. As we follow that trail, we find believers who saw and welcomed the promised Christ from a distance, anticipating His ministry of mercy and peace through the shedding of blood. This act of worship, offered by Noah, was not just any aroma, but a *soothing* aroma to the Lord who accepted Noah's Gospel-centered worship. Here we have, in Noah, an example of family worship. He served God in a manner that reflected the ideal standards given to the first Adam:

- *Noah served God in the domain of responsibility that God had entrusted to him. Noah ignored the voice of his culture: a culture that resoundingly denied the true worship of God. Noah also enjoyed the pleasures of marriage, food, and drink, but he did so as a means to the greater end of the worship of God. His servitude became a judgment to the whole unbelieving world.*[295]

- *Noah guarded his ministry by means of the Word of God. He had been entrusted with God's spoken revelation for the preservation of his family, and for the preservation of the promises of God regarding the coming Christ. As the head of his home, he diligently labored with*

---

[295] Heb. 11:7.

meticulous detail, reverently building a boat that was perfectly engineered by the plan of God. His family's preservation depended upon his diligence to the truth of God.

- *Noah practiced a leadership that was Gospel-centered. This is especially evidenced when he offered a sacrifice (in faith) that produced a soothing aroma to the Lord. His sacrifice was offered in view of the promises of God, for Noah saw and welcomed the promises of God concerning Christ at a distance (Hebrews 11:13-16).*

THE FIRST PROMISE

JOB

Job 1:1
There was a man in the land of Uz whose name was Job;
and that man was blameless, upright, fearing God and turning away from evil.

JOB

Our next example of godliness and leadership in the home, comes with the example of Job who also labored diligently on behalf of his family as their spiritual head[296]:

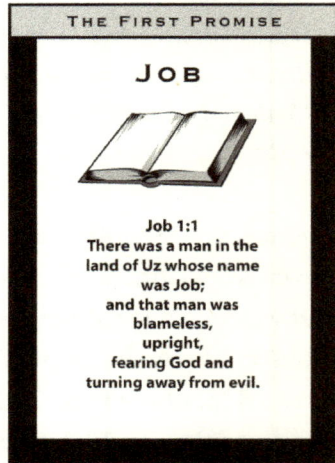

Job 1:1-5: 1 There was a man in the land of Uz, whose name was Job, and that man was blameless, upright, fearing God, and turning away from evil. 2 And seven sons and three daughters were born to him. 3 His possessions also were 7,000 sheep, 3,000 camels, 500 yoke of oxen, 500 female donkeys, and very many servants; and that man was the greatest of all the men of the east. 4 And his sons used to go and hold a feast in the house of each one on his day, and they would send and invite their three sisters to eat and drink with them. 5 And it came about, when the days of feasting had completed their cycle, that Job would send and consecrate them, rising up early in the morning and offering burnt offerings according to the number

---

[296] Ezekiel 14:20 "...even though Noah, Daniel, and **Job** were in its midst, as I live," declares the Lord God, "they could not deliver either their son or their daughter. They would deliver only themselves by their righteousness." [Bold, italics mine].

of them all; for Job said, "Perhaps my sons have sinned and cursed God in their hearts." Thus Job did continually.

There are four qualities of spirituality given to us concerning Job in this first chapter. These must be investigated in order to understand his activities of worship; after all, any man can be religious, but this does not necessarily mean that he is a worshipper of the one true God. However, Job's religion was true, for he sought to worship the Lord in spirit and truth:

- *He was **Blameless:** The word blameless (ṭām) speaks of completion, as in the completion of a full day, represented in the sunset. This word was also employed to describe Noah who was said to be blameless (ṭāmiym).[297] This is perhaps the broadest word that could be used to describe Job's overall spirituality. As an upright and God-fearing man, who turned away from evil, he was complete in the sense of having a right standing before God through the Lord's sovereign mercy and grace.[298]*

- *He was **Upright:** The word used here is (yāšār) which means straight. Job was an upright man, meaning that he lived a life that followed the straight path of God. Being upright means practicing righteousness: Psalm 11:7 "For the Lord is righteous; He loves righteousness; The upright (yāšār) will behold His face." God loves those who know His righteous ways and practices them. Uprightness is a quality that cannot exist without a knowledge of the truth.*

- *He was **a God fearer** [Psalm 36:1 "...Transgression speaks to the ungodly within his heart; There is no fear of God before his eyes."]: The man who fears God will bear the fruit of wisdom and humility, unlike those foolish and proud boasts of the ungodly. Job feared God and*

---

[297] Gen. 6:9.

[298] Job 1:8-10.

prospered under His hand. As a child of God, he feared the Lord with the filial fear that is clearly prescribed in God's Word.[299]

- ***He turned away from evil:*** *The internal qualities of his heart were evidenced through his actions. Job was a man who forsook the evil that surrounded him. Like Noah, he walked the narrow path of godliness, pursuing righteousness, and forsaking the evil of the world that surrounded him.*

These qualities help us to understand the nature of Job's habits concerning family worship. Though his children had accrued enough wealth to become self sufficient, having homes of their own, their spiritual needs were still the consummate concern for Job such that he consecrated his children unto the Lord when he arose early in the morning for worship.

Job 1:5 And it came about, when the days of feasting had completed their cycle, that Job would send and consecrate them, rising up early in the morning and offering burnt offerings according to the number of them all; for Job said, "Perhaps my sons have sinned and cursed God in their hearts." Thus Job did continually.

His devotions were centered in the message of the Gospel: Job offered sacrifices for *all* of his children, seeking their sanctification to God from sin. Consider the following observation from Matthew Henry in his commentary on the Bible:

"Job, like Abraham, had an altar for his family, on which, it is likely, he offered sacrifice daily; but, on this extraordinary occasion, he offered more sacrifices than usual, and with more solemnity, according to the number of them all, one for each child. Parents should be particular in their addresses to God for the several branches of their family."[300]

---

[299] Psalm 34:9.

[300] Henry, <u>Commentary on the Whole Bible</u>, Job.

The prayers and worship of Job were said to be continual, but we must not miss the extent of this expression's meaning, literally [*yāsĕh 'iyôḇ kăl-hāyămiym*]: *Job continually did [this] all the days.* When we consider the quality of Job's godliness, we must not underestimate the extent of his faithfulness in providing spiritual leadership for his family: he continually worshipped the Lord in this manner *all the days* of his life. This shows us the heart of the man indeed. He loved the Lord with all his heart and sought Him with a diligence which stands as an example to any husband/father who seeks to lead his family in the Lord.

ABRAHAM

THE FIRST PROMISE

ABRAHAM

Genesis 18:19
"...I have chosen him, so that he may command his children and his household after him to keep the way of the Lord by doing righteousness and justice, so that the Lord may bring upon Abraham what He has spoken about him."

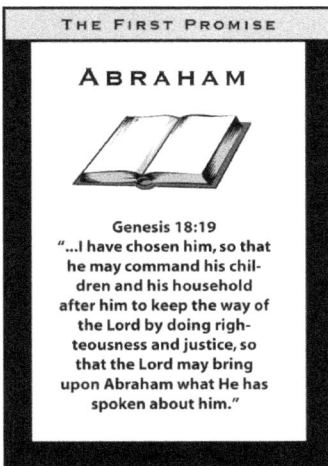

Both Abraham and Sarah are heralded in the NT as being examples of faith and piety. Abraham is called the spiritual father of all who believe[301] and Sarah is referred to as the spiritual mother of all women who exhibit the piety of fearless submission.[302] At the heart of the story of Abraham and Sarah is the gem of their genuine faith and worship, the examples of which are hard to deny or ignore. In addition to their many good examples, they also had no shortage of flaws, reminding us that all marriages since the fall can only offer a faint reflection of that pre-fall marriage of Adam and his wife. Man's sinful

---

[301] Gal. 3:7.

[302] 1 Peter 3:5-6: 5 For in this way in former times the holy women also, who hoped in God, used to adorn themselves, being submissive to their own husbands.6 Thus Sarah obeyed Abraham, calling him lord, and you have become her children if you do what is right without being frightened by any fear.

condition taints every aspect of every marriage to the extent that there will always be conflict and difficulty, even among those who worship the true God. Sarah's example was already considered in Chapter 3 (*The Spirit Filled Wife*), but our reflections are presently centered upon the leadership of Abraham.

The story of Abraham is really the story of God's gracious work of bringing about His promise concerning His promised seed.[303] The Lord had given the promise to Abram, that in him the nations would be blessed (Genesis 12:3); and that his descendents would be as numerous as the stars of heaven (Genesis 15:5). Through Abraham's seed, God would fulfill His promises:

> Genesis 22:18 "And in your seed all the nations of the earth shall be blessed, because you have obeyed My voice."

But we must remember exactly who this promised seed is. It is to this ultimate point that Paul instructs us:

> Galatians 3:16 Now the promises were spoken to Abraham and to his seed. He does not say, "And to seeds," as referring to many, but rather to one, "And to your seed," that is, Christ.

Abraham was entrusted with the promise of God's seed – Jesus Christ. By God's grace, manifested in Abraham's obedience to God's voice, the promise of God continued. The nations would indeed be blessed through the Seed of God, but it was Abraham's responsibility to walk in the light of God's promises, as he led his family in the path of God's revelation.[304] It is important to note that the fulfillment of God's promises were centered in Abraham's ordained responsibility to lead his family:

---

[303] Gal. 3:8-16.

[304] James 2:21-23.

Genesis 18:17-19: 17 And the Lord said, "Shall I hide from Abraham what I am about to do, 18 since Abraham will surely become a great and mighty nation, and in him all the nations of the earth will be blessed? 19 "For I have chosen him, in order that he may command his children and his household after him to keep the way of the Lord by doing righteousness and justice; in order that the Lord may bring upon Abraham what He has spoken about him."

Abraham's call to command his family is presented in this text as the instrumental means through which the promises of God would be fulfilled: the nations of the earth would be blessed ultimately through the Seed of God [Christ]. Through faith alone, and by God's grace alone, Abraham was to exercise a spiritual leadership in his home, directing family worship so that it would be centered on God's promised and coming Seed. Consider the following breakdown of Abraham's responsibilities, as articulated in Genesis 18:17-19:

- *He was chosen of God to command his children. It is interesting to note the word employed here concerning Abraham's prescribed responsibility of leadership. The word command comes from the Hebrew word zāwāh, the root word of which is used mostly to speak of the laws and commandments of the Lord. This is why the translators chose to use the word command to speak of the nature of his leadership of both his children and his household. This text clearly reveals that there was a calling upon Abraham to offer a demonstrative spiritual leadership for his children, and overall household, in order to procure their blessing and the blessing of the world through the coming Christ. Here again, we have an important message of God's calling of men to offer spiritual leadership, not only for their children, but to their households overall.*

- *He was chosen of God to command his household: Abraham was commanded to lead his children and his household. This is in keeping with the very priorities of the God-ordained marital roles from the very beginning. Sarah was not his co-leader, and their marriage was not a place of partnered rule. Rather her calling was to be Abraham's helper in all that he was called to do. Abraham was called upon by the Lord to command (or direct) his children and he was called upon to do the same for his whole household, which included Sarah. This is why Sarah is presented in Scripture as an example of piety for women, seeing that Sarah obeyed Abraham without fear.[305]*

- ***He was to direct his family to keep the way of the Lord:*** *Abraham's responsibility to keep the way of the Lord was patterned after the responsibilities of Adam: The word "keep" comes from the Hebrew word šāmār; the very same word employed to describe Adam's ministry of guardianship of the garden via the Word of God. Like Adam, Abraham had been entrusted with God's divine revelation, and with this, Abraham was called upon to guard (or keep) the way of the Lord through the priority of family worship. Their devotion was based upon the same simple principles of servitude, guardianship, and a pedagogy that directed them to the promises of God concerning His Seed.[306] With these responsibilities before him, Abraham was to lead his family in Gospel-centered worship.*

Abraham's priority for his family was the priority of the worship of God. This is perhaps most dramatically illustrated in that key moment when Abraham was instructed to offer up his son of promise as a sacrifice to the Lord, and yet with this, Abraham believed in God's power and promises:

Genesis 22:7-8: 7 And Isaac spoke to Abraham his father and said, "My father!" And he said, "Here I am, my son." And he said, "Behold, the fire and the wood, but where is the lamb for the burnt offering?"8 And

---

[305] 1 Peter 3:5-6: 5 For in this way in former times the holy women also, who hoped in God, used to adorn themselves, being submissive to their own husbands.6 Thus Sarah obeyed Abraham, calling him lord, and you have become her children if you do what is right without being frightened by any fear.

[306] Gal. 3:16.

Abraham said, "God will provide for Himself the lamb for the burnt offering, my son." So the two of them walked on together.

Hebrews 11:17-19 *17 By faith Abraham, when he was tested, offered up Isaac; and he who had received the promises was offering up his only begotten son; 18 it was he to whom it was said, "In Isaac your descendants shall be called." 19 He considered that God is able to raise men even from the dead; from which he also received him back as a type.*

We are reminded that at the heart of this story is a man who commanded his household by means of great faith. That he even obeyed God to the point of offering up his son Isaac is a remarkable climax of true faith and obedience, and this he did believing in God's promise to provide a blessing to the nations. What an example of trust and faith Abraham is for all believers, and what an example of a man who *commanded* his children and household for the glory of God!

SUMMARY

The early history of Genesis could be likened to the observance of the vast and spacious heavens, filled mostly with an incomprehensibly expansive void of darkness, but occasionally sprinkled with a bright star here and there. In the case of biblical history, the darkness of human wickedness is vast, and yet we see the occasional lights of true piety shining through as beacons of hope. Noah, Job, and Abraham are but a few stars in the universe of redemptive history. The radiance of their lives, in many ways, was enhanced by virtue of the darkness of corruption that surrounded them. These beacons of hope show us that there are clear principles of family worship that remain true for every generation, and will continue to stand until the return of our Lord.

THE FIRST INSTITUTION

FOR FROM HIM AND THROUGH HIM AND TO HIM ARE ALL THINGS
TO HIM BE THE GLORY FOREVER. AMEN. ROMANS 11:36

Index

G

Proverbs 3:5-18:

5 Trust in Jehovah with all thy heart,
And lean not upon thine own understanding:
6 In all thy ways acknowledge him, And he will direct thy paths.
7 Be not wise in thine own eyes; Fear Jehovah, and depart from
evil: 8 It will be health to thy navel, And marrow to thy bones. 9
Honor Jehovah with thy substance, And with the first-fruits of
all thine increase: 10 So shall thy barns be filled with plenty, And
thy vats shall overflow with new wine. 11 My son, despise not
the chastening of Jehovah; Neither be weary of his reproof: 12
For whom Jehovah loveth he reproveth; Even as a father the son
in whom he delighteth. 13 Happy is the man that findeth
wisdom, And the man that getteth understanding. 14 For the
gaining of it is better than the gaining of silver, And the profit
thereof than fine gold. 15 She is more precious than rubies: And
none of the things thou canst desire are to be compared unto
her. 16 Length of days is in her right hand; In her left hand are
riches and honor.17 Her ways are ways
of pleasantness, And all her
paths are peace.
18 She is a
tree of life
to them that
lay hold
upon her:
And happy
is every
one that
retaineth
her.

www.ingramcontent.com/pod-product-compliance
Lightning Source LLC
Chambersburg PA
CBHW031826090426
42741CB00005B/144